A COMMENTARY ON
SHAKESPEARE'S RICHARD III

WOLFGANG CLEMEN

A Commentary on Shakespeare's Richard III

ENGLISH VERSION BY
JEAN BONHEIM

METHUEN & CO LTD
11 New Fetter Lane, EC4

First published in Göttingen, 1957 under
the title Kommentar zu Shakespeares Richard III
by Vandenhoek & Ruprecht
© 1957 by Vandenhoek & Ruprecht
First English language edition published
1968 by Methuen & Co Ltd
11 New Fetter Lane, EC4
English translation © 1968 Methuen & Co Ltd
Printed and bound in Great Britain by
Butler & Tanner Ltd, Frome and London

CONTENTS

List of editions of *Richard III* which have been consulted:

Al.   *Complete Works*, ed. P. Alexander, Collins (1951);

Arden   *The Arden Shakespeare: The Tragedy of King Richard the Third*, ed. A. Hamilton Thompson, London (1907);

Churchill   *The Tudor Shakespeare: The Tragedy of King Richard III*, ed. G. B. Churchill, New York (1902);

Evans   *The Tutorial Shakespeare: King Richard III*, ed. B. I. Evans, London (n.d.);

F   *First Folio* (1623)

H. Spencer   *The Arden Shakespeare: The Tragedy of King Richard the Third*, ed. Hazelton Spencer, Boston, Heath (1933);

Hudson   *The New Hudson Shakespeare: King Richard the Third*, ed. Henry Hudson, rev. ed. E. C. Black, Boston (1916);

J.D.W.   *The New Shakespeare: Richard III*, ed. John Dover Wilson, Cambridge (1953); 1961 second impression with further corrections;

Q   *Quarto* (*Q1: Quarto* Edition of 1597; *Q6: Quarto* Ed. of 1622);

Var.   *A New Variorum Edition of Shakespeare: Richard III*, ed. H. H. Furness (1908);

Warwick   *The Warwick Shakespeare: The Tragedy of King Richard the Third*, ed. Sir George Macdonald, London (n.d.);

Wright   *The Tragedy of King Richard the Third*, ed. W. A. Wright, Oxford, Clarendon Press Series (1880).

The following texts of pre-Shakespearian plays have been used in this commentary:

for *Alphonsus King of Aragon, The Battle of Alcazar, Campaspe, David and Bethsabe, Edward I, Friar Bacon and Friar Bungay, James IV, King Leir, Locrine, Orlando Furioso, Selimus, True Tragedy* (*The True Tragedy of Richard III*), *The Wounds of Civil War* the text as found in the *Malone Society Reprints*.

for *Cambises, The Foure PP, Gorboduc: or Ferrex and Porrex* the text as found in J. Q. Adams, *Pre-Shakespearian Drama* (1924);

for *Gismond of Salerne* and *Misfortunes of Arthur*, the text as found in
Early English Classical Tragedies, ed. J. W. Cunliffe (1912);
for *Thersytes* the text as found in A. W. Pollard, *English Miracle Plays*
(1890);
for *The Spanish Tragedy* the text as printed in *Minor Elizabethan Drama*,
I (Everyman, 1910/1959);
for *The Troublesome Reign of King John* see the edition of I. Gollancz
(1913); for *Woodstock. A Moral History* see the edition of A. P. Rossiter
(1946).

For Marlowe's plays *The Works of Christopher Marlowe*, ed. C. F.
Tucker Brooke (1910) has been used.

The following abbreviations have been used for frequently quoted
books and for those periodicals with which the general reader will
perhaps not be familiar:

Boswell-Stone	*Shakespeare's Holinshed, The Chronicle and the Historical Plays Compared* by W. Boswell-Stone (1907)
DUJ	*Durham University Journal*
Hall	Hall, *The Union of the Two Noble and Illustre Families of Lancastre and Yorke* (1809)
Hol.	*Holinshed's Chronicles of England, Scotland and Ireland*, 6 vols. (1808), vol. III
MissQ	*Mississippi Quarterly*
A. Schmidt	*Shakespeare-Lexicon* by A. Schmidt, revised by G. Sarrazin (1902)
UMPEAL	*University of Miami Publications in English and American Literature*
UTQ	*University of Toronto Quarterly*
YSE	*Yale Studies in English*

The titles and authors of other books have been given in full only
when first mentioned in the footnotes.

PREFATORY NOTE

This book is a condensed English version of my *Kommentar zu Shakespeares Richard III*, which was first published in Germany by Vandenhoeck & Ruprecht, Göttingen, in 1957. For the sake of abridgement the sections on Shakespeare's treatment of his sources have been omitted, as a good deal of the material given there may now be found in Volume III of Geoffrey Bullough's *Narrative and Dramatic Sources of Shakespeare*, published in 1960. References to articles in German periodicals, to German dissertations and monographs have been curtailed; instead, a list of Munich dissertations on aspects of Shakespeare's dramatic art made use of in this commentary has been added. No attempt has been made to incorporate references to all the material published on *Richard III* since the commentary appeared in 1957, though a few additional articles have been consulted and are mentioned in the footnotes. The text used is that of Peter Alexander, available in the *Complete Histories of Shakespeare* (Collins, London, n.d.). This text adopts some readings from John Dover Wilson's edition of *Richard III* (*The New Shakespeare*, Cambridge 1954) to which the author is also indebted for many suggestions. Single editions of the play consulted in the commentary are listed on p. xi. The works cited in the footnotes are in each case quoted from the editions which I was using at the time.

I should like to express my gratitude to Mrs Jean Bonheim who drew up the text of the present English version and to Miss C. A. M. Sym who had previously prepared a literal full translation of the German book. As, however, a number of changes and abridgements had to be made shortly before the book went to press, the author bears the responsibility for the final text. Many thanks are due to Mr Rhys John Evans and Fräulein I. Bungartz for checking and revising the manuscript. I also wish to record my obligation and appreciation for advice and help received in Germany more than ten years ago during my work on the original book from

L. L. Schücking and E. Th. Sehrt and in England and U.S.A. from John Dover Wilson, Una Ellis-Fermor, Peter Alexander, Harold Brooks, J. C. Maxwell, Robert Birley, Alfred Harbage, and Oscar James Campbell. I should also like to renew my thanks for the generous support given me by James McManaway and Louis B. Wright of the Folger Shakespeare Library in Washington. My greatest obligation, however, is to my former students and the members of my Shakespeare Seminar at Munich whose names are included in the list of Munich dissertations and of whom several have in the meantime become professors and lecturers in German universities.

INTRODUCTION

What questions should we bear in mind when reading a scene in a play by Shakespeare? What methods should we apply in a close study of a single play? On what should we fasten our attention? What observations on style, characterization, theme and imagery, composition and dramaturgy will lead us to a fuller understanding of a play? To these and similar questions the present scene-by-scene commentary tries to give answers. Indeed, the author hopes that by integrating various approaches and methods of textual analysis into a running interpretation of the play, and by considering one of Shakespeare's well-known Histories against the background of Elizabethan drama, he has provided a general introduction to Shakespeare's early dramatic art.

The author's aim has not been to present a book on Shakespeare to be read at one sitting, a new monograph presenting the play in a radically new light. The purpose has been rather to provide a useful and informative commentary which offers a basis for further study, and which may even be used as a book of reference by any student interested in the all-round study of one of Shakespeare's plays. Such a student will have no difficulty in finding specialist studies as well as general books on Shakespeare. But he may feel the need for a book which helps him to apply the various possible approaches to the text before him, which shows him how, in going through a play scene by scene, he can draw upon the results of his own reading. To ensure that we are scrutinizing the text of a play with a sufficiently sharp eye, we must often change our perspective, looking first from one angle and then from another, applying at various levels the tools of analysis and comparison. But the tools and the materials must be at hand. One of the aims of this commentary has been to provide these tools as far as they are needed for the understanding of a single passage, a speech, or a scene.

The observation of characteristic features in the language,

construction, and dramaturgy of a scene are, however, only the first step in our study of the play. We must also recognize the interdependence of these various elements. In a Shakespeare play, as indeed in all great drama, there is no such thing as language independent of character-portrayal, or construction independent of theme: the student who tries to interpret a scene in the light of his own findings will eventually realize that all these different elements: style, character, construction, and subject-matter, are dependent on each other, and combine to form an indissoluble whole.

This is not to deny the value of specialization, which has yielded many stimulating investigations of particular aspects of Shakespeare's drama. However, specialist study tends to isolate the different elements of Shakespeare's art and to examine them separately, so that critics who analyse Shakespeare's language and style often do not pay much attention to problems of structure or to questions of theatrical impact. Even some of the monographs on individual plays examine them with emphasis on one or two aspects only. The problem with which Shakespeare studies are faced today is therefore the same as in all other fields: the more specialization there is, the more it is necessary to integrate the separate branches of research into a comprehensive whole.

Such comprehensive treatment, however, is what a scene-by-scene interpretation of a Shakespeare play must inevitably involve. Different methods must be brought to bear on a particular scene so that it becomes a meeting ground for varying types of analyses. Analysis of detail takes its place side by side with the consideration of wider issues. By taking the single scene as the unit of interpretation the commentary may appear to overestimate the individual scene as opposed to the continuous action, within which the scenes often follow so closely and smoothly upon one another that we scarcely notice the transition. For the sake of providing a suitable working basis, however, this – sometimes perhaps too rigid – system of subdivision had to be adopted.

As a rule, the commentary on each scene contains a short summary of its subject-matter; an examination of its construction and its position within the plot; a discussion of the scene as an example of a recurrent type and an assessment of its significance for the whole drama. This is normally followed by an examination of the manipulation and grouping of the characters, of their rôle and the degree to which they are individualized. This in turn generally involves questions of dramaturgy and production, the treatment of time and place, the stage-business and the 'theatrical impact' on the audience.

On a different level we are concerned with the use of language, the function of rhetoric and stylistic devices, the structure of the speeches, and the employment of verse and prose. Analysis of language naturally includes the examination of imagery, recurrent key-words, ambiguity, and versification. These are treated in relation to the characters and situations as well as in terms of their bearing on the total pattern of the play. Thus language is constantly bound up with form. The many instances of tragic irony and anticipation which careful study of the linguistic texture brings to light, often function as structural links; moreover, irony as well as anticipation play an important part in the technique of preparation, which operates in this play on several levels at once. In a similar fashion the underlying themes of this history-play find expression in its form and structure. In O. J. Campbell's phrase, the 'moral architecture' is visible in the tectonics of the drama.

When Shakespeare wrote *Richard III* he had before him the rich variety of Elizabethan drama, which offered him a colourful mixture of dramatic types, styles and modes of presentation. Indeed, *Richard III* may be regarded as a focal point where many elements of pre-Shakespearian drama combine with innovations introduced by Shakespeare himself. Thus this early play provides us with an excellent illustration of the way in which Shakespeare used existing conventions and stylistic patterns, his amazing capacity to integrate and amalgamate the dramatic traditions of his times, to turn outworn devices to new uses and combine heterogeneous forms in a unified dramatic structure. There is hardly another play in which we can so well study this interplay between tradition and originality, the gradual emergence of a new style out of the inherited forms. It has therefore seemed appropriate to examine Shakespeare's art in this first important stage of its development against the background of Elizabethan drama.

Richard III abounds in established conventions, traditional patterns, typical themes, situations and 'set pieces', so that the question of how these elements were handled in pre-Shakespearian drama is pertinent. Thus comparison is a frequent means of defining the position of *Richard III* within the history of Elizabethan drama.

But comparisons between *Richard III* and contempory plays do more than simply provide further arguments for the commonplace contention that 'Shakespeare surpassed his contemporaries', that his mode of dramatic presentation was more concrete and more complex. Comparison helps us to arrive at clearer standards, and often provides new perspectives from which we can assess Shakespeare's artistic achievement and investigate the exact nature of his dramatic intentions and his originality.

Furthermore, such inquiry gives us an insight into the complex development of Elizabethan drama. It is hoped, therefore, that the many references to the earlier drama will enable the student interested in following the evolution of dramatic technique from the beginning of the Elizabethan era up to the time of Shakespeare to trace certain trends and to follow the changing use of particular dramatic features and conventions.

It has been thought appropriate to discuss the 'meaning' of the play and other questions relating to the play as a whole only after enough textual evidence had been collected to make such considerations meaningful. Thus such matters as the significance of the drama as a whole, the conceptions of tragedy and fate which it implies, the degree of moral intensity which it conveys, are briefly considered only in the latter part of this book and then in connection with concrete observations. The author is nevertheless aware that the systematic approach he is attempting here carries with it its own limitations, and that there are qualities in this play, particularly where its total impact is concerned, which a detailed analysis can do little to illuminate, and which would be brought out more satisfactorily in a shorter appreciation.

This commentary has, of course, a different aim from that of existing critical and annotated editions of Shakespeare's plays, where the main emphasis is on the explanation of words or meanings, on the elucidation of obscure or disputed passages, on illustrations of points in the text concerning history, folk-lore, or allusions to contemporary literature, politics or social events. Observations on style, on dramatic technique and characterization do occasionally occur in such texts, but usually as a by-product of other considerations. In view of the detailed information on linguistic points provided by these annotated editions, and in order that as much as possible of the available space be devoted to the continuous interpretation, such explanatory matter has been strictly curtailed. Where, however, an explanation is called for, references are given to the existing editions of *Richard III* to which the present writer is indebted. For similar reasons, no effort has been made to treat in detail the intricate problems of textual criticism. The subject is too vast to be adequately dealt with within the framework of an interpretative commentary. In any case, the textual questions arising from *Richard III* have been discussed by several excellent authorities (D. L. Patrick, John Dover Wilson, Alice Walker, W. W. Greg, Peter Alexander, K. Smidt) so that it would have been presumptuous to take up this matter again in a book which has a different aim. Problems of textual criticism have, therefore, been dealt with only where they are involved in questions of meaning.

The critical methods and approaches used in this commentary owe a great deal to recent Shakespearian studies in England and the U.S.A., but they have also been influenced by the textual interpretations as carried out by classical philology and by the 'explication de texte' method as developed in France. In particular, Harley Granville-Barker's *Prefaces to Shakespeare* acted as a powerful stimulus to the plan of a scene-by-scene commentary; indeed, every scholar embarking on a running interpretation of a whole play must feel a debt of gratitude to Granville-Barker. In recent years a number of books on single plays have appeared and an increasing number of critics are concentrating their attention on individual plays. Though it is hoped that the present commentary will offer helpful suggestions to those carrying out detailed studies of other plays, it cannot serve as a model; for the methods to be employed in each case must arise out of the unique nature of the individual plays.

Act I

⚜

SCENE ONE

General Structure

This first scene – and indeed the whole play – is dominated by the figure of Richard.[1] He opens and closes the scene with a soliloquy, and keeps a constant steering hand on the direction of the dialogue. These two soliloquies make a frame for Richard's encounters with Clarence and Hastings, which are separated from each other by yet another short monologue. The central episodes (Clarence going to prison and Hastings leaving it) are also similar in content: in both Richard meets a future, unsuspecting victim; in both he dissembles, then explains the purpose of his deceit in the soliloquy that follows. Thus the first scene with its symmetrical construction introduces a technique used in various forms throughout the play and indeed throughout Shakespeare's early work. In *Richard III* this symmetry is still very obvious, almost obtrusive: Richard's twice-repeated show of hypocrisy before two of his future victims has an artificial flavour about it. Yet at the same time, the careful construction of this scene suggests the work of a highly conscious author unwilling to admit any fortuitous element into his plot, preparing well in advance for future developments. Themes and characters introduced here will not remain unutilized in future scenes.

[1] Throughout this commentary Richard of Gloucester is called *Richard*. In the play he is called *Gloucester* up to IV, i, and *Richard* only after his coronation (IV, ii).

The Opening Soliloquy (1–41)

The great opening soliloquy, delivered in prologue-like fashion by Richard alone on the stage, falls into three distinct parts: in lines 1–13 he surveys the situation; in 14–27 he describes his own appearance and character; and in 28–40 he tells us of his future plans. What is here presented in one speech furnished in pre-Shakespearian drama the subject-matter for three: the prologue revealed the opening situation; the monologue of exposition and self-introduction presented the main character; and the 'planning monologue' (the soliloquy in which the speaker announces his future plans) prepared for future events. These three motifs did not normally follow one upon the other. It is something new for *one* monologue of moderate length to fulfil these three functions.

The soliloquy (and the play) begins in the same tone with which *3 Henry VI* had ended. King Edward, in the concluding lines of the earlier play (V, vii, 42 ff.), had spoken of the *stately triumphs* and the *mirthful comic shows* in which the court would spend its days now that the Lancastrians had fallen: a season of *lasting joy* was about to open. And now Richard contrasts this joyful time with the period of war which has just ended. Richard's opening references to a season of sunny peace – ironic in the light of his later actions – remind the audience that England is actually enjoying an unclouded prospect free from civil and foreign wars. In other plays the opening situation provides grounds for the hero's subsequent action;[1] but nothing in the external world serves to explain Richard's aggressive behaviour.[2] The motive for his actions must be sought solely in his character, his will.

That Richard's sympathies are in fact for war is emphasized in: 'this weak piping time of peace' (24), and in his admission: 'And hate the idle pleasures of these days' (31). Lines 10–13 contain a disdainful criticism of the warrior's unmanly peace-time behaviour (the *he* in line 12 surely refers to this hypothetical soldier,

---

[1] e.g. *The Spanish Tragedy*, *The Jew of Malta*.

[2] Cf. Frank W. Cady, 'Motivation of the Inciting Force in Shakespeare's Tragedies', *Elizabethan Studies and other Essays in Honor of George F. Reynolds* (University of Colorado Studies, Series B. Studies in the Humanities, vol. II, No. 4, 1945).

with a possible hint at Edward IV[1]); the choice of the word
capers for what the warrior does in a lady's chamber (12)[2] underlines Richard's low opinion of this particular amusement. But,
more important, the striking and concrete description following
the more conventional lines on the passing of war and coming of
peace infuses the passage with movement and vivacity.

These first thirteen lines differ from the usual passages of introductory exposition in sixteenth-century drama[3] in that they contain hardly any names or historico-political detail; instead, images
of war are juxtaposed with images of peace in an extended contrast. The ponderous chronicling of facts which burdens so many
opening scenes is replaced by evocative description incorporating
a number of conventional expressions common in Elizabethan
drama.[4] These first thirteen lines, rich in rhetorical devices,[5] are
marked by a stately, ceremonious tone in striking contrast with
what follows. The *gravità*, *maestà*, and *dignità*[6] which, according to
Castelvetro, should characterize tragedy, lend their weight to
Richard's opening words. But here style is suited to content;
elevated rhetoric appears only where it is appropriate. As soon as
the soliloquy takes on a more personal note (14 ff.), the diction too

[1] Wright believes this *he* to refer to 'War, still personified as a rough
soldier'. But both H. Spencer and J.D.W. believe that, in spite of the ante-
cedent *war* (*War*), the *he* refers to the notoriously lascivious king, Edward IV.
Cf. J.D.W., p. 168.
[2] Cf. the use of *caper* in *2 Henry VI*, III, i, 365, *L.L.L.*, V, ii, 113.
[3] Cf. for instance *Locrine*, I, i; *Misfortunes of Arthur*, I, i; *The Spanish
Tragedy*, I, i.
[4] Cf. 'winter of our discontent' with 'winter of my miserie', Sidney,
Astrophel and Stella (Steevens). With 'grimvisag'd war' cf. Sackville's *Induction*, 386 f. (J.D.W.), and with 'bruised arms', cf. *Rape of Lucrece*, 110
(Malone). For the contrast between 'marches' and 'measures' cf. Lyly's
Campaspe, IV, iii, 32 ff. (Wright); and for the contrast between war and the
'delicate tunes and amorous glances' of peace, see II, ii, 35 ff. of the same work
(Reed). A. H. Krappe suggests that the metaphor 'winter of our discontent'
goes back originally to Claudian's *De Bello Gothico* (151 f.) (*Anglia*, LII, 1928,
p. 174 f.).
[5] Cf. the anaphora, the alliteration (2, 4-5, 7-8, 11, 12-13), the balanced
lines with their contrasting pairs of words (7, 8). Cf. the parallel gram-
matical construction of the line endings (adjective followed by noun, 5,
7-11).
[6] Cf. M. J. Wolff, 'Die Theorie der italienischen Tragödie im 16. Jahr-
hundert' *Archiv*, CXXVIII (1912), pp. 161 ff., 339 ff.

grows more personal; tempo and language adjust themselves to the new tone.[1]

And yet a personal note emerges even in these first thirteen lines. When Richard speaks of the 'glorious summer' which has been ushered in by 'this sun of York', the *this* (referring to his brother, Edward) has a disparaging ring. In any case, the pun on *sun=son* (suggested by the Yorkist badge, the sun-in-splendour[2]) is ironic, for Edward, the sun of York, is fast fading and near death; moreover, Richard lacks belief in both the radiance of this sun and the present *glorious summer*. It is typical of Richard, too, that these lofty images of sunrise, of summer's victory, of clouds *in the deep bosom of the ocean buried*, are evoked not by feelings of contentment, but by dissatisfaction. Thus Richard's feelings are the opposite of the sentiments seemingly expressed in these resounding opening lines. Nor is the subjective description of the warrior's antics what we should expect from an impersonal prologue. It has even been suggested that the high rhetoric of the opening lines is Richard's particular way of mocking the sentiments expressed.[3]

The second section of the soliloquy opens with Richard's *But I,* which stresses his isolation while it detaches him from the *our* which had linked the earlier lines on conditions at court and in the country.[4] It also forms a natural bridge (both syntactically and

[1] J. W. Draper's work on tempo in Shakespeare's plays is largely based on the proportion of 'slurrings of words or phrases' to the expressions uttered without slurring; he too concludes that lines 13–32 show a marked increase in tempo ('Patterns of Tempo in *Richard III*' *Neuphil. Mitteilungen*, L, 1949).

[2] Cf. A. Venezky, *Pageantry on the Shakespearean Stage* (1951), p. 181: 'In the opening passage of the play, Richard employs a favorite device of the royal entry pageant when he rejoices that the recently crowned sun-king has dispersed . . . all the clouds that lowr'd upon our house.' Cf. also the same image used in *Battle of Alcazar*, II, i. And similarly, *Mirror, Richard Duke of Gloucester*, 238. On the heraldic significance of the badge cf. C. W. Scott-Giles, *Shakespeare's Heraldry* (1950), p. 172 f. The 'sun emerging from a cloud' was Richard II's special badge. Cf. *Richard II*, ed. J.D.W., p. xii.

[3] Cf. J. Palmer on the opening of the soliloquy: '. . . while, across the play of intellect restfully aware of itself, runs a vein of mockery which, with a precise and amusing exaggeration, flouts the easy rhetoric as it marches to a conclusion. All those preliminary adjectives have, as it were, an elfin smile in their delivery – *glorious, victorious, dreadful, delightful*' (*Political Characters of Shakespeare*, 1945, p. 77 f.).

[4] Cf. H. Glunz, *Shakespeare und Morus* (1938), p. 150; Th. Spencer, *Shakespeare and the Nature of Man* (1942/49), p. 72.

logically) from the more general survey of the situation to the picture he then draws of himself. In pre-Shakespearian drama the various sections of the monologue had usually followed one another without any connecting link.

The seven-fold repetition of the word *I* in the second section, like the repeated use of *our* in the first section, lends the pronoun a special emphasis;[1] moreover, four of the *I*'s occur in the stressed position at the beginning of a line. In the first section the sentences were relatively short, but this section consists of one extended sentence, in which three relative clauses precede the eventual appearance of the verb. The third of these clauses, with its agglomeration of past participles all conveying a negative image of Richard (*curtail'd, cheated of feature, deform'd, unfinish'd, scarce half made up*), accelerates the pace of the speech and increases the bitterness of tone. For Richard, self-observation is clearly a fascinating activity.

The scornful way in which Richard makes fun of the lover's rôle[2] is striking. This particular tone – mocking and sarcastic, indeed spiteful – will make itself felt in many later passages. Here and elsewhere in the play he describes himself as though he were looking in a mirror: he enumerates individual imperfections (19–21) and dramatizes his disabled state in his account of the dogs barking at his approach (22–23). 'Deform'd' from birth, he feels 'cheated' by *nature*[3] – the same nature that had, as he says in the next scene, endowed Anne's murdered husband, Edward, with

[1] At the same time these lines extend Richard's 'I am myself alone' (*3 Henry VI*, V, vi, 83).

[2] Cf. *3 Henry VI*, III, ii, 146 ff.

[3] This conception of nature as creating men and imparting certain gifts and a certain outward shape to them is recurrent in Shakespeare (s. A. Schmidt, *nature*, 1). In his *Faerie Queene* (VII, vii, 5–6),[1] Spenser had shown that nature can be double-faced and is fundamentally ambivalent. Cf. also John F. Danby, *Shakespeare's Doctrine of Nature* (1949). On *Richard III* specifically, see pp. 58–67, though this particular passage is not cited. J.D.W. (cf. also Warburton, Malone, etc.) understands 'dissembling nature' to suggest 'hiding my real greatness under a deceptive appearance'; thus, keeping in mind the Renaissance insistence on the dual rôle of nature (cf. Danby), 'dissembling nature' may mean: hypocritical, perfidious, treacherous, deceitful, false. Cf. A. Schmidt, 1a; Johnson, Wright, Furness. On the Goddess Natura in the classical period, the Middle Ages, and the Renaissance, cf. E. R. Curtius, *European Literature and the Latin Middle Ages* (1953), ch. 6.

such 'prodigality' (I, ii, 243), whereas he himself is later addressed by Margaret as the 'slave of nature and the son of hell' (I, iii, 30).

Critics have been rather too ready to treat this second section of the soliloquy as though it were a modern exploration of the psychological roots of Richard's misanthropic attitude; line 19 ('Cheated of feature by dissembling nature') and Richard's subsequent statements on the reasons for his villainy are interpreted by such psychologically oriented critics somewhat as follows: Richard's physical deformities, which exclude him from the enjoyment of love, cause him to seek compensation in his villainous undertakings; not Richard himself, therefore, but the twisted body foisted upon him by nature, must be held responsible for his criminal behaviour. In fact, however, the main purpose of these lines is to make clear that the leading character *is* a villain, and, moreover, that he freely *chooses* to be a villain ('I am determined to prove a villain' 30).[1] His decision leads inevitably to his tragic end. These lines, then, introduce the theme of guilt and expiation that is to pervade the play. In Shakespeare's main source, Holinshed – More, and in Bacon's *Essay 44*[2] (cited by Wright in his discussion of these lines) an evil disposition is taken to result from a deformed body; but the connection is not seen to be inevitable and does not prohibit the exercise of the free will. These writers do not, then, suggest that a twisted body absolves its owner from the moral responsibility for his evil acts; this is a modern, not an Elizabethan,[3] concept. However appealing modern

---

[1] For a divergent interpretation of *determined* see: D. S. Berkeley, ' "Determined" in *Richard III*, I, i, 30' *SQ*, XIV (1963), pp. 483–484.

[2] 'Deformed persons are commonly even with Nature. For as Nature hath done ill by them; so doe they by Nature: Being for the most part, (as the Scripture saith) *void of Naturall Affection*; And so they have their Revenge of Nature' (*Of Deformity*).

[3] Cf. R. L. Anderson, *Elizabethan Psychology and Shakespeare's Plays*, Univ. of Iowa, Humanistic Studies, III, 4 (1928), pp. 146–147. Cf. also M. C. Bradbrook, *Themes and Conventions of Elizabethan Tragedy* (1935), p. 57: 'Most of the villains are given some kind of defect which embitters them and cuts them off from humanity. This is no justification for their behaviour, for the Elizabethan mind was not accustomed to distinguish between crimes which were the result of choice and those which were the result of heredity.' Cf. also A. Harbage: 'Nearly always the physical trait is also a moral symbol – in extreme cases a stigma like Richard the Third's hump' (*As They Liked It. An*

psychological interpretations of Richard's motivation may be, it is the content of the play itself that proves most helpful in interpreting difficult passages. Thus to view Richard's choice of evil as 'compensation', ignoring both his freedom of will and his subsequent guilt, is to view the play from an alien standpoint – and this notwithstanding the fact that modern psychoanalysis is particularly familiar with the psychological state hinted at by Richard.

If Richard's motives for his villainy fail to convince us that the passage is as Freudian as Freud suggests,[1] they are nevertheless a thoroughly convincing expression of Richard's own character. Just as later he is never at a loss for an explanation, brazenly and cynically justifying each of his crimes in turn, so here at the very outset he finds an apparently logical reason for being what he is.[2]

The last section of the soliloquy (32–40)[3] discloses the speaker's designs in the manner usual for a planning monologue (see below). Richard's methods of intrigue become immediately apparent: instead of openly confronting his enemies, he covertly seeks to

---

Essay on Shakespeare and Morality, 1947, p. 20). Hardin Craig (*An Interpretation of Shakespeare*, 1948, p. 70) mentions in connection with this soliloquy the Platonic doctrine 'a fair soul in a fair body', and its opposite application, 'a crooked and evil soul in a deformed and crooked body'.

[1] Sigmund Freud is one of the many who have commented on this monologue: 'I think, therefore, that Richard's soliloquy does not say everything; it merely gives a hint, and leaves us to fill in what it hints at. When we do so, however, the appearance of frivolity [imparted by Richard's explanation of his motive for doing evil] vanishes, the bitterness and minuteness with which Richard has depicted his deformity make their full effect, and we clearly perceive the fellow feeling which compels our sympathy even with a villain like him. What the soliloquy thus means is: Nature has done me a grievous wrong in denying me the beauty of form which wins human love. Life owes me reparation for this, and I will see that I get it . . . I may do wrong myself, since wrong has been done to me . . .' (S. Freud, *Imago, Zeitschrift für Anwendung der Psychoanalyse auf die Geisteswissenschaften* IV, 6, 1916, p. 320).

[2] Towards the end of *3 Henry VI* Richard makes a similar choice of villainy, and gives the same reason for his attitude:

> 'Then, since the heavens have shap'd my body so,
>   Let hell make crook'd my mind to answer it.' (V, vi, 78 f.)

[3] A change of stress at the beginning of line 32 marks the opening of the new section: 'Plots have I laid . . .'.

divide them and sow dissension among them. His self-portrayal (37) – intended for the audience's ear – and his objective description of King Edward[1] as *true and just* are carefully balanced in intentionally contrasting phrases (*if he be . . . As I am . . .*) so that the self-portrayal is less direct than, for instance, that in Marlowe's *Tamburlaine*. The key-word *hate*, heard twice in this section, frequently recurs later in the play contrasted to *love*.

The soliloquy closes with the traditional address to the speaker's own thoughts, 'Dive, thoughts, down to my soul. Here Clarence comes' – a reminder that Richard's secret thoughts, though revealed to us, must remain unknown to the other characters in the play. In his early plays Shakespeare made frequent use of this obvious and unrealistic device from pre-Shakespearian drama. Equally primitive and unrealistic is the way in which a character mentioned in the dialogue (in this case, Clarence) promptly appears on stage. It is true that in later plays characters continue to appear at precisely the right moment, but the wires by which they are drawn are more decently obscured than in *Richard III*, where the identity of each new arrival is carefully announced ('But who comes here? The new-delivered Hastings?' 121) in phrases which vary little from case to case.[2]

Never again after *Richard III* did Shakespeare choose to open a play in so direct a manner – with a soliloquy in which the hero introduces himself and provides necessary information for the audience. And yet the conventional aspects of this soliloquy[3] are not intrusive. On the contrary, it seems entirely appropriate that Richard, whose experience has been that of isolation and whose personality dominates the play, should step forward on an empty

---

[1] On the villain's self-revelation in his monologues and on his objective assessment of heroic figures, cf. L. L. Schücking, *Character Problems in Shakespeare's Plays* (1959), p. 59 ff.

[2] Cf. I, iii, 17; I, iii, 339; II, i, 45; II, iv, 38; III, i, 24; III, i, 95; III, iv, 22; III, v, 13; III, v, 21; III, vii, 55; III, vii, 82; IV, i, 1; IV, i, 12; IV, ii, 46; IV, ii, 68; IV, iv, 456.

[3] S. L. Bethell has discussed, with reference to this soliloquy, the convention of 'informing the audience' (*Shakespeare and the Popular Dramatic Tradition*, 1944, pp. 71–73). A new interpretation of this matter is given by Nicholas Brooke, 'Reflecting Gems and Dead Bones. Tragedy versus History in *Richard III*', *The Critical Quarterly* VII (1965), p. 129.

stage to address us. Moreover, the image of Richard which emerges from this monologue is in no way blurred by the interwoven factual and expository detail.

Such a subtle and convincing portrait at the very outset of *Richard III* would hardly have been possible without the foundations provided by the careful preliminary sketch in *3 Henry VI*.[1] The audience, who may be assumed to know the earlier plays in the tetralogy, thus re-encounter Richard in an opening soliloquy where traits merely suggested before are now revealed as parts of a sharply defined, fully realized character.

The Pre-Shakespearian Opening Soliloquy

In morality plays and in certain Elizabethan dramas,[2] and even in *Romeo and Juliet*, *2 Henry IV*, and *Henry V*, the prologue was spoken by a figure not taking part in the action itself. Such prologues, by conveying necessary facts and preparing the audience for the opening situation, simplify the otherwise overburdened opening scene. But even in older plays a soliloquy rather than a prologue often opened the proceedings or introduced a new stage in the action;[3] in many other cases (right up to Marlowe's *Faustus* and *The Jew of Malta*) the play begins with both a prologue *and* an opening soliloquy, the soliloquy spoken by one of the characters but designed primarily to convey information. The opening soliloquy also has roots in the naïve self-introductions of characters in medieval drama (*Deus sum*). In some of the earlier pre-Shakespearian comedies – for instance Nicholas Udall's *Ralph Roister Doister* – the opening soliloquy serves to characterize its speaker and to describe other characters. The interludes and farces

---

[1] Cf. in particular *3 Henry VI*, I, ii, 22–34; III, ii, 124–195; V, vi, 61–93. And cf. *2 Henry VI*, V, i, 213–214, 216. Cf. too the characterization in J. Palmer, *Political Characters of Shakespeare* (1945), p. 66 ff., and Hardin Craig, *An Interpretation of Shakespeare* (1948), p. 68 ff. Craig reminds us that there is little in the Richard of *2 Henry VI* to suggest his later character, which took shape in *3 Henry VI*, III, ii. Indeed (as A. Leschtsch has pointed out in *Richard III, eine Charakterstudie*, 1908), the Richard of *Henry VI*, Parts 2 and 3 is in some respects the opposite of the Richard in our play. Certainly the character is not developed along altogether consistent lines.

[2] e.g. *Conflict of Conscience, Locrine, Gismond of Salerne, Battle of Alcazar*.

[3] e.g. Bale, *King John*.

often begin with a monologue in which the speaker introduces himself, provides necessary background material, and discloses future plans.[1] Villains in pre-Shakespearian drama[2] always reveal themselves in a planning-monologue at the outset of the play or at the end of the first scene in which they appear.[3]

Critics have pointed to the long introductory soliloquies spoken by the leading characters in many of Seneca's plays (*Medea, Octavia, Oedipus, Hercules Oetaeus*) as the model for Richard's first soliloquy.[4] It is true that in *Richard III* the device of the Senecan opening soliloquy (also incorporated in English classical drama[5]) has been retained; and, indeed, *Richard III* may be said to belong to the tradition of tragedy rather than to that of the chronicle play, where an opening soliloquy by a leading character was not the rule. But in style and content Richard's soliloquy bears little resemblance to those of Seneca. Richard's cool and objective description of his own state of mind, his appearance, and his present situation is at the same time a complex character study, whereas the tumultuous Senecan outbursts of feeling convey only a general impression of an agitated personality. The Senecan soliloquies occasionally contain factual information on past events and future plans (*Hercul. Fur., Medea*), but such passages remain subordinate to the extended rhetorical outbursts of emotion; moreover, the expository material itself often turns out to be irrelevant, whereas in Richard's monologue every detail has its importance in the light of later events, and the monologue is an actual part of the opening scene, rather than the separate preface found in so many Senecan dramas. Seneca, then, cannot be said to have influenced either the content or the method of composition of Richard's opening monologue.[6]

[1] e.g. *Thersytes, The Play of the Wether, Johan Johan, The Foure PP.*

[2] Cf. C. V. Boyer, *The Villain as Hero in Elizabethan Tragedy* (1914).

[3] *Selimus*, 231 ff.; *Edward II*, 1 ff. For further examples cf. note 3, p. 18. Another example from Shakespeare's early works is York's monologue at the end of I, i in *2 Henry VI*. Cf. M. C. Bradbrook, *Themes and Conventions of Elizabethan Tragedy* (1935), p. 115.

[4] Cf. Hardin Craig, 'Shakespeare and the History Play', *Joseph Quincy Adams Memorial Studies* (1948), p. 57 f.

[5] e.g. *Gismond of Salerne; Misfortunes of Arthur.*

[6] Howard Baker (*Induction to Tragedy*, 1939) discusses the overestimate of Senecan influence on pre-Shakespearian drama.

There are also important differences between Marlowe's and Shakespeare's treatment of the opening soliloquy. Thus Guise in his opening speech in Marlowe's *The Massacre at Paris* puts all his cards on the table (whereas Richard only partly reveals his dark designs). But save for one quality – ambition – Guise remains a hazy figure; his soliloquy abounds in abstract reflection, in contrast to Shakespeare's concrete portrayal of a human situation.

Barabas's opening speech in Marlowe's *The Jew of Malta* is, on the other hand, an unusually vivid, if less pure, example of the monologue of self-introduction. Barabas is portrayed, not through the primitive method of self-description, but dramatically through his actions: counting his money, looking over his treasures, watching his weathervane and thinking of his argosies. The world in which he lives and the values by which he lives are thus depicted with economy and verve. There is none of the usual dull recounting of related material. The language[1] is fully as dramatic and vigorous as that of Richard's soliloquy – indeed the mid-phrase opening is more dramatic than Richard's studied and prologue-like lines. The monologue possesses a dramatic intensity and, in some respects, a modernity greater than that of Richard's more formal utterance.

Marlowe's 47 lines (which in fact put before us a short counting-house scene) all treat the same theme—the world of Barabas; Shakespeare's 41 lines, on the other hand, cover a much wider field – the political situation at court with its emotional overtones, Richard's personality in relation to this background, and his plans and intentions. Richard's soliloquy thus prepares for and is carefully linked to future events, whereas that of Barabas lacks any such precise connections; Marlowe is carried forward by his own sonorous and richly allusive diction.

Dialogue-Technique in the Episodes with Clarence and Hastings (42–116; 122–144)

Richard's two victims-to-be meet their future murderer in the central section of the first scene. In pre-Shakespearian drama,

[1] Cf. F. P. Wilson's discussion of it in his *Marlowe and the Early Shakespeare* (1953), p. 58 ff.

c

whenever friend and foe, victim and murderer met, something happened, the action moved forward. Even when one party was, as in the present case, less than honest with his opponents (*The Spanish Tragedy*, *The Jew of Malta*, *The Massacre at Paris*), more seemed to happen than here – something was arranged or planned, emotions were aroused, arguments developed. But Richard's victims have no idea of Richard's perfidious nature; everything, therefore, goes on below the surface. On the face of it, this is no more than a casual exchange of remarks; and that, moreover, is all that Clarence and Hastings are conscious of.

This new technique of suggestive (rather than explicit) dialogue had been foreshadowed in the plays of Kyd, where something happening on the stage, the significance of which was clear to the audience, might be understood by only some of the participants. Moreover, comedy had fully exploited the fact that a speaker may intend something quite different from what his partner understands him to mean; Lyly's characters, for instance, are masterful practitioners of dissimulation, ambiguity, and verbal trickery. Serious drama, however, had (with the exception of Kyd) made little use of these possibilities. In *Richard III* Shakespeare introduces this game of understanding and not-understanding into his histories and tragedies, with a resultant heightening of dramatic tension.

This new, subtler form of dialogue, evident in I, i and perfected in I, ii, makes it possible for Richard to retain the conversational lead while seeming to pose only harmless questions, the answers to which allow him to put forward certain malicious suppositions designed to arouse suspicion against a third party in the mind of the hearer. Thus he leads the others along without their noticing it. In his conversation with Clarence, for instance, Richard sympathetically questions his brother about the cause of his present unhappy situation, and, upon hearing that the King has ordered Clarence's imprisonment, confirms with seeming casualness ('Why, this it is, when men are rul'd by women', 62) Clarence's hatred and suspicion of the Queen. (Cf. also l. 130 f.)

But Richard, for all his subtle and careful cunning, sometimes throws overboard his hypocritical rôle of sympathetic, helpful friend and gives free reign to a brazen impudence which is a measure not so much of his recklessness as of an unending self-assurance and certainty of success. Thus, while ostensibly seeking to convince Brakenbury of the unobjectionable nature of his conversation with Clarence, Richard breaks into cynical, ironic praise of the King and Queen, and also of the physical charms of the King's mistress, then goes on (with a pun on *nought*) to further ambiguous and ironic remarks on Mistress Shore and her behaviour.[1] Such transparent yet at the same time uncompromising innuendos are among Richard's favourite conversational devices. In the same way he contrives to insult the King and Queen with a single, well-chosen word (*o'erworn widow* 81; *abjects* 106; *King Edward's widow* 109). To Brakenbury he presents an ironically distorted account of what he and his brother have just been saying, using some of the same words in a different context. Instead of 'the jealous o'erworn widow' (81), what Brakenbury hears is 'his noble queen, well struck in years, fair, and *not jealous*' (91 f.) and for: 'since that our brother dubb'd them *gentlewomen*' (82), we now have: 'the Queen's kindred are made gentlefolks' (95). Furthermore, his audience would have been familiar with the word *dubb'd* (cf. *OED*) in an obscene sense.

Forms of Irony in I, i

These ironic allusions, distortions, and echoes may be classed together as 'overt irony',[2] in that they are understood by at least one of the other characters on the stage. But Richard is also master of *implicit irony*, which is only understood by himself and the audience, not by his stage partner. Thus, after Clarence has made clear the absurdity of his arrest ('Because my name is George'), Richard takes up the theme and seems on the surface to be ironically stressing the flimsiness of this pretext still further;

---

[1] Since King Edward's mistress, Jane Shore, has no direct bearing on Richard, she is only referred to in this play, whereas she takes an important part in *The True Tragedy*.

[2] For the following remarks on irony the author is indebted to Hermann Fischer. See also general observations on dramatic irony in G. Sedgewick, *Of Irony Especially in Drama* (1948), and A. R. Thompson, *The Dry Mock* (1948).

but he is at the same time reminding the audience of his own plans for getting rid of Clarence:

> O, belike his Majesty hath some intent
> That you should be new-christ'ned in the Tower.
>
> (49–50)

These words conceal yet another irony of which Richard is unconscious; for they reminded the audience of the well-known tradition by which Clarence was drowned 'in a butte of Malmesey' [1]. The following examples also hide some 'ironic truth'; speaking to Clarence, Richard says:

> 'Tis not the King that sends you to the Tower;
>
> (63)

> . . . this deep disgrace in brotherhood
> Touches me deeper than you can imagine.
>
> (111–12)

> I will deliver you, or else lie for you.
>
> (115)

and

> We are not safe, Clarence; we are not safe.
>
> (70)

Besides the irony intended by Richard, this last remark also contains an element of tragic irony emphasized by Clarence's rejoinder, 'there is no man is secure' (71); for Richard, fated to fall in the end, feels himself as safe as do his victims. Clarence's words are an unconscious comment on all the destinies unfolded in this drama.

The short soliloquy separating the two encounters reinforces the hypocritical irony of Richard's attitude to his brother. But here, as in the opening soliloquy, Richard's irony is also directed against himself, as with wry cynicism he refers to his murderous intentions:

---

[1] Cf. J.D.W., *Introduction*, p. xxvi.

> Simple, plain Clarence, I do love thee so
> That I will shortly send thy soul to heaven,
> If heaven will take the present at our hands.
>
> (118–120)

This same cynical tone marks the passages in the concluding soliloquy, where Richard ironically describes his own future rôle in the murderous game. We might also note in connection with *simple, plain Clarence* the ironic effect, in this scene, of the manner in which people are addressed,[1] as, for instance, in the decreasing degree of reverence in Richard's names for Brakenbury (*Your worship, Brakenbury* 88; *man* 90; *fellow* 98; *knave* 102).

In *Richard III* the irony is by no means exclusively verbal: *situations* as well as words contain irony, and these situations may be ironic because of what has preceded them, or ironic in themselves. Within the first scene, for example, Richard's rôle of zealous advocate and affectionate brother contrasts ironically with his earlier disclosure of his intrigues against Clarence (32 ff.). Moreover, Richard's scornful references to lovers' antics in his opening monologue lead up to an effective ironic contrast in the next scene, where he emerges as a master of amatory strategy.

Richard is provided with the ideal foil for his irony in the person of Hastings, who, with his naïve confidence in his own security and his trust in Richard's kind intentions, provokes Richard to covert mockery. Hastings, when he says

> But I shall live, my lord, to give them thanks
> That were the cause of my imprisonment.
>
> (127)

does not, of course, intend to thank his enemies. But his intentional irony (*give them thanks*) is engulfed in a deeper stratum of tragic irony by Richard's ambiguous 'No doubt, no doubt; and so shall Clarence too' (129). Richard, linking the two men together, pretends to believe in a free future for both; but he has already decided that both must die.

---

[1] See the chapter on I, ii, under 'The Address as a Means of Irony', for a list of such ironic forms.

There is a fundamental affinity between Richard's rational-intellectual nature – surely one of the factors determining the whole tenor of the play – and the quality of irony with its shrewd underlining of allusive links, its cunning dialectic, and its often calculated subtleties. The contrasts between 'appearance and reality' [1] in which the play abounds have their counterpart in the many forms of irony permeating the play.

The Language of the Dialogue

The range of Richard's tone, including subtle irony, cynical suggestiveness, outright slander, and feigned brotherly affection, calls for a flexible verbal style, far removed from the dignified formality of Senecan tragedy;[2] whole passages dispense with rhetorical ornament and symmetrical design. Indeed, in the dialogue between Richard and Clarence we have something approaching a conversational tone: colloquial everyday phrases have replaced conventional declamation; and frequent parenthetical and confirmatory statements, interpolated questions and words of address give the language a particular sprightliness.[3]

[1] For a general study of the 'appearance and reality' theme in Shakespeare, cf. W. Clemen, *Schein und Sein bei Shakespeare*, Sitzungsberichte d. Bayer. Akad. d. Wissensch. (1959).

[2] On this stylistic transition, cf. Hardin Craig, 'Shakespeare and the History Play', p. 56; F. E. Halliday, *The Poetry of Shakespeare's Plays* (1954), p. 59.

[3] Cf. 'Yea, Richard, when I know' 52; 'Why, this it is . . .' 62; 'By heaven, I think . . .' 71; 'I'll tell you what –' 78; 'Even so' 88; 'We speak no treason. man; we say . . .' 90; 'How say you, sir?' 96; 'I tell thee, fellow, . . .' 98, And from the dialogue with Hastings, cf. 'No doubt, no doubt' 129; 'What news abroad?' 134; 'Now, by Saint John,' 138; 'Where is he? In his bed?' 142. The peculiar conditions governing the text of *Richard III* make it possible that some of the colloquialisms that occur throughout the play are in fact accidental and are actors' interpolations; for these are characteristic of the 'memorially contaminated text' of the *First Quarto* and were presumably not all eliminated in the *First Folio*. 'Many of these interpolations (interjections, connections, tags of one kind and another) were eliminated, but some may have survived' (A. Walker, *Textual Problems of the First Folio*, 1953, p. 27). Yet even if we accept this explanation for some of the colloquialisms, there still remains a large number which certainly derive from Shakespeare's own hand and which are clearly appropriate, both metrically and stylistically, in their particular contexts.

Strangely enough, rhyme as it is used in the dialogue, does not conflict with the informal tone. The rhyme in

> Humbly complaining to her deity
> Got my Lord Chamberlain his liberty.
> (76–77)

makes even more striking the ironically casual and disparaging tone with which Richard refers to Hastings. In other passages the rhyme obviously serves to emphasize some particular circumstance and imprint it on the memory (and this is especially true where the rhyme is repeated in later passages with a similar content). When Richard tells us of the prophecy which he is later to make use of to destroy his brother, the rhymes are the same[1] as those we hear sixteen lines later from Clarence, who describes in lengthier form the same prophecy (39–40 *G–he*; 55–59 *G–G–he–G–he*).

The dialogue is also varied by alternation of line lengths and changes of tempo – the tempo slackening as the speaker arrives at some detailed description or enumeration and gathering speed immediately after. The lines preceding and following the detailed listing often contain a large proportion of monosyllabic words, inviting a rapid delivery; the resulting directness and conciseness is close to that of real conversation:

> We say that Shore's wife hath a pretty foot,
> A cherry lip, a bonny eye, a passing pleasing tongue;
> And that the Queen's kindred are made gentlefolks.
> How say you, sir? Can you deny all this?   (93–96)

The relish with which Richard dwells on the description of Mistress Shore (the second line exceeds the normal pentameter by a couple of feet) contrasts with the sharper, more angular rhythm of the third line;[2] the last line with its two rapidly ejaculated questions

---

[1] J.D.W. has pointed out that the prophecy here has the same rhyme as it had had in the *Mirror for Magistrates* (*Clarence*, 181–186) (J.D.W., p. xxv).

[2] Cf. E. Guest, *History of English Rhythms* (1838), p. 272 (*Var.*). At line 95 J.D.W. reads *Kin* for *Kindred* (F, *Q*), taking *Kindred* to be an error echoing line 72. This reading would do away with the metrical irregularity. For the remarks on metre the author is indebted to Thomas Finkenstaedt.

leads naturally into the ambiguous exchange between Richard and Brakenbury. Another instance of a sudden change in tempo occurs when Richard in his dialogue with Hastings almost upsets the flow of the blank verse with his abrupt yet purposive questions which betray to the audience the real direction of his concerns ('What news abroad?' 134; 'Where is he? In his bed?' 142).

Richard's ability to modulate the language, to change key and mode of expression, is shown to be an important component in his many-sided makeup;[1] for on this mastery of language and gesture, which he practises with a secret, spiteful zest, with, indeed, a thoroughgoing enjoyment,[2] depends his success in mastering others.

Richard's Soliloquies (117–121; 145–162)

The two soliloquies preceding and following Richard's dialogue with Hastings supply a commentary on his real plans for the victims he has just been duping. Kyd, Peele, and Greene all wrote soliloquies designed to reveal the villain's designs, but their soliloquies made little attempt to depict his character.[3] In the present play, however, the soliloquies reveal not only Richard's plans, but his nature as well: the amused contempt in his exclamation *Simple, plain Clarence*, the sarcasm in his declared intention of 'sending' his victim's 'soul to heaven' (118–120; 146), especially the flippancy of *Till George be pack'd with posthorse up to heaven* (146), all point to an ice-cold immorality. Equally characteristic are his mocking, even blasphemous references to heaven and God both here (120, 151 f.) and throughout the play, and his use of the verb *to bustle* (152) to describe his own projected activities on earth. Even the way in which Richard announces his intention of marrying *the wench* Anne[4] tells us something about the sort of man he is. The rhetorical device of repeating a particular phrase, made use

[1] The first scene thereby refutes the familiar contention that in *Richard III* the style is stiff and rhetorical throughout.
[2] J.D.W. points out that this characteristic is not derived from the source.
[3] Cf. *Edward I*, v, 180–190; vii, 66–99; *Spanish Tragedy*, III, ii, 208–227; III, iv, 310–321; 349–359; *James IV*, 2078 ff.; *Orlando Furioso*, 249–272; *Battle of Alcazar*, II, i, 451 ff., 489 ff.
[4] Line 157 'not all so much for love' also prepares us for the next scene.

of by Richard in the final soliloquy (*her husband and her father* 154, 156), expresses both a love for cynical paradox and an almost unbelievable callousness. And finally, the closing lines of the soliloquy suggest another facet of Richard's flawed nature –

> But yet I run before my horse to market.
> Clarence still breathes; Edward still lives and reigns;
> When they are gone, then must I count my gains.   (160–162)

The jargon of trade in these lines reveals a cautious, calculating streak in Richard, which protects him from the rashness of reacting merely emotionally.

The *secret close intent* (158) which Richard mentions as his real reason for seeking to marry Anne is usually thought to refer to the crown;[1] but this interpretation has justifiably been called in question,[2] for the marriage with Anne, even though it allies Richard with the Lancastrians, hardly seems a direct way of fulfilling such an ambition.[3] Somewhat more convincing seems the explanation that through this marriage Richard might hope to gain custody of Clarence's two children, then in Anne's charge.[4] Richard's *secret close intent* may, however, have been left obscure on purpose: it may have been placed there with the sole purpose of suggesting that the wooing-scene which follows is related to Richard's rise to power, although exactly *how* the scene advances Richard's career might be hard to define: 'Thus Shakespeare palms off on the audience a highly effective scene which "does not advance the action, i.e. the career of Richard, in the least".' [5]

The concluding soliloquy is concerned less with character-portrayal than with plot: it arouses expectations and places the encounters with Clarence and Hastings, as well as the news of the King's illness, in the context of a more exactly defined future. To close a scene with a planning-monologue leading over into the

[1] Wright; *Warwick*.
[2] H. Spencer; H. N. Hudson (*School Shakespeare*). – In *3 Henry VI* Richard openly declares that he aspires to the crown. It seems unlikely that he would choose to disguise the same aim here.
[3] Cf. also Wright (*Var.*).
[4] H. Spencer; Warner (*Var.*).
[5] J. D. Wilson, quoting Herford (J.D.W., p. 173).

next scene was, in any case, a popular dramatic convention of the time.[1]

Exposition within the Scene

The prologues or opening scenes of pre-Shakespearian chronicle plays and popular dramas,[2] and in particular of plays on the Senecan model, had tended to be weighed down with a mass of factual background material. Similarly, in the three parts of *Henry VI* we tend to lose our way in a jungle of data. In *Richard III*, on the other hand, the background information is kept to a necessary minimum and is distributed over the whole of the first act. Only gradually do we learn about the past with its complicated family feuds, about the political state of affairs, about the intrigues at court.

This gradual introduction of background material has one great advantage: from the very outset our attention is fixed on the true focal point of the play – the character of Richard.

And indeed it is Richard's character that determines the whole exposition; information about what is going to happen comes only *after* Richard's initial self-revelation. Yet this exposition of plot is unobtrusive, so that we are scarcely aware of how many different things we have learned in the first scene. Besides what we hear about the characters who actually appear on the stage – Richard, Clarence, and Hastings – we learn much about King Edward, the Queen and her faction, and the situation at court.

In *Richard III*, then, the exposition is woven into the body of the play, and not conveyed, as in most earlier plays, through some expository device such as a prologue, a dumb-show, or the utterances of a ghost. When, in classical drama, such information was contained within the play it was usually in a monologue, whereas popular drama frequently used dialogue for this purpose.[3] Marlowe was the first to use a combination of soliloquy and dialogue for purposes of exposition. His *Jew of Malta* opens with

---

[1] Cf. e.g. *The Spanish Tragedy*.

[2] Cf. W. Clemen, *English Tragedy before Shakespeare* (1961), passim.

[3] e.g. *Edward I*, *Friar Bacon and Friar Bungay*, *Woodstock*, *Troublesome Reign of King John*.

an expository soliloquy[1] by the chief character, followed by short
passages of dialogue which supplement the exposition of character in the soliloquy by adding information about the current
situation. The pattern (both in *The Jew of Malta* and in *Edward II*)
is the same as in *Richard III*: monologue – dialogue with secondary
characters – a long aside amounting to a monologue – further
dialogue – concluding monologue. But in both of these Marlowe
plays the secondary characters are nameless figures indistin-
guishable one from the other and of no importance in the play.
Clarence and Hastings, however, far from being mere receivers
and conveyers of information, play an important part in the
events with which the play is concerned.

Moreover, in Marlowe's plays the connection between the
monologue (with character-portrayal as its central concern) and
the dialogue (centring on plot and background) is much less close
than in *Richard III*. Finally, both in Richard's monologues and in
the dialogue the details are 'purposive', they will be taken up
again later and are related to future happenings;[2] plans and anticipations are in the course of the play translated into actualities.
Marlowe's plays, however, are not nearly as close-knit. The plans
which his heroes unfold in their opening soliloquies are less
detailed, less revealing of the future. What Marlowe's heroes
strive for (and, in particular, Tamburlaine and Faustus) is something eternal, universal – indeed, beyond their reach. Marlowe's
heroes are less concerned with a particular goal than with the
exercise of will itself,[3] and Marlowe's exposition reflects this fact;
it is less tightly constructed, less purposeful, than is Shakespeare's
in the opening scene of *Richard III*; here, with unprecedented
economy and richness of relevant detail, the groundwork is laid
for all that is to come.

[1] But the soliloquy is, in deference to the earlier tradition, preceded by a
prologue spoken by Machiavelli.
[2] Cf. p. 65.
[3] Cf. Una Ellis-Fermor, *Christopher Marlowe* (1927), passim.

SCENE TWO

This second scene, a fully developed episode complete in itself, opens with a soliloquy by Anne, but it is nevertheless dominated by the figure of Richard. Anne is for Richard a mere object, and not a real 'antagonist'. Her function in the scene is largely that of revealing Richard's character. Moreover, the scene, which lacks any basis in the source, is curiously unrelated to the main action of the play,[1] for Anne and the marriage for which Richard strives are of very little importance later on. We may well ask why Shakespeare, otherwise so faithful to his source, placed this particular scene – a scene of great dramatic and psychological daring, even in an age which was used to seeing extraordinary events enacted on the stage – at the outset of his play.

Part of the answer may lie in the fact that here, before the action of the play is fairly under way, Shakespeare shows Richard in a situation displaying not only the intellectual superiority of the hero but also his mysterious personal fascination. The audience is likely to feel that the man who can bring off a venture as fantastic as this one can surely accomplish anything.[2] Moreover, his triumph is not achieved through violence or intrigue, but simply by virtue of a compelling personality, a power to charm. His ability to control and corrupt the minds of others is thus displayed before the action of the play itself shows him as a brutal murderer, a Machiavellian intriguer. The scene opens, admittedly, with a reminder that he *is* a murderer; the corpse of Henry VI is borne in, and against this mute background the persuasion-scene unfolds. But violence is only a background here:[3] what Shakespeare is

---

[1] This lack of a link with the main action has led many critics to suggest that the scene is of later origin than the wooing-scene with Elizabeth (III, iv) and had been inserted into the plot at some subsequent stage. For a comparison of the two wooing-scenes cf. L. L. Schücking, 'Über einige Nachbesserungen bei Shakespeare', *Berichte über die Verhandlungen d. Sächs. Akad. d. Wiss. zu Leipzig*, Phil.-hist. Klasse, vol. 95 (1943), I, p. 24 ff.

[2] Cf. also H. B. Charlton, *Shakespearian Tragedy* (1949), p. 26.

[3] Not, however, simply because of the influence of Senecan drama or in

concentrating on is not violence itself but what led up to it and what follows from it. Thus the 'tragedy of blood' has undergone a considerable modification.

The whole incredible conversion, brought about in mere minutes under wellnigh impossible conditions, is in keeping with the taste for sudden violent changes and sensational contrasts that characterizes the Elizabethan theatre. Indeed, this highly theatrical quality serves to mask and neutralize the psychological improbabilities of the scene. Given a good performance, we are convinced, and only when the scene is read or subsequently analysed does it seem illogical.[1] We should not conclude, however, that Shakespeare's dramatic skill masked a primitive psychology. This scene manages, in fact, to blend rare psychological insight with other elements which are conventional or merely theatrical.

A heightened tension distinguishes the scene from the preceding one. Richard's dissimulation, his skill in handling his partner, and the cynicism with which he observes himself in action – these traits were present in I, i; but here the emotional pitch has risen considerably and the tension mounts.

Like I, i, the present scene is bounded by two soliloquies:[2] the opening monologue of Anne and the concluding speech of Richard in which, as in the speech closing the first scene, he enlarges upon his own rôle and announces his future plans. We have, then, the same rhythm as before: first we see Richard the dissembler, then Richard as he in fact is; first we have a high-flown, stylized diction, then the freer speech of the ensuing dialogue.

---

obedience to the classical convention whereby acts of vengeance were performed *off* stage. Clarence, for instance, is murdered *on* stage. Cf. W. Clemen, 'Tradition and Originality in Shakespeare's *Richard III*' *SQ*, V (1954), pp. 247–257.

[1] This has been commented upon especially by E. E. Stoll in his various publications. The opinions of other critics on this scene have, however, varied widely: Coleridge and others denied that it was by Shakespeare at all; but Charles Lamb praised the genius for persuasion with which Shakespeare imbued his hero.

[2] The first act contains six out of a total of ten monologues in the play.

Anne's Soliloquy (1-32)

Unlike Richard's opening monologue this soliloquy is linked with
a 'spectacle',[1] a solemn funeral procession with the King's corpse
– the same sort of procession, in fact, with which *1 Henry VI* had
begun (*Dead March. Enter the funeral of King Henry the Fifth*). Such
Shakespearian spectacles carry a symbolic significance. Here, the
open coffin containing the King's corpse plays an intrinsic part in
the scene: not only does the dead man cast a deep shadow on
what is to follow, but his presence is felt throughout, reminding us
of the preposterous and paradoxical nature of the situation. The
spectacle has, in fact, become a symbol. Anne's lament too, unlike
so many pre-Shakespearian speeches of this kind, refers to what is
actually going on at the time. But while Richard's first soliloquy
bore the stamp of his personality, Anne's is impersonal, telling us
little about herself. Her speech shows the influence of the conventional set speech of lament in earlier drama;[2] its ritualistic and
formal qualities are evident, for instance, in the elevated rhetoric
of the second line – a conditional clause added in parenthesis, the
word *honour* taking up the *honourable* of the line before. Expressions
such as *shrouded, hearse, obsequiously, untimely fall, virtuous Lancaster*
belong to the language of the formal elegy, and the three lines of
address that follow do so still more, with their similar pattern and
careful balance. Anne's identification of herself ('poor Anne,
wife to thy Edward') bears the stamp of the conventional lament
in which the speaker describes and at the same time observes
himself.[3] But the apostrophes (always a traditional part of the
lament), instead of being addressed to Fortuna or Heaven or some

[1] Such 'spectacles' were frequent on the Elizabethan stage. Cf. for instance
Wounds of Civil War, V, i; *2 Tamburlaine*, III, ii; *The First Part of Hieronimo*,
III, iii; *Massacre at Paris*, 1252. Cf. also A. S. Venezky, *Pageantry on the
Shakespearean Stage* (1951), p. 21; Th. Spencer, *Death and Elizabethan Tragedy*
(1936), p. 184; A. I. P. Wood, *The Stage History of Shakespeare's King Richard
the Third* (1909), p. 31.
[2] Cf. W. Clemen, 'The Dramatic Lament and Its Forms' in *English Tragedy
before Shakespeare*, p. 211 ff.
[3] 'The characters are always dramatizing themselves and their situations'
(M. C. Bradbrook, *Themes and Conventions of Elizabethan Tragedy*, 1935, p. 120).
For examples of self-description in particular, cf. l. 9 f. and l. 12 'Lo, . . .'.

other supra-human power, are to the dead man himself; thus the
lament is kept from extending, as it so often did, beyond the
situation of the moment. The next two lines (12–13), although
they contain elaborate paraphrase and antithesis, show this same
tendency to restrict the limits of their reference.

Now Richard himself becomes the subject of Anne's monologue; her curse against the 'self-same hand that made these
wounds' provides a natural transition to her outburst against the
dead King's murderer and prepares us for Richard's reappearance.

In pre-Shakespearian drama (and particularly in Senecan drama),
lament and imprecation were often joined in one speech, the two
themes receiving parallel but separate treatment. The movement
from lament to imprecation was far less skilfully handled than
in this scene, and the traditional phrases often lacked any connection with the precipitating circumstances.[1] Thus in Marlowe's
Tamburlaine, the frequent curses are inadequately motivated and
swell to the proportions of independent tirades.

In Anne's speech, however, we are not for a moment allowed to
forget the hero. The three words *hand*, *heart*, and *blood* draw attention to Richard as murderer – and *blood* in particular is a key-word
that recurs throughout the play. In a similar manner the names of
animals – 'adders,[2] spiders, toads, Or any creeping venom'd thing
that lives!' – anticipates a series of animal images later to be
applied to Richard himself.

Poison and *venom*, too, will be repeatedly associated with him.[3]
The curse against any child he may father (21–25) directs our
attention to Richard's own warped body; his deformity is to
descend to his offspring. (The theme of the deformed offspring –

---

[1] Cf. e.g. *Selimus*, 1802–1806:

> Bajazet: Leaue weeping *Aga*, we haue wept inough,
>   Now Baiazet will ban another while,
>   And vtter curses to the concaue skie,
>   Which may infect the regions of the ayre,
>   And bring a generall plague on all the world . . .

Cf. also *Selimus*, 1314 ff.

[2] *adders*: Q., Camb., Al.; *wolves*: F. and J.D.W., who notes that in the
Mirror, Richard is called a *wolf*. L. 20 'Or any creeping venom'd thing' would
in the latter case refer only to *spiders* and *toads*, and not to *wolves*.

[3] Cf. I, ii, 146, 147; I, iii, 291; III, i, 14; IV, i, 62.

with reference to Richard himself – is touched on again in I, iii, 229 ff.) Finally, Anne's curse against Richard's future wife (26 ff.) bears poignantly upon both the present and the future; for she is in fact cursing herself. That her curse is later fulfilled in a way she little dreams of exemplifies Shakespeare's tragic and prophetic use of irony – rare in pre-Shakespearian drama and never so deliberately employed. At the same time these lines refer back to I, i, 153–156, which had foreshadowed the action of this second scene and which the audience may well recall, especially when Anne exclaims: 'If ever he have wife.' [1]

The last four lines, addressed again to the bearers of the coffin, recall the opening lines of the soliloquy, and thereby connect the speech once more to what we see happening (the corpse being carried by) and, through the references to real place names and events, to actual historical matters. The scene has, as we know, no source in history; but several details – the removal of the corpse to Chertsey Abbey and the brief rest at St Paul's – are in fact noted by Holinshed. The soliloquy of lament, then, is no longer simply an interpolation as in earlier tragedy, but has become an integrated part of the texture of the play.

[33 ff.] The verbal interchange between Anne and Richard is preceded by a clash between Richard and the men with the corpse (Richard attempting to obstruct their progress). The manner of Richard's entry into the scene and into Anne's affairs reveals a new facet of his character: he is imperious, overbearing, no longer the jovial flatterer of the first scene. And in fact, an examination of Richard's various entries helps throw light on the different sides

---

[1] Anne's wish that Richard's future wife be made miserable by his *death* makes no sense (*Qq* 1–6, 'As miserable by the death of him'; *F*, adopted by Alexander, 'More miserable by the death of him'). Nor does the following line (28), in which she names her husband as well as Richard as the cause of her misery. As J.D.W. points out, 'Any wife of such a monster would be happy, not miserable, at his death, while it is not Prince Edward and King Henry who make Anne miserable but *their* death.' J.D.W.'s conjectured *life* for *death* (27) and his 'Than I am by my young lord's death and thee!' (28) (based on IV, i, 76–77) seem convincing. The illogicality of the existing texts may result from a psychologically explicable printer's error: the conventional assumption that a wife is miserable at her husband's death – appropriate to a lament – may have been unwittingly introduced by the printer.

of his character. Richard storms in like this again at I, iii, 42,
IV, iv, 136, 148, and V, iv, 7; in other scenes his entry is suave and
diplomatic.

Richard's behaviour during this episode with the halberdier
contrasts effectively with his behaviour towards his brother in
I, i, and, immediately afterwards, towards Anne. Contrast is, of
course, a favourite technique of dramatic construction, and plays a
rôle in the language of the scene as well: Anne's soliloquy
is strikingly different from the subsequent exchanges between
Richard, Anne, and the halberdier. Anne's rhythmic, stately: 'Set
down, set down', that had ushered in the lament, is entirely different from Richard's peremptory: 'and set it down' (33) and 'Villains,
set down the corse' (36); with her agitated question: 'What, do
you tremble? Are you all afraid?' (43) Anne, too, forsakes her
earlier tone of speech.

The Address as a Means of Irony

In Shakespeare's hands the address becomes a sensitive index of
the changing relationships between one character and another.
Often the various forms of address convey a subtle irony:[1] the
contemptuous names Richard uses in addressing the procession
guards, for instance, contrast with his flattering words when he
then speaks to Anne (*villains* 36; *unmanner'd dog* 39; *beggar* 42; – *sweet
saint* 49; *lady* 68; *sweet lady* 149; *fair creature* 132); and these in turn
are very unlike the epithets which Anne hurls at him (*thou dreadful
minister of hell* 46; *foul devil* 50; *thou lump of foul deformity* 57; *villain*
70; *hedgehog* 102; *homicide* 125).[2] These speeches also contain a
differentiated use of *thou*, *thy*, *you*, and *your*. When he speaks to
Anne, Richard usually chooses *you* and *your*, which Shakespeare
and the Elizabethans generally regarded as the more polite,

---

[1] In order to avoid a scene-by-scene discussion of the ironic use of address,
here is a list of the most significant instances from later scenes: II, 1, 46 ff.;
II, ii, 101, 151; III, i, 1–2, 18, 102, 113; III, ii. 35; III, vii, 227, 247; IV, i, 5–6;
IV, iii, 24, 28; IV, iv, 412, 431. In the present scene, cf. the following instances of address in addition to those mentioned in the text: 75, 78, 81, 83,
114, 138, 172, 184.

[2] Speaking of the style of *Richard III*, E. K. Chambers comments 'There
is much violent and vituperative speech' (*William Shakespeare* I, 1930, p. 302).

D

reserved form of address. Anne, up to the moment of her 'conversion', employs the more impassioned and emotional *thou* and *thy* to express her contempt and loathing.[1] Such pointed use of address is far more common in *Richard III* than in the later works.

The variety of names applied to a particular character in the course of the play builds up a compound picture of that character (a technique which Shakespeare later employed extensively in *Antony and Cleopatra*[2]). A stage in the construction of such a multi-faceted image can be observed in I, ii. Anne begins by calling Richard a fiend; she then curses him and calls down God's vengeance upon him.[3] All this contrasts sharply with the successful ending of the wooing-scene. At the same time her epithets stress those demoniac qualities which enable Richard to accomplish a feat beyond normal powers of persuasion. The appellation *thou dreadful minister of hell* will take on further significance in the interpretation which sees Richard as an instrument of Divine Justice (see p. 52).

Anne's Speech of Imprecation (50–67)

This speech of Anne's is an extension of her monologue of lament and imprecation. There, and in set forms, she had arraigned an absent enemy; here she curses him to his face, and the murdered King's wounds begin to bleed afresh as if to reinforce her words. Her five-fold reiteration of the word *blood* fixes our attention on the bleeding corpse on the stage and foreshadows the violence which is to come.

The opening invocation to God to avenge the King's death is no empty formula; it introduces the idea of 'Divine Vengeance'

---

[1] For distinctions in usage between *thou* and *you*, cf. Sister St Geraldine Byrne, *Shakespeare's Use of the Pronoun of Address, its Significance in Characterization and Motivation* (1936). On *Richard III*, see pp. 26–31. A recent German investigation of the subject is by Th. Finkenstaedt, *You and Thou. Studien zur Anrede im Englischen* (Quellen und Forschungen zur Sprach- und Kulturgeschichte der Germanischen Völker N.F. 10), 1963.

[2] Cf. W. Clemen, *The Development of Shakespeare's Imagery* (1951), p. 167.

[3] Cf. the echoes of Biblical phrases noted by Noble in connection with lines 47–48 (Matt. x, 28); 63 (Gen. iv. 11); 45 (Ps. cvi. 17); 106–110 (Luke ix. 62) (R. Noble, *Shakespeare's Biblical Knowledge*, 1935, p. 131).

which pervades the play.[1] But the prayer addressed to the earth
(63) and especially the demand: 'Or, earth, gape open wide'
correspond to a conventional formula common in pre-Shakespearian drama and derive from Seneca's 'Dehisce, tellus' (*Oed.*
868).[2] Similarly, the invoking of heaven and earth together in a
speech of lament and imprecation was another convention much
used in plays on the Senecan model (cf., for instance, *The Spanish
Tragedy* II, v, 331 ff.). Shakespeare adopts it here, but links it with
the events of the play, and in particular with Richard, the murderer of the King (66–67).

Anne's acquiescence following the dialogue between herself and
Richard is bound to seem psychologically implausible according
to modern standards, and critics have regarded the scene as no
more than a brilliant bout of verbal fencing. But within a psychologically improbable framework Shakespeare has succeeded in
achieving an effect both dramatically skilful and even humanly
convincing. How, in a scene that opens with Anne's curses and
vengeful cries and ends in her: 'with all my heart' and half-
acquiescent 'farewell', is this change of feeling brought about? In
the first place, Richard's wooing of Anne does not follow directly
upon her outcry against him. The past must first be clarified
through an exchange of accusation and defence, allowing us to
view Richard's character not only, as in I, i, through his own
words, but in the light of the spectacle and of Anne's lament.
And so both sides have their say, Anne accusing and Richard
defending; only then does Richard proceed with his wooing.
Thus the dialogue fulfils several functions: it points to the future[3]

---

[1] Cf. Sister Mary Bonaventura Mroz, *Divine Vengeance: A Study in the
Philosophical Backgrounds of the Revenge Motif as it Appears in Shakespeare's
Chronicle History Plays*, 1941 (esp. ch. II). Lily B. Campbell, 'Theories of
Revenge in Renaissance England' *MP*, XXVIII (1931).

[2] Cf. e.g. *1 Tamburlaine*, 2023 'Gape earth, . . .'; *Edward I*, 2448: 'Gape
earth'; *Spanish Tragedy*, II, v, 333; *Gorboduc*, IV, i, 11 ff.; *David and Bethsabe*
1497 'Ope earth, . . .'; Kyd, *Cornelia*, V, 39 'O earth, why op'st thou not?'.
Also Seneca, *Thyestes*, 1007.

[3] This pointing to the future is sometimes fraught with tragic irony. For
instance, Richard's reply to Anne's angry mention of hanging, 'By such
despair, I should accuse myself' (85), points to Act V, Scene iii, where the
ghosts call out to him to despair and die, and where (in line 200) Richard
himself cries 'I shall despair'.

and carries the action an important step forward; but first, it looks back to the past and through a violent altercation reveals incidents of significance both for the exposition and for our picture of Richard.

The Technique of the Dialogue (43–224)

In the earlier half of the dialogue there is no real conversation – only a violent clash of conflicting and seemingly irreconcilable points of view. But, as in the pre-Shakespearian love-dialogues that echoed and played upon certain words, the wording used by one character is woven into the speech of the other; each makes use of the other's expressions and phrasing to frame his own rejoinder, giving it a new sense by some change in the order or the content. This sort of dialogue, when used by two lovers (as in Shakespeare's earlier comedies, for instance), emphasized the concord between them; in the present case, however, where a murderer is wooing a future victim, there is something almost paradoxical in the use of the same technique. Nevertheless Richard's reference to 'this keen encounter of our wits' (115) suggests that Shakespeare had in mind the witty verbal skirmishing of the comedies. Certainly the effect here is quite different from that of the love-dialogues in the comedies, where the puns, the verbal echoes, and the antitheses are decorative, tending to mask what lies below the surface, part of a predictable game. Here, however, in a scene steeped in black cynicism, reproaches and facts unadorned by metaphorical trimmings are set side by side, and the words spoken reveal the gulf that separates the speakers rather than their nearness.

This technique, which may at first seem alien to tragedy, should not be judged the result of a desire to experiment; the links and echoes in the language serve to emphasize the absence of any inner relationship between the two protagonists. On the other hand, the change in Anne's relationship with Richard from an outer, merely verbal compliance with his mood to a final inner yielding to the man is suggested by her altered rôle in the dialogue: her initial passivity (50, 70, 78, 83, 86, 99, 131, 136 ff.) gradually passes over to a more active participation in the verbal sparring match (73, 120, 133, 145, 148, 150). It is possible, then, to see in the parallels linking Anne's speeches with Richard's an ironic anticipation of the later close association which will in fact exist between them. The more obvious interpretation, of course, is to see in Anne's mimicking and twisting of Richard's words a scorn that strikes back at and unmasks the enemy by means of his own words.[1] Moreover, the sententious and proverbial utterances, weapons of this particular verbal duel, impart a special impact to the clash.[2]

The rhetorical devices in this dialogue are not limited to stichomythia. Indeed, after Richard's: 'And fall somewhat into a slower method' (116), there is almost no repartee or word play, but questions and answers, short and to the point, are exchanged in an almost everyday prose. Some broken lines in the earlier part of the dialogue (89, 91, 101, 142, 144) had already foreshadowed this transition. These sections are given especial emphasis by the division of the individual line between two speakers. They constitute not only pauses but also climaxes and turning-points in the conversation. It is also striking that a change of tempo always occurs in these passages.

The dialogue gains in liveliness through the introduction of two longer speeches among the many shorter ones and through metrical variations, which result in a changing tempo. The effect of rapidity achieved by the emotional intensity and variety of the dialogue is, of course, appropriate and useful in a scene where as much happens as in this one; at the same time the sharp pace of the exchanges helps make less obvious the rashness of Anne's *volte-face*.

Richard's Tactics

Richard avoids making lengthy observations during the early part of the dialogue; again and again during the first hundred lines, his interjections, arguments, and assertions provoke Anne to

---

[1] '. . . whenever he mockingly gives her a cue, she answers with some true observation about him' (H. Glunz, *Shakespeare und Morus*, 1938, p. 155).

[2] e.g. 71, 73, 86, 106, 149f. Cf. H. Weinstock, *Die Funktion elisabethanischer Sprichwörter und Pseudosprichwörter bei Shakespeare* (1966), pp. 125-127.

increasingly impassioned outbursts and accusations.[1] Earlier commentators considered this behaviour to be an intentional psychological manœuvre on Richard's part, contending that he adds fuel to Anne's rage in order that, when the blaze of emotion has burned itself out, she may be guided into other avenues of thought.[2] But we have already noted that the discussion of past events in this first section of the dialogue also functions as a necessary preparation for and a gradual transition to the real wooing-scene that follows.

Richard's breathless leap from dissimulation to open avowal of his own misdeeds causes Anne to accept his candour as genuine; and so she believes in his remorse, his contrition, his subsequent declaration of love, and finally his professed grief over the dead King (211). He exploits her vanity, her pride at the thought that she is reclaiming a contrite sinner;[3] he exploits, moreover, the psychological distance which separates Anne's wish for his destruction and the actual performance of the deed. He varies his tactics of surprise attack with unexpected confessions and sheer effrontery (101, 111, 146), now cautiously feeling his way and now calmly refuting her assertions, skilfully leading the dispute to where Anne can find no answer or, at best, a weak one (112, 114,

[1] Out of 80 lines (34–114) Anne has 50 to Richard's 28; but later the proportion is reversed, for out of 110 (115–225) Richard speaks 82 and Anne 28.

[2] W. Richardson: 'He knows that her feelings are violent; that they have no foundation in steady determined principles of conduct; that violent feelings are soon exhausted; . . . All that he has to do, then, is to suffer the violence of one emotion to pass away, and then as skilfully as possible to bring another, more suited to his designs, into its place. . . . In order, as soon as possible, to exhaust her temporary grief and resentment, it is necessary that they be swollen and exasperated to their utmost extent.' (Richardson, *Essays on Shakespeare's Dramatic Characters*, London 1797, p. 18 *Var*.). On the psychological significance of the scene cf. also G. Goetze, 'Die Richard-Anna-szene in Shakespeares *Richard III*' *Anglia*, XLI (1917), p. 1 ff. – H. Oppel interprets the scene from a different angle in 'Zur Problematik des Willenskampfes bei Shakespeare' *SJ*, 89 (1953), p. 72.

[3] Cf. Heinrich Heine: 'King Richard speaks of his sufferings, of his grief, so that Anne cannot withhold her pity, all the more because this wild being is far from being a plaintive nature. . . . And this wretched murderer has qualms of conscience – speaks of repentance – a good woman might perhaps lead him to the better path if she would sacrifice herself for him!' (*Shakespeare's Maidens and Women*, in: *Works*, transl. C. G. Leland, 1891, p. 346).

145). Above all, however, he employs this dialogue to focus Anne's interest and curiosity on himself.[1] From now on he takes the lead in the dialogue, whereas Anne's replies tend to grow shorter and less assured.

The 'Conversion-Speech' (151–183)

As in pre-Shakespearian drama, the real change of heart occurs in the course of a long speech, the 'conversion-speech', for which the foregoing dialogue is a preparation. Whereas Anne's last words before this speech constitute a prayer for Richard's destruction (150),[2] her first words after it are: 'Arise, dissembler . . . ' (184). Richard's speech contains neither arguments nor logical reasons to account for this change of heart; he simply compares the emotional state brought about by Anne's beauty with his hardheartedness in a past episode.[3] These real happenings in the past, referred to in a short interposed epic passage, are couched in language of a conventionally rhetorical and poetic kind that contrasts sharply with the abrupt quality of the dialogue that has gone before. The studied antithesis between *mine eyes* (148) and *thine eyes* (149), and the elaboration of the theme of eyes in lines 155–166[4] recall Shakespeare's earlier style, rich in conceits and anti-

---

[1] As, for example, in lines 141–145. Anne's 'Name him' (142) seems to mark a new attentiveness on her part, and the first slight softening towards Richard.

[2] Though a few short remarks had in fact contained the germ of compliance (cf. note 1), and so had her question 'Where is he?' (144).

[3] Richard in *3 Henry VI* had already referred to his ability to shed hypocritical tears:

> And wet my cheeks with artificial tears,
> And frame my face to all occasions.
> (III, ii, 184 f.)

Earlier in the same play, however, Richard had disclaimed this talent (II, i, 79–85). B. Spivack notes that Richard's feigned tears are a constantly reappearing motif in *Richard III* (I, iii, 328; I, iv, 242; II, ii, 23; III, v, 24) and never fail to produce the desired effect (*Shakespeare and the Allegory of Evil*, 1958, p. 397).

[4] Cf. Wright, p. 134. Lines 155–166 occur only in the *Folio*. Since $Q1$ is assumed to be a 'reported text' (perhaps a reconstruction from memory by members of Shakespeare's own company), the absence of these inessential lines may be the result of cuts in the prompt-copy. For an assessment of

theses. We catch echoes, too, from the sonnets, where images of *eyes* and *tears* often occur; and the image of the cheeks wet with tears 'like trees bedash'd with rain' (there is a parallel phrase in *Titus*, III, i, 111) is reminiscent of the earlier style. But this passage is not simply a decorative addition. The fact that Richard uses a theme drawn from courtly love-poetry stresses once again the irony of such a 'wooing'. In addition, Richard's speech adds to the self-portrait started in the soliloquy of Scene i; but now his purpose is no longer objective self-revelation. Rather, self-description has become a means of achieving his ends in his encounter with the bereaved Anne.

The rhetorical finesse of the conversion-speech is solidly backed by a lively sense of what makes good drama. Thus Richard's sudden gesture of baring his chest for Anne's sword-thrust[1] contrasts vividly with the more conventional qualities of the earlier part of the same speech. Such transitions from verbal persuasion to visible action on the stage[2] are not to be found in pre-Shakespearian conversion speeches (see below, pp. 39–42.)

Psychological Development

Richard, in placing a false choice before Anne (by saying *no* to one alternative she is to commit herself to the other), shows consider-

---

Q1, cf. J.D.W., p. 140 ff. For the relation between Q and F texts of *Richard III*, cf. Greg, Patrick, Walker, and also L. L. Schücking, *Über einige Nachbesserungen*, p. 24 ff.

[1] Cf. Seneca, *Phaedra*, 616 (V. K. Whitaker, *Shakespeare's Use of Learning*, 1953, p. 66). Th. Vatke (*SJ*, IV, 1869, p. 67) drew attention to a corresponding scene in Seneca's *Hercules Fur.*, 332 ff., in which Lycus woos Megara after murdering her father. For further parallels between 171–190 and Seneca's *Phaedra* (and *Richardus Tertius* by Th. Legge – written ca. 1573 under the influence of *Phaedra*), cf. F. Wilhelm, 'Zu Seneca und Shakespeare (*Richard III*)' *Archiv*, LXVI (1912), p. 69 ff.

[2] The sight of Richard with bared breast kneeling as suitor before Anne, who stands with sword in hand ready to avenge the double murder, brings home to us the full contradiction of the situation. Furthermore, we are shown one of Richard's fundamental traits: he is a reckless gambler, staking all to win all. Cf. V, iv, 9 f.

> Slave, I have set my life upon a cast
> And I will stand the hazard of the die.

able psychological insight. He at once exploits Anne's rejection of
this false choice (she wishes his death but will not act as execu-
tioner) by offering to kill himself if she will give the order.

> This hand, which for thy love did kill thy love,
> Shall for thy love kill a far truer love;
>
> (189–190)

Thus he woos her, playing on the word *love* (a key-word throughout the play) four times in the course of two lines.[1] At this point
Anne hesitates; for the second time she fails to act according to her
own earlier words. Richard has indeed acted shrewdly: by calling
on Anne to carry out judgement herself, he has appealed to her
better nature, to something beyond her outbursts of rage and
hatred; he has caused her to draw back and look dispassionately
at the man she has been cursing. Thus the conflict between
Richard and Anne is supplemented by the suggestion of a further
struggle within Anne herself – a struggle between her hatred of
Richard and her natural charity and moderation.[2] Richard's
strategy for converting Anne is a true offspring of his diabolical
nature: he conquers by appealing to the best in the person he is
seeking to win over – but to a 'best' that is often at the same time
a weak spot which he quickly and cunningly exploits. The actual
moment of conversion is marked by Anne's: 'I would I knew thy
heart' (192) – a psychologically convincing and genuinely human
utterance.

'I would I knew thy heart', the turning-point of the scene, is
the first of eleven short, similarly constructed lines, each containing three stresses. These lines, despite the stichomythia, succeed in conveying through their tone, their metre, and their
avoidance of marked contrast, the new understanding, the half-
reconciliation.[3] The action – the putting away of the sword and

[1] These lines remind us of Richard's words towards the end of *3 Henry VI*:

> And this word 'love', which greybeards call divine,
> Be resident in men like one another,
> And not in me!   (V, vi, 81)

[2] For a full treatment of this point, see H. Oppel, 'Zur Problematik des
Willenskampfes' in: *Shakespeare* (1963), pp. 62–106.

[3] For a different interpretation of this transitional passage cf. V. K.
Whitaker, *Shakespeare's Use of Learning* (1953), p. 70.

Anne's acceptance of the ring – symbolically emphasizes the same thing. But Anne's short, simple sentences (cf. 187, 192, 194) contrast with the lofty rhetorical style of Richard's protestations of love in the ensuing lines (203–208).[1] Besides, Anne's symbolic acceptance of Richard's ring contains ironic undertones: her ambiguous answer, 'To take is not to give' (202), echoes a well-known proverb of that period, 'To give a thing and take a thing is to wear the devil's gold ring'[2] – a proverb which Richard's next words (203) also seem to hint at. Thus below the obvious meaning of 'to take is not to give'[3] lies a suggestion that Anne's acceptance of the betrothal ring has something of the diabolical about it.

Richard's request that he be allowed to join in the mourning for the King is psychologically astute; it also helps make more credible Anne's changed feelings which, had they been embodied in a clear statement instead of being merely hinted at, would have been far less convincing. In pre-Shakespearian conversion-scenes the person won over always expressly states that his heart has been changed, but here much remains unexpressed, even at the end. In spite of the unreality of the central situation, Anne's hesitation and indecision are successfully rendered without the crudity of explicit statement. Anne's consigning of coffin and guards to Richard (whose *villains* of line 36 now, in line 224, becomes *sirs*) results in a symbolic rearrangement of the characters on the stage, emphasizing in a visual image a change which the scene itself has already accomplished in fact.

Richard's Concluding Soliloquy (227–62)

The fantastic and outrageous nature of the preceding events is firmly underlined in a speech which, though it is delivered by Richard,[4] embodies Shakespeare's own commentary. Here

---

[1] 'Even so thy breast encloseth my poor heart' (204) is a 'stock protestation of lovers' (J.D.W.). Cf. M. P. Tilley, *Dictionary of Proverbs* (1950), p. 565.

[2] Cf. G. L. Apperson, *English Proverbs and Proverbial Phrases* (1929), p. 247, A 17; H. Weinstock, *Die Funktion elisabethanischer Sprichwörter*, p. 126.

[3] Cf. Sir George MacDonald's rendering (*Warwick*, p. 151). The line is absent from *F* but most editors accept it. Cf. J.D.W., p. 145.

[4] Cf. J. Palmer: 'All that has ever been urged against the success or likeli-

Richard's comment is unmistakably moral:[1] Anne's capitulation is retrospectively condemned, and the virtues and charms of her murdered husband are reviewed. These moral comments are delivered within the conventional framework of the 'villain's monologue' with its objective comment on the adversary and on the speaker himself.[2] Richard's judgement of the situation inevitably arouses in him feelings of contempt for his gullible fellow men – his victory over Anne fully confirming the mean opinion of humanity that he had already expressed in his first soliloquy.

Moreover, his successful accomplishment of this unlikely feat has obviously fed his self-esteem. The world of virtuous-seeming men from which he, hunchbacked scoundrel, feels cast out, is not after all so virtuous that he cannot seduce and conquer it with his devilish arts. The tone of triumphant mockery in his questions and exclamations, the cynical and yet exuberant way in which he gloats over his own success,[3] his wry 'I do mistake my person all this while . . . ' (252), his talk of employing tailors and his plan: 'to study fashions to adorn my body' – all this conveys Richard's own view of his machinations as an amusing game; and his virtuosity and paradoxical irony are so entertaining that at times we forget how morally reprehensible it all is. Richard's aloofness in commenting on himself and on others reflects a lack of feeling for the sufferings of his victims, and an indifference to his own baseness. He remains a spectator of himself up to the last act, where a change finally takes place. Such aspects of Richard's character are related to the tradition of the *Vice*;[4] yet Richard's impartiality and coldness strike us not simply as mere conventional graftings; they are the genuine expression of his twisted soul.

---

hood of the enterprise is put into Richard's own mouth' (*Political Characters of Shakespeare*, 1945, p. 82).

[1] On this point cf. A. Harbage, *As They Liked It. An Essay on Shakespeare and Morality* (1947).

[2] Cf. L. L. Schücking, *Character Problems*.

[3] Cf. Nicholas Brooke, 'Reflecting Gems and Dead Bones: Tragedy versus History in *Richard III' The Critical Quarterly*, 7 (1965), p. 128.

[4] Cf. C. V. Boyer, *The Villain as Hero in Elizabethan Tragedy* (1914). Ambidexter in *Cambises* is an early example of the type, revelling in his own misdeeds. Cf. D. C. Boughner, 'Vice, Braggart, and Falstaff' *Anglia*, LXXII (1954), p. 35 ff.; B. Spivack, *Shakespeare and the Allegory of Evil* (1958).

Richard, in his first soliloquy (I, i, 24–27), tells us that to contemplate his own shadow in the sunshine 'and descant on mine own deformity' is, since he cannot hope to enjoy the pleasures of love, one of his few pastimes. This same *shadow* theme now recurs at the end of a scene in which, to his surprise, the woman he desires has clearly overlooked his deformity so that he himself can no longer view his physical flaws as he had done in I, i; further-more, he has successfully played a new rôle (that of the devoted suitor) – a rôle quite outside the former range of his successes and indeed one which he himself had expressly renounced (I, i, 14 ff., 28).[1] Thus the repetition of the shadow image, by reminding us of Richard's earlier speech, once more brings home to us the unexpectedness of his success with Anne. Moreover, these con-cluding lines hint at a further victory – the victory won by Richard over his own crippled body which need no longer be supposed an insuperable obstacle to amatory undertakings.

Richard's contemplation of his own shadow is at the same time symbolic of his isolation and self-centredness. 'I am myself alone', he had said at the end of *Henry VI* (*3 Henry VI*, V, vi, 83). And despite the successful wooing of Anne, his shadow continues to be his sole companion. The image of the shadow – frequently and subtly used by Shakespeare[2] – here becomes a means of reveal-ing character. Moreover, Richard's apostrophe to the 'fair sun' contains elements of irony; for what Richard wishes to have illuminated is the darkness of his own shadow, the sign of his villainy. The sun is to illuminate a Richard moving from one dark crime to the next.

The shadow image, which in this scene is associated with Richard, is in the context of the play as a whole used to represent what is dark and evil, in contrast to the light. Darkness and shadow are generated where the figure of Richard occupies a portion of sunlit space. Thus the image of *sun and shadow* would seem to epitomize the polarity of good and evil that pervades the whole play. Here, as is so often the case in Shakespeare, we cannot say with any certainty which of these possible interpretations and

[1] Cf. also *3 Henry VI*, III, iii, 148–164.
[2] Cf. Maria Wickert, 'Das Schattenmotiv bei Shakespeare' *Anglia*, LXXI (1953), p. 274 ff.

allusive links are intended. Nevertheless the symbols function – as
true symbols always do – on various levels.

Conversion-Scenes and Wooing-Scenes in Pre-Shakespearian Drama

Scenes involving a conversion (or persuasion) occur frequently
in Elizabethan drama.[1] Such scenes cover a wide range of situations; wooing-scenes in particular had a firmly established place
in earlier sixteenth-century drama. In morality plays there had
been scarcely any technique of persuasion; the important thing was
not *how* the character made his choice between good and evil, but
that he made it; and this choice was made suddenly and abruptly.[2]
Rhetorical tragedy, on the other hand, took over the Senecan
long speech, which made rich use of rhetorical figures and was
particularly well suited to the purpose of persuasion. Up to
Marlowe's *Tamburlaine* this speech was usually the means by which
the conversion was brought about,[3] so that Richard's persuasion
speech (I, ii, 152–183) may be considered a late example of this
particular form. Conversion, before the time of Greene and
Marlowe, had usually been effected by logical argument, the persuader appealing in particular to his partner's reason. Rational
argument had been characteristic of Seneca's persuasion scenes,[4]
though his works also include instances where conversion is
brought about by an appeal to pity (*Troades*, 690 ff.), a threat of
suicide (*Hercules Fur.*, 1312 ff.), and an interpolated narrative
(*Medea*, 225–251; *Hercules Fur.*, 1252 ff.; *Troades* 210 ff.); all of
these techniques play a part in the present scene (49, 68 ff.; 191;
153 ff.). To appreciate Shakespeare's innovations we must keep

[1] Cf. L. L. Schücking, *Shakespeare und der Tragödienstil seiner Zeit* (1947),
p. 48 ff.
[2] For persuasion-scenes in morality plays cf. *Youth; Hyckescorner; Mundus
et Infans; Magnificence; An Interlude of the Four Elements*.
[3] Cf. *Gorboduc*, II, i; *Gismond of Salerne*, II, ii; *Wounds of Civil War*, 537 ff.,
1814 ff.; *Promos and Cassandra*, III, iv; *Battle of Alcazar*, 722 ff.; *2 Tamburlaine*,
2510 ff. Cf. also I, ii of *Misfortunes of Arthur*. Here, though the influence of
classical tragedy is still strong, the conversion is brought about in a dialogue
involving stichomythia, each of the two speakers taking an equal share.
[4] Cf. F. L. Lucas, *Seneca and Elizabethan Tragedy* (1922).

in mind that in earlier plays the partner's change of heart had
taken place not only quite suddenly but for the most part with no
outer signs of growing uncertainty or wavering. The persuader,
moreover, not only accomplished the job in one long speech, but
showed himself to be in control of the situation from the beginning; the resulting change of heart was then openly acknowledged.[1]
Thus Tamburlaine brings about the conversion of Theridamas
in a single long speech (*1, Tamburlaine* 360 ff.), following which
Theridamas, completely won over, declares:

> Not *Hermes* Prolocutor to the Gods,
> Could vse perswasions more patheticall.
>
> (405 f.)

Young Mortimer, in Marlowe's *Edward II*, trying to win over the
lords to Gaveston's recall, is given not *one* long speech but several;[2]
nevertheless his partners remain largely passive.[3] (*Edward II* is also
remarkable in that it presents for the first time a persuasion-scene
that is mimed rather than spoken. We do not hear the Queen herself win over young Mortimer; instead the scene is watched and
its progress described by the onlookers.) Shakespeare, however,
was the first to give the partner in the conversion-scene an
opportunity to express his opposition; conversion comes about
through a balanced dialogue rather than through the persuasive
powers of a single speaker.

Another difference between pre-Shakespearian persuasion-
scenes and the Richard–Anne scene is that the former were all
appreciably shorter than this one – naturally enough, for the
extent of the ground to be covered between the opening and the

---

[1] In a work as late as Greene's *James IV*, the King is persuaded to murder
his royal consort after a mere twenty lines (IV, iv; cf. also II, ii); and he
freely and unexpectedly announces his new state of mind.

[2] Moreover, Mortimer appeals to the emotions of the lords, and not simply
to their reason; he makes use of various means of persuasion.

[3] *Doctor Faustus* is the only play of Marlowe's in which the person to be
converted (Faustus himself) plays an important part in the conversion-
scene. But the scene does not really show a completed conversion; rather it
consists of a series of short episodes in which Faustus is warned by the good
angels, tempted by the bad ones (98 ff., 447 ff., 622 ff., 691 ff.). The influence
of the moralities is still strong in this play.

conclusion of the Richard–Anne scene was without precedent. If today the scene appears too short for what it embraces, in its own day it must have seemed very long indeed. To make his scene convincing, Shakespeare had to use more than the usual amount of dialogue, as well as techniques more varied than those used by his predecessors.

The really important achievement in this persuasion-scene as opposed to earlier ones, however, is that up till this time such scenes had as a rule proceeded smoothly, without variations in the level of intensity and without particular moments of crisis, along a 'single track', using only *one* method of persuasion and appealing to only *one* side of the person (in general to his intellect alone). Shakespeare uses a variety of means, including gesture and spectacle,[1] he makes Richard appeal to both reason and feeling and shows the gradual and tentative process of conversion.

If we now turn to 'wooing-scenes' before Shakespeare, although in most of these the partner yields abruptly,[2] we find that in pre-Shakespearian comedy there are instances of a certain psychological subtlety as well as of indirect and sophisticated use of language. Lyly with his witty airy talk of love, his ample use of play upon words and of verbal echoes, of metaphor and imagery,[3] is the best example of this sort of thing. But as has already been pointed 'out, the dialogue in a comedy springs from a situation quite unlike the one in which Richard and Anne find themselves; the degree of verbal fencing and decorative ornament to be found in a Lyly comedy would be inappropriate in the scene between Richard and Anne, where exposure rather than 'hide-and-seek' sets the tone.[4]

---

[1] Much of this gesture, stage-business, and symbolic grouping on the stage is indicated in the words of the characters; cf. 1, 12 f., 29, 33–43, 54–55, 144, 171, 174–179, 181, 183–184, 196, 201, 221, 224–226, 260–261).

[2] In *Cambises* (881 ff.) the king is struck by Cupid's arrow, sees a lady, and at once woos her in a long speech. The lady hesitates, the king threatens, and the lady at once yields. The rapid, naive reversal is quite in keeping with a style ignorant of transitions.

[3] e.g. *Campaspe*, III, i; III, iii; *Sapho and Phao*, III, iv; *Mother Bombie*, II, iii; *Gallathea*, III, ii; IV, iv.

[4] Pre-Shakespearian wooing-scenes are not strictly confined to a technique involving stichomythia and verbal exchanges. In Kyd's *Soliman and Perseda*, for instance, there are long wooing speeches; and the same is true of Greene's

The wooing-scenes in the chronicle plays and tragedies resemble those of the comedies,[1] making use of subtle hints, allusions, and prettily worded antitheses. Shakespeare had already
provided just such a 'keen encounter of our wits' in *3 Henry VI*,
where King Edward woos Lady Grey (III, ii).[2] The scene might
almost be a preliminary study for the Richard–Anne scene; here
too we have a widow[3] who first rebuffs (indeed, fails to grasp) the
King's demands. Here, too, there is stichomythia, with matching
words and phrasing, interrupted by dialogue in different rhythms,
by longer speeches of several lines, by terse and direct statements.
Yet the scene will not bear comparison with that in *Richard III*: it
lacks the diabolical undertones, the sharp brilliance, and the
breathtaking impetus of Richard himself.

SCENE THREE

The break between Scenes ii and iii is sharper than that between
the first two scenes; these had been linked by Richard's revelation
at the end of Scene i of his plan to marry Anne, followed by her

---

Orlando Furioso (I, i), and *A Looking Glass* (I, i, 60), and Peele's *David and
Bethsabe* (I, i, 99–120). Marlowe, too, favours a speech full of pathos and
passion without a trace of wit (*Dido*, 747 ff.; *1 Tamburlaine*, I, ii). When
Tamburlaine woos Zenocrate, the lady hardly manages to speak at all and is
obviously overwhelmed by her suitor's stupendous flow of rhetoric. Theridamas's wooing of Olympia, comparable in some respects with the Richard–
Anne scene, is also devoid of stichomythia and verbal fencing. Olympia,
mourning her slain husband, tricks Theridamas, the 'enemy' suitor, into
killing her (*2 Tamburlaine*, IV, ii).

[1] e.g. *James IV; Locrine; Wars of Cyrus.*

[2] In the earliest wooing-scene in Shakespeare's Histories (*1 Henry VI*, V,
iii, 45–130), the partners at first seem to be talking to themselves, and even
though actual conversation develops towards the end, there is no real
stichomythia.

[3] The wooing of a widow was a favourite theme in Elizabethan drama;
cf., for instance, *2 Tamburlaine*, IV, ii. Cf. N. Weisman, *The Wooing of Widows
in the English Drama 1558–1642*, unpubl. M.A. thesis, Columbia Univ. (1948).

entry at the beginning of Scene ii. Now, however, the court, the Queen and her associates, take the stage. Richard remains important, but his domination is less complete than in the earlier episodes. It is Margaret who assumes the pivotal rôle, Margaret whose entry overshadows even Richard's presence; for the first time we are confronted with a figure Richard's equal in stature. In the first two scenes our attention had been closely focused upon Richard, but now we see him among his enemies in the larger world of the court. Thus in this third scene the play's perspective broadens: the revelation of character continues, but our attention is now drawn to certain political and historical circumstances important for our understanding of the action.

In the wider focus of Scene iii soliloquy and dialogue are naturally enough replaced by conversation among several speakers. The broader social context is also reflected in the forming, dispersing, and subsequent reforming of new groups, and in the frequent entries and exits. Scenes i and ii had each dealt with a single incident, with one basic theme; but here there is more than one centre of gravity, and the various concerns overlap. It is hardly surprising that this scene with its swollen cast is longer than any other in the first three acts.[1]

Structure

A total of twelve characters (including the two murderers) takes part in the scene. The stage fills up gradually; the first three characters are joined by further groups (17, 42), until Margaret's entry (alone) completes the company and the scene rises to its climax, the great passage-of-arms between Margaret, Richard,

[1] The longer 'ensemble' scenes in *Henry VI* are noticeably less well constructed than this one; the component episodes, succeeding and overlapping with one another, rarely build up to a central climax; rarely does a single span of tension unite an entire scene. Moreover, Shakespeare was not always able to devise lines for each of the many figures on stage. Here, in *Richard III*, such technical problems have found their appropriate solution. The ensemble scenes in *Henry VI* (all three parts open with one) are remarkable for the way in which groups of characters take up positions symmetrically opposed to one another, entering and leaving the stage together; a simultaneous entry of groups from opposite sides of the stage at the outset of the scene often serves to clarify the distribution of factions (e.g. *2 Henry VI*, i, 1).

E

and the rest. While Margaret is present, no one enters or leaves and there is no action on the stage – a suspension of activity which gives the passage particular emphasis. The latter part of the scene resembles the opening; the stage empties by degrees: Margaret leaves first, then the courtiers, and finally Richard is left alone for the short closing conversation with the murderers. Two sections, then, of entrances and exits enclose the more static central episode.[1] The scene begins and ends with three speakers conversing confidentially, while the central section is, in contrast, louder, more melodramatic.

Although Margaret is the central force in Scene iii, the vivid portrayal of Richard's duplicity remains a primary dramatic object, and the structure of the scene is to some extent dictated by the two-fold picture of Richard which is to be conveyed – first Richard in Machiavellian action, then Richard undisguised. Richard's soliloquy following the court sequence, besides providing an accurate account of his behaviour in the central sequence, fixes our full attention once more on the villain himself and so again emphasizes his leading position in the play. The short interview with the murderers, appended as it were to the main scene, shows us, much as the soliloquy had done, Richard as he really is, whereas in the middle section Richard the dissembler had held the stage. The alternation of appearance and reality, here as elsewhere in the play, helps to shape the scene.

The Opening Episodes (1–41)

The scene opens in the middle of a conversation – a device already employed more than once in *Henry VI* (cf. in particular the dialogue between this same Rivers and Queen Elizabeth in *3 Henry VI*, IV, iv). The Queen is pessimistic about the outcome of the King's illness (of which Richard was pleased to learn in I, i), and the atmosphere of foreboding is only strengthened by the hollow comfort offered by the two courtiers.[2] Such words as *comfort, cheer, merry, comforter, joyful,* used in such a context, appear

---

[1] The structure of IV, iv, is similar; see below, p. 176.
[2] The starkness of the rhyme (*son–gone,* 9–10) reinforces the lack of conviction which these lines convey.

merely ironic, and the Queen, urged to keep her spirits up, responds with: 'If he were dead, what would betide on me?' (6) showing clearly the direction of her thoughts.

Following Derby's and Buckingham's entrance, the King's illness is again discussed, and mention is made of court intrigue and opposition to the Queen (the Countess of Richmond, mentioned in this context, is Buckingham's aunt, and the mother of the future Henry VII;[1] but only readers of the chronicles would have been aware of these relationships[2]). The Queen's words concerning the Countess of Richmond, 'And loves not me . . .' (23), echoing line 13, 'A man that loves not me', reveal her unenviable position as a woman surrounded by enemies. The court is racked with hate and envy, circumstances most suitable for exploitation by Richard Gloucester.

Buckingham's hopes for the King's recovery, and the prospect he voices of reconciliation among the courtiers (36 ff.), slows for a moment the otherwise relentless advance of the tragedy. But the moment passes, leaving the Queen as sorrowful and despairing as ever, and her former anxiety now crystallizes into true premonition:[3]

> Would all were well! But that will never be.
> I fear our happiness is at the height.
>
> (40–41)

Richard's Entry and Behaviour (42–109)

Richard now bursts onto the stage, his presence and manner changing the whole tone of the discussion. The conciliatory and friendly note discernible until his entry vanishes. Richard's mid-scene entries, whether characterized by a hypocritical affability (II, i, 46; III, iv, 22) or constituting a tyrannical and inconsiderate intrusion (III, iv, 61; IV, iv, 136), are always thoroughly dramatic; they command attention.

---

[1] Cf. notes in Wright and J.D.W.

[2] Cf. J.D.W., p. 179.

[3] P. Reyher sees this passage as an example of the 'conception fataliste des événements et de la vie que cette image de la roue de Fortune suppose' (*Essai sur les idées dans l'œuvre de Shakespeare*, 1947, p. 248).

Richard's first speech after his entrance, addressed to no particular person but skilfully framed as a pseudo-monologue in which he poses as the victim of unjust accusation and complaint,[1] attracts general attention. Richard (who tends to dispense with the crude method of directly attacking his enemies, preferring rather to defend himself against the supposed attacks of others) rails against unnamed enemies and calumniators. In this way he hopes to forestall any complaints against himself: 'I do the wrong, and first begin to brawl' (324).[2] He attempts to isolate his enemies, to sow dissension in the court party; he is, indeed, a master of the Machiavellian arts.[3] Even his insolent behaviour – his *blunt upbraidings*, *bitter scoffs*, and *gross taunts* (104, 106) – may be a calculated move to deceive his listeners; for his outward belligerence blinds them to a far greater danger, that of an underlying murderous malice.

Richard's claims that he is incapable of flattery, of deceit, that he is just a 'plain man' (51), are, like many of his other statements in this scene, clearly ironic,[4] for we have just witnessed his well-developed ability to 'flatter and look fair' (47). His assertion that others have attacked and persecuted him is an early example of one of his favourite devices – the ironic reversal of a situation (III, vii).

Richard has, in fact, little real interest in what he is complaining about: the 'promotions' of the Queen's faction and the slights suffered by the older nobility (79–82; 70–72). But he adroitly uses court dissatisfaction with the Queen's party to introduce the

---

[1] He may, of course, have overheard part of the foregoing conversation, a possibility strengthened by his 'love them not' (44), which echoes the 'loves not me' that occurs twice at the beginning of the scene (13, 213).

[2] In his note on this line, J.D.W. quotes the Elizabethan proverb: 'Complain to prevent complaint'.

[3] Cf. the quotation from Gentillet, p. 62, note 2.

[4] e.g. 142: 'I am too childish-foolish for this world'. Cf. also 140–141, 149–150, 263, 307, 311, 315 f. The contrast between his unmannerly and outrageous behaviour and his subtle irony makes such lines particularly effective. Cf. Coleridge: 'In Richard there is a predominance of irony, accompanied with apparently blunt manners to those immediately about him, but formalised into a more set hypocrisy towards the people as represented by their magistrates.' 'Shakespeare's English Historical Plays': '*Richard III*' (in: *Notes and Lectures*, ed. 1881, p. 183).

insinuation that the Queen had helped bring about the imprisonment of Clarence and Hastings (Richard had hinted as much in
his earlier conversation with them); the audience is thus reminded
of the earlier appearance of these innocents and prepared for the
scene to follow. He then proceeds to mock at the Queen's marriage with the King. The Queen defends herself with some force
and dignity against Richard's insolence, but at the close of the
encounter she is even more isolated and forlorn than in her first
conversation with the courtiers. Her wish 'I had rather be a
country servant-maid | Than a great queen' (107 f.) was a
commonplace in plays of the period.[1] The same idea appears in
lines 83–84 where the Queen contrasts the 'careful height' of her
present position with the 'contented hap' of her earlier days.

Richard's Use of Language

Richard reveals himself to us in his speech – even when he is
dissembling. He has an eye for gesture and behaviour and a
ready, if cynical, tongue, able to portray a general characteristic
with a few individual touches.[2] The accumulation in the opening
lines of his pseudo-monologue of graphic and striking verbs and
adjectives, such as *cog* (48) and *silken* (53) to describe the appearance of a flatterer, recalls the diction of the play's opening soliloquy, with its realistic use of images based on bodily movement,
where, for instance, war 'capers nimbly in a lady's chamber' (12).
In Scene iii the impatient questions and exclamations (56 ff., 93,
100), the use of colloquial turns of phrase (e.g. 57, 70, 93), the
introduction of puns (*noble* 82; *marry* 100), the pious oaths (*by holy
Paul*, 45) and invocations (59, 77), are all characteristic of his use
of language, as is his way of taking up a word, parroting it in a

[1] Cf. e. g. *3 Henry VI*, II, v, 21, 42 ff. On this subject cf. E. M. W. Tillyard,
Shakespeare's History Plays (1948); W. F. Schirmer, 'Glück und Ende der
Könige in Shakespeares Historien', *Arbeitsgemeinschaft für Forschung des
Landes Nordrhein-Westfalen*, vol. 22 (1954).
[2] Compare for instance the concrete vividness of lines 47–49 with the
treatment of the same theme in *A Mirror for Magistrates*, Anthony Lord
Rivers, 435 f:

> A noble hart they say is Lyon like,
> It can not couche, dissemble, crouch nor fayne.

mocking fashion (93, 100 f.), 'running it to death' in order to
cheapen it, and often giving a sudden twist to its meaning (100).
Typical, too, is his habit of interrupting others (93, 234).[1]
Richard's speech[2] – realistic, natural, and rough, yet at the same
time flexible and expressive – lends the whole scene a new tone
and tempo quite unlike that which had prevailed before his entry.

Margaret (110–303)

With the entrance of Margaret – an almost mythical figure
emerging from a distant past – the play takes on a new dimension.
The action no longer unfolds purely on the level of personal interplay, for historical and even supernatural overtones now make
themselves felt. Shakespeare's dramas rarely contain mythological
figures or allegorical abstractions, but characters occasionally
embody some of the attributes of Ate and Nemesis in classical
tragedy; in Margaret traces of such origins remain. She is not a
'dramatic character' in the same sense as the others in the play,
but rather a choric figure. Through her we see how the chorus's
function may continue to be carried out even after the chorus
itself has disappeared.

Margaret stands outside the action, her only activity is to
accuse, to call down curses, and, not least, to prophesy. Yet she
dominates the action more than might at first appear, for everything that happens later fulfils her curses and prophecies. She
seems almost to be an instrument of providence, coming from
some higher sphere, possessing a knowledge of the past through
which she plumbs the present and foresees the future. But at the
same time she is an old woman consumed with hate and grief, far
too human to be considered a mere choric observer. She alone in
the play is Richard's equal in demoniac and elemental force, suggesting that there exist opposing powers which are neither duped
by Richard's trickeries nor prepared to bow to his will.

The various elements in Margaret's nature seem, each in turn,

[1] Cf. for instance III, iv, 76; III, v, 15; IV, ii, 107.
[2] Cf. M. C. Bradbrook, *Shakespeare and Elizabethan Poetry* (1951), p. 133.
As early as 1908 A. H. Thorndike had called attention to Richard's speech:
'In the main he speaks with a naturalness and directness far greater than was
usual in tragic heroes' (*Tragedy*, 1908, p. 122).

to dominate her behaviour: standing in the background before advancing to join the others (110–157), she is a choric figure; then, in the imprecation-scene, she is both Ate herself and a suffering, guilty victim of fate – a fate born of the wars between York and Lancaster; finally, in her beseeching words: 'O, serve me well, and teach yourselves that duty!' (253), as in her appeal to Buckingham: 'O princely Buckingham, I'll kiss thy hand' (280), gentler, more human traits emerge. In seeking supporters for her cause she is, for a few moments, neither judge nor unearthly demoniac being, but simply the outcast Queen appealing for human sympathy.

Margaret and the Stage Action

Margaret's lonely rôle in the play receives symbolic expression in her initial position at the back of the stage (110–158). Unseen and unheard by the rest, she listens to Richard's speech and to the replies of Rivers and Elizabeth, occasionally interpolating observations of her own. These remarks, which on the printed page may appear to be interruptions of the other speakers, are in reality a running commentary on what is being said[1] and are intended only for the audience, which thus becomes witness to a double scene. The situation is, of course, contrived and artificial; but realism is not a standard one can usefully apply to *Richard III*. Moreover, Margaret's appearance is supposed to strike the audience as partaking of the supernatural and prodigious.

Simultaneous Staging in Pre-Shakespearian Drama

The pre-Shakespearian 'eavesdropping-scene'[2] is the principal model for this kind of dual-scene; a monologue or dialogue is overheard by a third person (possibly more than one) who is himself unobserved. This person's remarks are interpolated, as in the present case, in the conversation or monologue, like a counter-point or accompaniment. These interpolations often comment on

---

[1] R. Flatter gives examples of simultaneous speech from other plays in *Shakespeare's Producing Hand* (1948), p. 55 ff.

[2] e.g. *James IV*, 282 ff.; *Alphonsus of Aragon*, IV, ii; *King Leir*, sc. vii.

what is being said, using language almost identical with that overheard, but producing a quite different meaning. The interpolation may take up some phrase and echo it in a new context. The most striking and technically brilliant dual-scene is perhaps the one in Kyd's *Spanish Tragedy* (II, ii); here Balthazar and Lorenzo interpolate their lines into the dialogue of the lovers Bellimperia and Horatio, and by almost echoing what they hear, add a new meaning to the lovers' statements.

Similarly in the present scene: Margaret's interpolated remarks contradict Richard's hypocritical and misleading assertions, unmask his lies, and show up what is paradoxical and specious in his words.

Linguistic Structure

Antithesis is used in this dual-scene to express genuine contrasts and paradoxical contradictions, and to illuminate the discrepancies between appearance and reality (cf. 125/126, 133/134, 136/137). The much-criticized artificiality and rhetorical extravagance of the diction in Scene iii,[1] far from being mere virtuosity, effectively conveys by means of balanced phrasing the characters' position in relation to each other. The Queen, for instance, had emphasized her joylessness by play upon the word *joy* (a 'leit-motif' throughout the play, cf. I, iii, 18, 110); now Margaret continues the word play with:

> A little joy enjoys the Queen thereof;
> For I am she, and altogether joyless.
>
> (155–156)

—laying claim both to the rank of queen and to the state of joy-lessness (cf. 111, 172–173). Again, when she replies to the presumptuous reproach of Rivers, 'Were you well serv'd, you would be taught your duty' (250) with 'To serve me well you all should do me duty . . .' (251), her answer is not only skilful repartee but also a convincing rebuttal; for by changing only a few words she reveals what would be appropriate to the situation.[2] Another

---

[1] Cf. for instance H. Spencer, p. 171; *Var.*, p. 92.

[2] In a similar way Margaret seizes on the words *shame* and *charity* from

such revelation follows Richard's proud reference to the eagle
brood (meaning his own House of York) who nests 'in the cedar's
top'[1] and 'scorns the sun'. Margaret continues:

> And turns the sun to shade – alas! alas!
> Witness my son, now in the shade of death,
> Whose bright out-shining beams thy cloudy wrath
> Hath in eternal darkness folded up.
>
> (266–269)

She applies the image of the sun, which Richard not only *scorns*
but has also darkened, to her own son, slain by Richard; and she
makes use of the symbol of the shadow, with which Richard has
already been associated (cf. I, ii, 263). Richard is not only a
creature of the shadows; he casts these shadows over others.

Everyday patterns of speech are not crowded out of this scene
by the rhetorical flourishes. As in the earlier scene between
Richard and Anne, the rhetorical diction is shot through with
colloquial expressions, and the even flow of the blank verse is
varied and interrupted by irregularities, short or incomplete
lines, and marked rhythmical variation. Such contrasts are used
to most effect at moments of crisis. For instance, Margaret's
crescendo of curses against Richard, expressed in a series of
regular lines, is suddenly cut off when Richard breaks in with the
word *Margaret* and pretends to take Margaret's closing *Richard*
as the beginning of a fresh remark addressed to him. The result
is a most effective syncope, a momentary suspension of the action
on the stage, and almost a reversal of the situation in that the
curser becomes the cursed.

Richard as the Instrument of Nemesis

Richard, in his exchange with the Queen and Rivers, reminds
them that, whereas he had supported Edward before he was king,

---

Buckingham's admonition 'Peace, peace, for shame, if not for charity!' (273),
and by applying these words to the behaviour of the others and to her own
situation, she gives them a different meaning (274–278).

[1] Cf. J.D.W., p. 183, note. Cf. also Hazlitt, *Richard III* in: *Characters of
Shakespeare's Plays*, 1817 (ed. 1903, p. 141).

they had sided with Lancaster.[1] He compares his own and the Queen's former position with their present state in a forcefully expressed and rhythmically striking passage (121 ff.). Finally, in recalling Clarence's disloyalty to Warwick, he implies a connection between his brother's past guilt and his present incarceration.

Richard's arguments are of course one-sided, and ignore his own misdoings; but he does lay his finger on the moral weakness of the others, on the source of their guilt. Thus the historical material drawn into this drama is not included simply for purposes of exposition; rather the illumination of past events reveals the guilt of Richard's future victims. For Richard, this guilt is no more than an excuse for his savage actions; nevertheless he functions – even if unconsciously – as an instrument of Divine Providence, of the Nemesis behind history.[2] Moulton has discussed the connection between the 'Nemesis Action' which will later engulf Richard himself, and the earlier minor Nemesis Actions to which his victims succumb.[3] In this scene, the discussion of the past makes us aware of the cycle of guilt and expiation in which Richard himself will soon be caught up.

Margaret's curses, which are at the same time accusations of her enemies (195 ff.), suggest that the fates befalling Richard's victims are not altogether unjust; yet she too, as she stands there, banished and bereft of her rights, is shown to be subject to the very same cycle of guilt and expiation. Richard's short, epic description of Margaret's past guilt, inserted in the middle of a violent altercation, is so convincing that the others unite in condemning her inhuman act. The characters have regrouped themselves; opponents join forces in their hatred of Margaret, and Margaret herself draws attention to this change, making use of the animal imagery so prevalent in this scene:[4]

[1] This contradicts *3 Henry VI*, III, ii, 1–7, but agrees with Holinshed; cf. J.D.W., p. 181.

[2] Cf. E. M. W. Tillyard, *Shakespeare's History Plays* (1948); Lily B. Campbell, *Shakespeare's 'Histories'. Mirrors of Elizabethan Policy* (1947).

[3] R. G. Moulton, *Shakespeare as a Dramatic Artist* (1885), ch. V.

[4] Cf. W. Clemen, *The Development of Shakespeare's Imagery*, p. 51; A. Yoder, *Animal Analogy in Shakespeare's Character Portrayal* (1947); G. C. Taylor, 'Shakespeare's Use of the Idea of the Beast in Man' *SP*, XLII (1945).

> What, were you snarling all before I came,
> Ready to catch each other by the throat,
> And turn you all your hatred now on me?
>
> (188–190)

Margaret's ensuing curses introduce a third time-dimension –
that of the future – to the consideration of the relationships
between past and present which, up until this point, have played
a dominant part in the scene.

Past and Future Dramatically Portrayed

Shakespeare includes past and future in his drama to a much
greater extent than did his contemporaries. English classical
drama had included much information about the past in the form
of reports, both because the material itself was of interest and
because such reports summarized action which would otherwise
have had to be dramatized on the stage. In other pre-Shakespearian plays, glimpses into the future usually come from characters'
references to future plans or from anticipations of coming events
designed for the audience's enlightenment (in prologues or by
preparatory dumb-shows). Shakespeare replaces such superficial
links between past and present by more fundamental connections:
every present moment is shown to have its roots in the past and
to carry within itself the seeds of the future. Thus references
backwards and forwards in time in Shakespeare's plays are
usually of great dramatic power, no longer isolated reports or
predictions, but closely bound up with the situation on the stage.
In the later tragedies the character's consciousness ranges freely
beyond the immediate present. In the Histories, however, the
references to the past are designed to suggest causes for what we
see before us on the stage; the past evoked is not just any past, but
that particular time when the sins were committed which must
be expiated in the present and future.[1] Destiny, then, has its roots
in the past and is shown working itself out in a chain of historical
circumstances stretching into the future. It seems probable that
Renaissance concepts of the workings of Providence in history,

[1] Cf. W. Clemen, *Past and Future in Shakespeare's Drama*, Annual Shakespeare Lecture of the British Academy 1966 (Oxford, 1967).

the cycle of guilt and expiation (concepts on which, for example, the *Mirror for Magistrates*[1] is built), may have provided some of the ideas which Shakespeare put to use in the structure of his plays.

The Curses (195-303)

The curses which give this scene its distinct character are based on both past and future events. Richard's references to the curse called down by his father upon Margaret – a curse now taking effect – causes his former opponents to unite in condemnation of Margaret, and the key-word *revenge* rings in our ears as Margaret begins her speech of imprecation. She, who has suffered from a curse, knows their power:

> Can curses pierce the clouds and enter heaven?
> Why then, give way, dull clouds, to my quick curses!
>
> (195-196)

The effect of curses is mentioned elsewhere in the scene: Margaret asserts that 'they ascend the sky | And there awake God's gentle-sleeping peace' (287-288). Here, as so often in Shakespeare, a particularly important point in a scene – in this case the power of curses – is returned to and expressed in somewhat altered form.

Margaret curses in turn the King, Prince Edward, the Queen, Rivers, Dorset, Hastings, and Richard himself. All these curses (except the one against Dorset) take effect later in the play, and on each occasion the victim remembers Margaret's words.[2] Buckingham receives only a warning, which, however, later proves to have been valid. With her curses Margaret assigns every major character in the play to his appropriate place,[3] and provides a novel kind of prophetic exposition that covers the rest of the

[1] Cf. E. M. W. Tillyard, *Shakespeare's History Plays* (1948); Lily B. Campbell, 'Theories of Revenge in Renaissance England' *MP*, XXVIII (1931); W. Farnham, *The Medieval Heritage of Elizabethan Tragedy* (1936); Sister Mary Bonaventura Mroz, *Divine Vengeance*; P. Reyher, *Essai sur les idées*; H. B. Charlton, *Shakespearian Tragedy* (1949), p. 34 f.

[2] Cf. III, iii, 15; III, iv, 94; IV, i, 46; IV, iv, 78; V, i, 25.

[3] She has already cursed Clarence with her parenthetical 'Which God revenge!' (137).

action; her curses, then, prepare for and anticipate later events,[1] perhaps all too obviously.

Finally, the curses are linked to the inescapable cycle of guilt and expiation that endures from generation to generation. Even remorse and heartfelt contrition are powerless to blot out guilt or to avert the punishments[2] which, except in Richard's case, are surprisingly harsh. For above and beyond individual guilt towers that of the whole tribe. The original wrongdoings lie far back in time,[3] but the fatal curse lives on from one generation to the next, handed down over the heads of its individual victims.[4] There is no need to emphasize how closely *Richard III* is bound up with the three preceding parts (*Henry VI*) of the tetralogy; that the two historical tetralogies are more than mere chronological sequences has often been stressed:[5] they are linked not only by certain reappearing characters, but by a theme that concerns itself with matters beyond the individual and his fate, that shows him, indeed, as the instrument and agent through which higher purposes are fulfilled. This theme is conveyed primarily through the figure of Margaret.

In Margaret's curses the inexorable quality of expiation that demands an eye for an eye[6] receives strong rhetorical emphasis: the curses are for the most part put into balanced phrases in which two contrasting parallel statements are so similarly worded as to achieve the effect of an echo (*king – king*, 197–198; *Prince of Wales –Prince of Wales*, 199–200; *a queen – a queen*, 202).[7] The individual

[1] See below, p. 112.

[2] On the significance of the curses and prophecies in Shakespeare's Histories, cf. P. Reyher, *Essai sur les idées*, p. 233 f.

[3] Cf. R. G. Moulton, *Shakespeare as a Dramatic Artist* (1885), ch. V.

[4] The classic example of a curse handed down in this way is the one that brooded over the Atrides. And yet there is a vital difference: the destiny that hangs over the Atrides is inevitable, bearing with equal harshness upon the innocent and involving them too in guilt; but in *Richard III* every victim of destiny bears his own weight of guilt and has at some time chosen to do evil.

[5] e.g. E. M. W. Tillyard, *Shakespeare's History Plays* (1948). Cf. J.D.W.'s introductions to *Henry VI* and *Richard III*.

[6] On the Old Testament conception of vengeance which finds expression here cf. Lily B. Campbell, *Shakespeare's Histories. Mirrors of Elizabethan Policy* (1947), p. 317.

[7] And cf. for instance the antithesis in line 272, 'As it was won with blood,

fates are carefully differentiated; they are not simply the destruction, utter ruin, and final damnation usually invoked in sixteenth-century drama (see below, p. 57 f.). The curses against the Queen, for instance, refer to quite specific vicissitudes in her life which in fact later take place, and which are a repetition of what Margaret herself has suffered.

The most far-reaching curse, the one set apart even on the printed page by Richard's interruption, is directed against Richard himself. For him the vengeance of heaven is to be kept back (217), till the sins 'be ripe' (219). That 'any grievous plague' be called down upon him was in keeping with the pre-Shakespearian tradition of dramatic cursing;[1] yet the curses that now follow are specifically related to what in fact comes about. The pangs of conscience Margaret wishes on him are certainly delayed for a long time; but although they play a far smaller part in this play than in the *True Tragedy*,[2] they do overtake him at the very end (V, iii, 193). All the other imprecations likewise refer to important stages and circumstances in Richard's future career.[3]

In a series of lines, five of which are related by the rhetorical device of anaphora, Margaret's curse works up in a crescendo of execration to a peak of emotional vehemence. Epithets of execration appear throughout the play, but they are especially frequent in this scene,[4] and particularly in this final passage of Margaret's

---

lost be it so!' The Biblical undertones (Gen. ix. 6, Matt. xxvi. 52) add additional weight to this passage (Noble, *Shakespeare's Biblical Knowledge*, p. 132).

[1] Cf. *Selimus*, 1806; *Jew of Malta*, 395.

[2] E. E. Stoll sees in Margaret's 'The worm of conscience still be-gnaw the soul!' (222) a return to an earlier conception of the play, in which Richard's pangs of conscience would have played a larger rôle (*Shakespeare Studies*, 1922, p. 222).

[3] Thus Anne's words in IV, i, 'But with his timorous dreams was still awak'd' (85), recall the 'tormenting dream' of Margaret's curse. These lines of Margaret's (226–227) also foreshadow the ghost-scene, not as Shakespeare actually wrote it, but as Holinshed reports it: 'a dreadfull and terrible dreame: for it seemed to him . . . that he did see diuerse images like terrible diuels, (cf. Boswell-Stone, p. 413).

On Margaret's curses, cf. Lily B. Campbell, *Shakespeare's Histories*, p. 316.

[4] Besides the epithets contained in Margaret's curse, Richard is addressed as *devil* (118), *murd'rous villain* (134), *cacodemon* (144), *gentle villain* (163), and *dog* (216). He calls Margaret *foul wrinkled witch* (146), and *hateful wither'd hag* (215).

curse against Richard. These insults, like the earlier curses, reflect the past, reminding us of Richard's ill-starred origin and congenital defect, thus once more bringing past, present, and future into the scope of a single speech.

Curses in Pre-Shakespearian Drama

The plays of Seneca may have served as models for the plentiful use of curses and for the arrangement of curses in rhetorical sequence. Seneca's curses, however, are used to express an abundance of hatred, frenzy, despair, and grief, rather than to serve dramatic (e.g. foreshadowing) ends. The most usual form of curse was an apostrophe to some supra-human power – to the Furies and gods, to earth, heaven, the elements, etc. In English drama based on Seneca the Senecan forms were varied with an exuberant inventiveness often resulting in exaggeration and in an emphasis on metaphor greater than that to be found in Seneca. The imprecatory formulas in Elizabethan drama, in particular cosmic curses and those calling down total annihilation, enabled characters to express their intensity of passion and strength of will.[1] Such imprecatory formulas are a characteristic feature of Marlowe's works, and especially of *Tamburlaine*, where the ever upward-striving will finds its true expression in these cosmic imprecations.[2] Curses always release vast, violent, destructive images in Marlowe: he is less concerned with the object of his curses, who will receive some concrete punishment, than with vividly imagining all the torments of hell and every variety of horror.[3] In the plays of the 'University Wits', in part influenced by *Tamburlaine*, this tendency to elaborate and to expand the curses by means of mythological concepts and extravagant imagery is stronger still; in *Locrine*, for instance, Humbert mobilizes the entire underworld and this world as well, in order to express in 30 lines of imprecation his hatred of the hero (III, vi, 1295 ff.); and in *Selimus*, Bajazet curses everything he can think

[1] Cf. L. L. Schücking, *Shakespeare und der Tragödienstil seiner Zeit* (1947), ch. IV.
[2] Cf. *1 Tamburlaine*, 2036 ff., 2071 ff.; *2 Tamburlaine*, 4393 ff., 4642 ff.
[3] Cf. *1 Tamburlaine*, 1995 ff., 1466 ff., 2006 ff.; *2 Tamburlaine*, 3523 ff., 3846 ff.

of;[1] in *Orlando Furioso* (1275 ff.) the extravagances of *Tamburlaine*
almost seem to be parodied. In addition to such extended imprecations, there are, of course, short, stereotyped expressions in
Tamburlaine and even more frequently in Marlowe's later plays,
and in those of Greene and other contemporaries.[2] But despite
the clearness of the detail in these plays, the curses – unlike those
in *Richard III* – remain fundamentally vague and unrealizable.[3]
Nor in the earlier plays are the curses structurally integrated into
the play, whereas Margaret's curses, exactly fulfilled and remem-
bered by the victim, occupy an important place in the general
design of the play and of the scene in which they occur.

In English classical drama the curses are to be carried out by
heathen powers – the gods, the Furies, and the Eumenides.
Shakespeare's characters call upon *God* to undertake the task of
retribution or they name God as the rightful executor of Divine
Vengeance.[4] The idea that God can make use of a tyrant or a
villain for His purposes of retribution was readopted during the
Renaissance[5] from Old Testament[6] and medieval sources, and

[1] Baiazet's curses conclude with the lines:

> And curse on all thing vnder the wide skie,
> Ah *Aga*, I haue curst my stomacke drie.
>
> (1824–1825)

[2] e.g. *1 Tamburlaine*, 903: 'And fearefull vengeance light vpon you both';
2 Tamburlaine, 2890: 'Hel and confusion light vpon their heads'; *Massacre at
Paris*, 1231 f.: 'the deuill of hell | torture his wicked soule'; *Edward II*, 199:
'For this offence be thou accurst of God'. Also of particular interest in
connection with *Richard III* is the passionate (but unprophetic) curse in the
True Tragedy, 1912 f.:

> Then vengeance, mischiefe, horror, with mischance,
> Wild-fire, with whirlewinds, light vpon your heads.

Cf. also *True Tragedy*, 1386 ff.

[3] This was also true of the curses in Shakespeare's earliest plays. Cf.
2 Henry VI, III, ii, 310–328; *Tit. Andr.* III, i; V, ii.

[4] Cf. ll. 137, 181, 182, 212, 271, 288, 303.

[5] *The Mirror for Magistrates*, 'Thomas Duke of Gloucester', 197–203, provides the classic example here:

> For blood axeth blood as guerdon dewe,
> And vengeaunce for vengeaunce is iust rewarde,
> O ryghteous God thy iudgementes are true,
> For looke what measure we other awarde,

Footnotes continued on opposite page

underlies Shakespeare's portrayal of Richard III. It becomes increasingly clear as the play progresses that Christian ideas, though obscured by other concepts, are of great importance in the play.

Warnings and Prophecies

The warnings with which Margaret follows up her curses lead to fresh prophecies and curses. Margaret warns the Queen (241), Dorset (255), Gloucester (266), and Buckingham (289). But they fail to understand her warnings and angrily reject them, whereupon Margaret prophetically conjures up 'another day' when Buckingham will recall her words 'and say poor Margaret was a prophetess' (301).

The warning addressed to the Queen is particularly rich in symbolic undertones and wider references. The two phrases with which Margaret addresses the Queen ('Poor painted queen, vain flourish of my fortune!')[1] suggest the shadowy nature of Elizabeth's existence; the Queen is playing a rôle that rightly belongs to Margaret. These two expressions sum up Margaret's earlier lines (155, 202) in which she had claimed for herself both the status of queen and a state of joylessness. In Act IV she reminds the Queen of her earlier warning, commenting on what she had said, and what has since come to pass (IV, iv, 82–115), so that the later passage serves as a gloss on her earlier words.

> The same for vs agayne is preparde:
> Take heed ye princes by examples past,
> Blood wyll haue blood, eyther fyrst or last.

Cf. also Mroz, *Divine Vengeance*, particularly ch. II, 7; Lily B. Campbell, 'Theories of Revenge in Renaissance England' *MP*, XXVIII (1931).

In George Whetstone's *The English Myrrour* (1586) God is said to appoint 'tirauntes to be the scourges of his ire'. And in a sermon by Thomas Lever (1550) we read: '. . . it is the sinnes of the people that causeth God to make these men youre rulers. The man is sometymes euyll, but the authoritie from God is alwayes good, and God geueth good authoritie unto euyll men, to punyshe the synnes of the euyll people'. (Quoted by Mroz, *Divine Justice* pp. 37, 38.)

[6] 'I will do vengeance on my enemies, by my enemies' (Deut. xxxii. 41).

[1] Cf. the use of *painted* in *King John*, III, i, 105; *As You Like It*, II, i, 3; *Tit. Andr.*, II, iii, 126; *Hamlet*, III, i, 53.

F

Margaret's warning picks up once more the theme of appearance and reality so prevalent in Scene iii. Although she enters like an apparition from the past and fades from the stage like a shadow, Margaret is in fact living nearer to reality than are the others, those blind and foolish ones whose world of imagination her words unveil. Thus Elizabeth, failing to recognize her own danger, leagues herself with that *bottled spider* Richard, ensnaring herself in his *deadly web* (241–246). An obviously appropriate animal image (one of the many used in connection with Richard[1]) is here extended to suggest that Richard's victims contribute to their own doom. The later warning to Buckingham ('take heed of yonder dog! Look, when he fawns, he bites; . . .') links another character-revealing animal image with a reference to poison which has already been associated with Richard.[2]

The portrayal of Richard continues throughout this scene – the hypocritical mask he presents to others is supplemented by a true image of his present and future conduct. Indeed, he reinforces Margaret's unflattering words when, alone again, he outlines his rôle in a soliloquy. This dual method of character-portrayal – Richard as he seems and Richard as he is – employs the technique of contrast through which the play achieves many of its striking dramatic effects.

Margaret, in answering Dorset's impertinent: 'she is lunatic',[3] refers to the misery caused by loss of honour – a misery which Dorset, member of the new, untried nobility, cannot recognize. The old, forsaken Queen speaks from her own experience, desiring only human sympathy; this new tone gains force as the episode draws to an end. She speaks with increased clarity of her own fate, the fate of those who fall from high and 'dash themselves to pieces' (260).[4] The Fall of Princes, a basic theme of late medieval

[1] Cf. W. Clemen, *The Development of Shakespeare's Imagery*, p. 51; A. Yoder, *Animal Analogy in Shakespeare's Character Portrayal*, p. 39 f.

[2] I, ii, 147.

[3] John Masefield considers 'Your fire-new stamp of honour is scarce current' one of the best examples supporting his contention that, by the time of *Richard III*, 'the poet's great confident manner was now formed' (*W. Shakespeare*, 1954, p. 71).

[4] Cf. IV, iv, 86. In *Richard II* this idea of a fall from on high was to occupy a central position. Cf. P. Reyher, *Essai sur les idées*, p. 285.

'tragedye', later befalls Richard himself. Margaret's words to
Dorset are, then, at once a choric utterance and a statement of her
own experience.

Margaret's Final Curse

Margaret's last two lines are not words of entreaty but a final
curse in which each of her hearers is assigned a place in a constellation of hate where all will be hated by God himself.[1] Our
last view of Margaret, like our first, is of a figure of savage
vengeance. The first words spoken after her exit express the
feeling of horror induced by her expressions of hate: 'My hair
doth stand on end to hear her curses' (304).[2]

That Richard should be the one to express sympathy and understanding for Margaret – even contrition – is, of course, profoundly ironic. One would expect him to return hatred for hatred.
With his hypocritical show of good-heartedness, however, he
takes the bite out of Margaret's imputations concerning his evil
nature. His dishonest words gain their special impact through
the fact that Richard, of all people, becomes the mouthpiece of
what is doubtless the audience's own sympathetic reaction to
Margaret's tragic appearance. Richard's hypocritical profession of
forgiveness towards those who put his brother in prison[3] (which
Rivers clearly takes at its face value, 316–317) prepares us for the
next scene.

The final reference to curses in this scene occurs in Richard's
crafty and devilish aside. Later scenes confirm the impression that
Shakespeare no longer employs the aside, as his predecessors had
done, simply for explanatory comment to the audience, but
instead allows the character to 'speak out' his thoughts.[4]

---

[1] Both curses and laments in *Richard III* seem to establish a relationship in
which the relative positions of the speaker and of each of those involved are
assessed. On this point see below under IV, iv, p. 181.

[2] The *Q2* reading, where this line is given to Hastings, who has already
called upon Margaret to 'end thy frantic curse' (247), is decidedly preferable
to that of the *Folio*, where it falls to Buckingham. Cf. J.D.W., pp. 147, 185.

[3] Cf. H. Spencer, note on 315.

[4] On the use of the *aside* in *Richard III*, see below, p. 104 f.

Richard's Soliloquy (324–339)

Richard's ensuing soliloquy, on the other hand, which follows
the pattern of the Machiavellian villain's monologue, *does* convey
information: he takes the audience into his confidence and lays
his cards on the table. Cynically he admits to masking his villainy
by quoting from the Bible[1] and to deceiving and dividing his
enemies by exploiting whatever tensions exist between them.[2]
But since everything that Richard says has been made clear by the
foregoing scene, the purpose of this monologue may be less that
of conveying information than of allowing us a further glimpse
into the workings of Richard's mind: Richard's satisfaction with
his own devilish arts is once more illustrated. He even describes
the method of deception which enables him not only to disguise
his real nature but also to feign behaviour the contrary of what
he really feels. His last words – 'I play the devil' – (echoing the
appearance-reality theme) draw attention to his histrionic pro-
pensities: he feels that both his deceit and the wickedness underlying it are ingredients in a rare performance which he observes
and applauds.

[1] Cf. R. Noble, *Shakespeare's Biblical Knowledge*, p. 132: 'Richard . . ., like
Satan tempting Christ, as in *Matt.* IV. and *Luke* IV., quotes sufficient
Scripture to suit his purpose and conceal his real intent'.

[2] In this Richard shows himself to be a pupil of Machiavelli (or rather of
'pseudo-Machiavelli' – Machiavelli as the Elizabethans understood him). In
1577 an English translation of a work by Gentillet had appeared (*A Discourse Upon the Meanes of Well Governing*), which reproduced a biased and
hostile version of the theories of Machiavelli: 'A vertuous Tyrant, to maintaine his tyrannie, ought to maintaine partialities and factions amongst his
subjects, and to sley and take away such as love the commonwealth' (Pt III,
Maxim 15). Cf. W. A. Armstrong, 'The Influence of Seneca and Machiavelli
on the Elizabethan Tyrant' *RES*, XXIV (1948), pp. 19–35. In *3 Henry VI*
Richard had claimed that he might 'set the murderous Machiavel to school'
(III, ii, 193). Several critics have seen Richard as Machiavellian *par excel-
lence* for the Elizabethans. Cf. E. Meyer, *Machiavelli and the Elizabethan
Drama* (1897); Kuno Fischer, *Shakespeares Charakterentwicklung Richards III*
(1889), p. 86; A. Hennecke, 'Shakespeares englische Könige im Lichte
staatsrechtlicher Strömungen seiner Zeit' *SJ*, 66 (1930), pp. 79–144. See
also note 1, p. 123.

The Interlude with the Murderers (339–356)

The short episode with the murderers picks up the thread of the action again and prepares us for the next scene in which the murderers carry out the orders received here. In Shakespeare's Histories, scenes consisting in the main of static dialogue frequently end with some livelier incident called for by the course of the action – this is the structure of both Scenes iii and iv. In pre-Shakespearian drama, indeed, the scene or act was often rounded off with a short passage in which a character received orders which he carried out later in the play.[1]

Incitement to Murder in Pre-Shakespearian Drama

Scenes portraying the hiring or commissioning of murderers were fairly common in pre-Shakespearian drama. In later plays the process of 'winning over' the murderers was depicted in some detail,[2] but in the more primitive versions (of which Marlowe's *Massacre at Paris*, 67–90, offers a late instance) no attempt was made to present the murderer as a person; he accepted his instructions as commands, without argument or hesitation. In *Edward II*, the murderer has some individual qualities. As in *Richard III*, he has already agreed to do the job before his first appearance on stage, and young Mortimer's question, 'Come forth, art thou as resolute as thou wast?' (2354)[3] is not unlike Richard's greeting to the murderers: 'How now, my hardy stout resolved mates!' (340). There too (2358) the instigator warns the murderer not to weaken at the sight of his victim. In *King Leir*, as in *Richard III* (348), a warning is given against the victim's persuasive tongue,[4] and the same motif appears yet again in the anonymous *Woodstock*, where the murderers are warned that on no account must they let the sight of their victim move them to pity (V, i, 17 ff.). Thus this

---

[1] Cf. e. g. *James IV*, I, ii; III, ii; *Friar Bacon and Friar Bungay*, I, i; *Jew of Malta*, 1129–1149.

[2] As, for example, in *King Leir*: both Gonorill and Ragan only gradually give the 'messenger' to understand that they would like him to murder their father, and they use skilful methods in the attempt to persuade him (xii, xvii).

[3] Cf. *Massacre at Paris*, 'Come on sirs, what, are you resolutely bent' (938).

[4] 'But see thou faynt not; for they will speake fayre' (*Leir*, 1346).

episode with the murderers contains much that was conventional. Some of the murderers' observations sound like trite proverbial truisms[1] to which their behaviour in the next scene gives the lie.

While Shakespeare does not turn his attention to making the murderers convincing and individual characters until Scene iv, this episode brings Richard's character into sharper relief. He displays his usual skill in varying his method of address to suit the particular moment (*my hardy stout resolved mates* 340; *sirs* 346; *lads* 355). His: '... do not hear him plead; | For Clarence is well-spoken ...' (347–348) evidences shrewd judgement and at the same time creates an element of suspense for the next scene. And the compression and bite of his concluding antithesis – 'Your eyes drop millstones when fools' eyes[2] fall tears' (354) perfectly express his ready tongue and sarcastic nature.

SCENE FOUR

The 'Self-Contained' Scene in Shakespeare's Plays

Scene iv (Clarence's dream and his murder) differs from the preceding, strongly expository scene, resembling rather the woo-ing-scene between Richard and Anne in presenting an event complete in itself. The scene is, in fact, almost a tragedy in miniature with a dramatic curve complete in itself: the foreshadow-ing of the tragic event, so common in Shakespeare's tragedies, takes the form of a prophetic dream; like so many tragedies, the scene contains a decisive moment when things might take a turn for the better; and the hero, like many of Shakespeare's tragic heroes, is blind to his real danger until the moment of revelation shortly before his death.

This scene reminds us that Shakespeare in his earlier plays, in common with most Elizabethan dramatists, often worked with the

---

[1] e.g. 351: 'Talkers are no good doers'.
[2] Cf. Richard's earlier reference to tears (I, ii, 153).

single scene as his unit rather than with the entire play. But whereas in pre-Shakespearian drama the short, self-contained episodes followed abruptly one upon the other with little or no concern for the unity of the whole work, Shakespeare took care that even the scenes constructed almost as independent dramatic entities be firmly linked to the plot, to the thematic structure, and to the general design of the play.

The first act of *Richard III* prepares us for what is to follow, not only, as in Scene iii, by conveying background material and hinting at future events, but through the device of interpolating into the complicated and fast-moving flow of action portraits of an individual in a character-revealing situation. Both Richard's opening monologue with the encounters which follow it and the subsequent wooing-scene provide 'portraits' of this kind. Here, in the fourth scene, the spotlight focuses in similar manner upon Clarence. But from Act II onwards the rapid advance of plot brings about a shift from the more static portrait scenes to mixed scenes combining character-portrayal and action; moreover the weaving together of the separate strands of theme and of plot and the construction of smooth transitions between scenes become, with the increase in narrative tempo, matters of greater concern to the playwright.[1]

The Place of the Scene in the Dramatic Structure

In Scene iii the complicated pattern of court life was reflected in the comings and goings on stage, in the large cast, and in the variety of episode within the scene. Scene iv returns to a more intimate setting, yet one markedly different in style and construction from those that have gone before. Here for the first time Richard is not present in person; nevertheless the knowledge that it is he who has planned this deed, he who is responsible for this first in a series of violent acts, keeps his figure before us, knitting the scene into the pattern of the play.

But it is not only Richard's invisible presence that links this scene to the larger design of the play. Clarence has been guilty of

---

[1] On the 'five movements' of the play see A. P. Rossiter, *Angel with Horns* (1961), p. 7.

the murder of a child and of the betrayal of his father: he becomes the first victim in a string of Nemesis Actions of which Richard is both instrument and victim. With this scene the first cycle of retribution is brought to its completion.

I, iii had ended with Richard's cynical account of his own dissimulation, and the very down-to-earth meeting with the murderers; the present scene opens on quite another note. Clarence's dream-vision, couched in poetic and imaginative language, carries us into a region beyond reality. It marks, moreover, a pause in the flow of scenes, a moment of reflection in the rapid sequence of action and verbal exchanges.

It also looks forward to what is to come. Not only does Clarence's nightmare exude an atmosphere of impending disaster, but from his vision of the other world the dominant theme of guilt and expiation rises like a black cloud to hang over the ensuing acts. Clarence's dream, like Richard's in the final act (V, iii) is of a suggestiveness and a richness which stems in no obvious way from the actual events of the dream. A detailed examination of the relationships between these two dreams must await a later section. Here suffice it to say that, whereas Clarence repents past sins, Richard remains unashamed and cynical to the end.

These few observations should not be considered as an exhaustive list of the links between Scene iv and the rest of the play. But perhaps they will serve to refute the view that the episode is insufficiently integrated into the fabric of the play.[1]

The Composition of the Scene

The scene is constructed round a striking contrast. The elevated, poetic language of Clarence's account of his dream is followed by the coarse jesting and laconic cynicism of the two murderers. Such contrasts in style and construction – occurring nowhere else in the play – raise the question as to whether the scene results from a combination of two originally unrelated parts.[2] The character-

[1] Cf. H. Spencer: 'This clumsy scene is typical of the loose-jointedness of the chronicle plays' (p. 175).

[2] Cf. L. L. Schücking, Über einige Nachbesserungen, p. 25 f.

ization of the two murderers in the prose section, for instance, is quite different from that which follows in the verse passage. But even if this scene represents a marriage of originally separated elements, we must give Shakespeare credit for recognizing the particular effects which a fusion would bring about. Since these diverse components do, in fact, add up to a convincing total impression, it cannot be said that the scene falls into two independent halves; nor can the murderer's prose dialogue be considered a comic insertion, an interlude designed only to amuse the audience but contributing little to the real content of the scene. The talk between the murderers carries on, in a different key, themes first sounded in Clarence's account of his ominous dream. Thematic modulation of this kind is a technique much used by Shakespeare.

Pre-Shakespearian tragedy had already contained examples of comic prose side by side with conventional, highflown rhetoric,[1] for instance in plays which were a mixture of English drama and tragedy on the Senecan pattern. Thus in *Locrine* scenes involving the clowns Strumbo and Trompart are set between scenes of high drama.[2] But in all such cases, though the two stylistic levels are placed side by side, there is no link between them. The passages of clowning are simply interruptions, in no way related to the tragic themes.[3] In our scene, however, the murderers' prose dialogue plays an effective part in the inner action of the play.

Clarence's Dream (1–75)

The account of the dream is prefaced by a short conversation between Brakenbury[4] and Clarence in which the latter's reactions

---

[1] Cf. W. Clemen, *English Tragedy before Shakespeare*, passim.

[2] e.g. where Alba's address to Fortuna, just before his suicide, is followed by Trompart's parody that turns the rhetorical style upside down (II, v).

[3] This is also true of the clowning in Marlowe's *Doctor Faustus*, though here we must take into consideration the state of the text and the disputed authorship of the comic passages. Cf. W. W. Greg, *The Tragical History of the Life and Death of Dr. Faustus. A Conjectural Reconstruction* (1950).

[4] For reasons to be found in the note to J.D.W.'s edition (p. 149), it seems preferable to follow *Q*, which identifies the keeper as Brakenbury from the start, and to reject the *F* reading (retained by Al. but not by most editors)

to his own dream are revealed. Before the dream is recounted, we are given a clear idea, through words, facial expression, and gesture, of the effect the dream has had on Clarence. The 'miserable night', 'ugly sights', 'fearful dreams', and 'dismal terror' of Clarence's report are made credible by his manner and appearance, to which our attention is drawn by the question 'Why looks your Grace so heavily to-day?' Such indirect stage-directions, employed by Shakespeare to indicate facial expressions, gesture, and demeanour, play a larger part in his plays than in those of his contemporaries.

Only after Clarence has portrayed his mood, then, does he go on to tell the content of his dream. It is a dream of death and of what follows after death; the two main sections are divided by the question which Brakenbury interposes at line 42. The first section recounts three episodes: the scene on shipboard, ending with the fall into the 'tumbling billows' (–20); the vision in the depths of the sea (–33); and the death-struggle (–41). The dream is prophetic and is not intended to be interpreted psychologically. At the same time, however, it is a 'genuine' dream in that the first part, at least, has an intuitive psychological accuracy. The second part, with its classically inspired epic description of the next world, is more strongly allegorical and literary.

The dream moves from circumstances familiar to Clarence to unknown and more remote areas of experience. It begins with a sea-crossing to Burgundy (10) but ends in the next world among the Furies and the torments of hell. But even here, the past, the 'thousand heavy times, | During the wars of York and Lancaster' (14 f.) lives on in the accusations of the dead (50, 55).

Clarence in his dream has broken out of prison; but by an ironical reversal this wish-fulfilling freedom leads only to his death. Richard's rôle in Clarence's dream, like his rôle in Clarence's life, is that of the seemingly sympathetic companion and friend – a friend who nevertheless lures Clarence from the security of his cabin up onto the deck where he strikes the blow that plunges

---

which distinguishes between a 'keeper' and Brakenbury whose *entry* is recorded at line 76. On Brakenbury in Holinshed and in Shakespeare, cf. R. A. Law in *PMLA*, LX (1945), pp. 694–695.

Clarence into the sea. Clarence recognizes Richard as the agent of
his dream-death, but not yet as its deliberate author; the recogni-
tion of Richard's real villainy comes later in the scene. The language of the dream thus allows Clarence to express a subconscious
sense of Richard's menace.

The sensation of falling, so frequent in dreams, and the experience of drowning are related with a convincing intensity
which appeals to all our senses. The horror and anguished
foreboding of a nightmare is accurately captured both in the
drowning sequence and in the following vision of the bottom of
the sea, where the images following fast one upon the other seem
to reflect thoughts racing through the mind of a dying man.

But what, we may ask, is a dream about drowning, the sea and
the sea-bed, doing in this scene? The subsequent dream-episode in
the world of the dead is not so unexpected: it follows the traditions
of the time in adopting as its model dreams from classical drama
dealing with conscience and judgement. That the escape dreamed
of by Clarence would necessarily involve a sea-crossing is one
very superficial explanation. More convincing is the suggestion
that the drowning is an ironic anticipation of Clarence's death in
the butt of malmsey-wine. Yet even this explanation fails to
account for the particularly suggestive quality of these lines – a
quality that seems to stem from the symbolic colouring of much of
the passage, and more particularly from the symbolic value
attached here to the element of water. In ancient mythology
water, because of its dissolving and transforming qualities, was a
symbol of death. Here, too, water is associated with death: Souls
were carried over the River Styx to the world of the dead, and
Clarence must pass through the medium of water before he arrives
at that other kingdom. He is conveyed from the lighter element,
from the 'air' of life, into the ominous, oppressive, fatal element of
water and is held there in an unfamiliar deathlike world. Water
thus seems to represent a transitional stage in the process of
disembodiment, in the passage from life to death.

There is symbolism too in Clarence's vision of the sea-bed as a
huge grave in which lie a thousand wrecks, a thousand corpses.
The skull-gem images serve, of course, to remind us of the
transitoriness of life. But beyond that, they point to the falsity of

wordly standards: the precious things which, while we lived, seemed the essence of beauty and worth (in Elizabethan sonnets gold and precious stones are used both in this sense and as a lofty image of feminine beauty) now lie about uselessly, heightening through their contrast with the surrounding rottenness the impact of this spectacle of death. And just as the enduring gems 'mock' the dead men's bones, and also, by implication, the transitoriness of life, so death mocks at all together; for now these treasures are without meaning, even they have become subject to the law of death. Their lover now is only 'the slimy bottom of the deep', which they 'woo' in place of the living lover – now nothing but bones. These lines bring to mind the medieval 'Dances of Death' with their opulently jewelled skeletons, and even seem to foreshadow the frequent juxtapositions of beauty and death in the metaphysical poets.

The image of jewels in the eye-sockets of skeletons recurs much later in *The Tempest*, where Ariel sings of Ferdinand's drowned father (I, ii, 396 ff.). There, however, the image takes on magical qualities. No longer are dead men's bones contrasted to jewels; instead, the corpse itself undergoes a 'sea-change'. The eyes turn into pearls, the bones into coral. Instead of dreadful decay, death brings about a mysterious and miraculous metamorphosis. Whereas the passage in *Richard III* is a rational description though conveyed through the medium of poetry, Ariel's song has a pure, lyrical quality of its own. Clarence's lines,

> Where eyes did once inhabit there were crept,
> As 'twere in scorn of eyes, reflecting gems,
>
> (30 f.)

contain a conscious comparison; but Ariel's 'Those are pearls that were his eyes' substitute for the comparison an immediate and direct equation. Brakenbury's question, 'Had you such leisure in the time of death | To gaze upon these secrets of the deep?' betrays the rational element which is also part of Clarence's description. It also marks the gulf separating the world of the dream from everyday reality, and Clarence from honest, stolid Brakenbury.

Clarence's sea-bed vision, revealing to him what may be seen only at the point of death, is the most imaginative and imagistically rich passage in the dream – indeed, in the whole play. Yet its connection with the action is less close than that of the first and last sections of this dream. Shakespeare, unlike his contemporaries, was prepared to construct his dream so that parts of it are self-justifying, with no purposeful relation to the plot. It was sufficient that such passages exercise an appeal to the audience's imagination. And certainly the imaginative force of the vision on the sea-bed is great; neither the revelation of Richard's evil in Scene ii nor the torments of hell described later in the play evoke an atmosphere so full of horror as does this underwater vision of universal death and destruction.

Several scholars have suggested, rather convincingly, that the sea-bed vision may in fact carry hidden references to the treasure-laden Armada,[1] the destruction of which had taken place shortly before Shakespeare wrote *Richard III*. The description in the *Faerie Queene* (III, iv, 22–23) of treasures scattered on the ocean's depths ('through the ouerthrow | And wrecks of many wretches') may have been partly influenced by this same historical event,[2] and, together with Spenser's description of Mammon's treasury (*F. Qu.* II, vii, 4–5), may conceivably have had some influence on Shakespeare's sea-bed spectacle; but such a connection can only be surmised. What is the most striking in this passage is, in any case, the rich, symbolic treatment of an historic event out of the then recent and still living past.

Clarence experiences his death-struggle less as a struggle to stay alive than as an agonized effort to free himself from his body. As elsewhere in Shakespeare,[3] the soul is depicted as a volatile substance, a breath enclosed within the body whose way to 'the empty, vast, and wand'ring air'[4] is barred by the restraining

[1] The Armada theory would support Wright's reading of *ingots* in place of *anchors* (26) – a reading adopted by J.D.W. in his text.

[2] Spenser handed the first three Books to the printer in November 1589, but he had begun work on the *Faerie Queene* in 1580.

[3] Cf. *Richard III*, IV, iv, 11; V, iii, 172; *2 Henry VI*, III, ii, 391; *3 Henry VI*, V, ii, 35; *Richard II*, I, iii, 195; V, v, 111; *King John*, V, vii, 28; *Romeo and Juliet*, III, i, 123. Cf. also A. Ackermann, *Der Seelenglaube bei Shakespeare*, Frauenfeld (1914).

[4] Most editors, including Al. and J.D.W., have followed F at this point: 'empty, vast, and wand'ring air'. This reading is preferable to *Q*'s 'empty

waves. Once again the physical agony accompanying a physical-
spiritual experience is forcefully conveyed; the immediate impact
of these lines is gained not only from the violence of such words as
panting, bulk, burst, belch, but also from their explosive alliteration.

The Journey to the Underworld

After Brakenbury's question 'Awak'd you not in this sore agony?'
(42), the last two words of which sum up the preceding tortured
lines, Clarence goes on to describe his soul's journey to the underworld. This second section is less vivid in its imagery, less
visionary, and altogether more derivative than the opening
section – the text itself hints as much with the words 'which poets
write of' (46). It has been suggested that Shakespeare may have
had the *Aeneid* VI, Dante's *Inferno* (III, 109), and above all the
Induction to the Complaint of Buckingham (*Mirror for Magistrates*)[1] in
mind. But there are no striking parallels in the wording, so that
any influence must have been of a quite general nature.[2] The
images of Charon, the Styx, the 'kingdom of perpetual night', the
'dark monarchy', and the Furies belong to the classical underworld rather than to the Christian hell, though Christian imagery
mingles with the classical in expressions such as 'a shadow like an
angel' (53).[3]

---

vast, and wandering air' (where *vast* = *waste*, n.), because it is precisely the
piling up of adjectives which gives the line its particular poetic effect.

[1] On this point cf. in particular J.D.W., p. xxvii ff.

[2] Details with a classical flavour could easily have been derived at second
hand: cf. *The Spanish Tragedy*, 'But churlish Charon, only boatman there'
(I, i, 20), or *Tamburlaine*, 'Where shaking ghosts with euer howling grones, |
Houer about the vgly Ferriman' (*1 Ta*, 2026 f.; cf. also 2037, 2245). Conceptions of the next world in Elizabethan drama are discussed by Th.
Spencer, *Death and Elizabethan Tragedy*. Spencer notes that images such as
'kingdom of perpetual night' (47) as well as many other Shakespearian and
Elizabethan references to night, darkness, and shadow as symbols for death
and the next world derive originally from the classics (p. 86 ff.).

[3] Th. Spencer also discusses the mixture of classical and Christian images
in descriptions of the next world in Elizabethan drama (*Death and Elizabethan
Tragedy*, 1936, pp. 118–120). The original meaning of *inferna* (*inferi* = 'kingdom of the dead', 'Hades'), and its later meaning ('place of perdition', i.e.
'hell') are both present in the underworld of the dream. Cf. P. Althaus,
'Niedergefahren zur Hölle', *Zeitschrift für systematische Theologie*, XIX (1942).

In this section the dead pass judgement on the living; two of the people he has wronged confront Clarence with their accusations and deliver him over to the Furies.[1] These accusing spirits are the voice of Clarence's own conscience. Clarence's earlier reference to 'a thousand heavy times, | During the wars of York and Lancaster' (14–15) takes on at this point more definite shape: both his murder of Prince Edward on the field by Tewkesbury (56) and his treachery towards his father, Warwick (already mentioned by Richard: I, iii, 135), belong to this dark period in his past. Clarence himself summons these accusing figures back into his memory and must suffer the unavoidable punishment for his crimes at the hands of the avenging Furies, just as later in the scene he will be punished through the agency of the murderers. Past and future are interwoven in varying ways in almost every scene; in this case Clarence's memories of past guilt arouse dread in the face of the inevitable expiation. Here, as elsewhere in the play, the linking together of guilt and punishment emphasizes their necessary connection. Besides, these memories of the past serve an informational as well as a thematic purpose.

Comparison with Richard's Dream in V, iii

We are reminded of the accusing figures in Clarence's dream when, in Act V, the spirits of Richard's victims remind him of his crimes and call for his end. In Richard's dream, too, the past is revived and guilt and expiation are shown to be inextricably bound together.[2] Yet Richard's dream consists entirely of the accusations of the dead; in place of the continuous dream-narrative with its shifting dream-landscape, a well-drilled succession of ghosts address themselves one by one first to Richard, then to Richmond, in morality play fashion.

Clarence's dream benefits from the fact that it lacks the symmetrical structure of Richard's dream, that the accusations made

---

[1] For examples of the Furies in Elizabethan drama cf. *1 Tamburlaine*, 1655, 1999; *Span. Trag.*, III, xiii, 1171; III, ii, 125; *Locrine*, III, vi, 1317. Cf. also Sackville's *Induction* to the *Mirror*, 109.

[2] A. Arnold in his article 'The Recapitulation Dream in *Richard III* and *Macbeth*' *SQ*, VI (1955), stresses the similarities between the two dreams.

by the dead are only one strand in its weave. In richness of texture, poetic subtlety, and range of theme it is superior to Richard's clean-cut nightmare. The first section and again the conclusion (where the *hideous cries* of the Furies following upon the shrieks of Clarence's accusers wake him from his sleep) have a genuinely dreamlike quality.

Dramatization of the Dream-Narrative[1]

In pre-Shakespearian tragedy, narrative passages were usually inserted into the drama without any attempt at dramatization; but here a first tentative step is made towards working a long, poetic account into a conversational setting: Clarence is provided with a conversational partner who interrupts the narrative with his questions. These infrequent and rather trivial questions of Braken-bury's show him to be emotionally quite uninvolved in Clarence's story, so that it cannot really be claimed that the narrative is thoroughly integrated into the conversation; the exchange is too one-sided for that. Nevertheless Brakenbury's opening question *does* serve as a quasi-conversational transition to Clarence's account of the dream, and his later questions, too, introduce an element of naturalness into what might otherwise seem an over-long, undramatic speech. It is, of course, possible that this 'failure' to provide Clarence with a partner who reacts to and comprehends what he is hearing is intentional; for the introduction of a listener of such little understanding makes Clarence appear even more alone than he would have been if there had been nobody with him at all. Brakenbury's questions have the additional effect of forcing Clarence to make several fresh starts; thus the division of the description into its component sections, each with its own poetic momentum, is underlined by the formal division brought about by Brakenbury's questions.

The Dream: Language and Versification

The dramatic quality of the narrative results not only from the introduction of a conversational foil, Brakenbury, but also from

---

[1] On what follows cf. K. Schlüter, *Shakespeares dramatische Erzählkunst*, Schriftenreihe der Deutschen Shakespeare-Gesellschaft, VII (1958).

the urgent manner in which the dream is recounted. Clarence tells
of the experience while still under the spell it has cast, so that
almost every line (especially in the first part) seems to be describing something actually taking place.

The measured beginning and gradually increasing momentum
of the account is in part attributable to the verse pattern of the
opening lines: thus the conclusion of the first sentence in the
middle rather than at the end of a line, and on an unaccented
syllable ('. . . Upon the hatches', 13) results in a slow, deliberate
pace. In the second sentence the pauseless run of the verse from
line 14 to line 16 brings about a gradual increase of tempo which
is sustained by the heightened suspense of the third sentence with
its insertion of 'that thought to stay him' into the middle of line 19.

But the pace of the three involved and parenthetical opening
sentences remains, in spite of such variations, rather measured.
With the fourth sentence (Clarence's cry of anguish as he remembers his terrible experiences: 'O Lord, methought what pain it was
to drown' 21) the mood and the flow of the verse changes utterly,
and the two exclamations which follow (22–23) convey with
undiminished intensity Clarence's renewed perception of the
tortures of drowning. The rhetorical character of these two cries
(parallel construction reinforced by anaphora) does not obtrude
itself on us as artifice; formal rhetoric is used in Clarence's dream
with restraint. A further example occurs at line 55: 'Clarence is
come – false, fleeting, perjur'd Clarence' echoes the earlier 'empty,
vast, and wand'ring air' (39) and introduces the rhetorical device
of epanalepsis (the use of the same word at the beginning and end
of the line); but, as in the earlier lines 22 and 23, the rhetoric does
not impose itself on our attention. The effect is appropriate and
unforced.

The lines describing the sea-bed vision, like the opening lines
of Clarence's account, gradually increase in tempo. The rather
slow pace of line 24 leads up to the rapid listing of objects in
lines 26–27 which then gives way to a fairly long and syntactically
more involved poetic elaboration.[1] In the first three lines of this
extended image (29–31) the two final stresses are syntactically

---

[1] For an appreciation of this passage cf. also F. P. Wilson, *Marlowe and
the Early Shakespeare* (1953), p. 123.

G

divided from the rest of the line, so that we feel the concluding effect of the final two lines, which, running together, round off this sub-section.

After Brakenbury's interruption (34–35), the verse pattern changes again, becoming more agitated. The enjambement of lines 36–38 (describing the death struggle) produces a strong, restless movement coming to a halt in the even beat of *empty, vast, and wand'ring* (39). The same effect is produced again in lines 58–62 (when Clarence is seized by the Furies). The unbearable strain of the final struggle with death is suggested in the alliteration and vowel-sequence of 'bulk ... burst ... belch ...' (40–41).[1] In contrast to such verbal violence, the stateliness of the lines that introduce the words of the murdered Edward ('Then came wand'ring by | a shadow like an angel, with bright hair | Dabbled in blood'; 52 ff.) are doubly striking. Despite such isolated excellences, however, the language and rhythm of the second part of the account fails to reach the heights of the sea-vision.

The impact of Clarence's speech is not, of course, dependent on rhythm and tempo alone: various stylistic devices add to the immediacy of effect. The piling up of transitive verbs (as in lines 37–41: *yield, stopp'd in, let it forth, find, smother'd, belch*) is one way in which the account is made vivid. A sense of immediacy is also achieved by the use of direct speech for reporting the words of the dead. Above all, the constant appeal to our senses, and in particular to our hearing, brings life to the passage.

In the dream-narrative the resources of language are stretched to new limits to permit the handling of previously unexplored regions of experience. And, moreover, one of the great themes of allegorical poetry – the dream-vision of the next world[2] – has here been successfully incorporated into drama.

[1] Noted by E. Guest (*History of English Rhythms*, 1838), see *Var.*, p. 121 f.
[2] 'The latest of a long line of English vision-poems going back to the *Roman de la Rose* of the thirteenth century, Clarence's Dream, as a fearful vision of the after-life, belongs to a special class of such poems, which drew their inspiration from the sixth book of the *Aeneid* and Dante's *Inferno* . . .' (J.D.W., p. xxvii).

Dreams in Pre-Shakespearian Drama

Shakespeare was not the first Elizabethan dramatist to make use of dreams in his plays to predict, to warn, and to anticipate; Greek tragedy, the epics of Horace and Virgil, and the works of Seneca[1] all contained useful models for later writers.[2] The *Mirror for Magistrates*, certainly known to Shakespeare, contains a warning dream which accurately captured the dream-atmosphere (*Anthony, Lord Rivers*, 470–487). In pre-Shakespearian drama the connection between the dream and the event for which it prepared or of which it warned was always made abundantly clear, and usually explicitly stated; the dramatists were, indeed, far more concerned with making plain the significance of the dream than with creating a dream-world or describing the experience of dreaming. Consequently their dreams, often mere outlines of allegorical fables or well-known stories, are much shorter than Clarence's, less keenly observed, thinner in content, and awkward in presentation.[3] Shakespeare seems to have been the first dramatist to reproduce the atmosphere of a dream, even if, seen from our modern vantage point, Clarence's dream is rather too rational to be altogether convincing. Nevertheless, the first part could really have been dreamed practically as Clarence recounts it. Most dreams in Shakespeare, however, are not very different from those of his predecessors, doing little more than to convey a warning,[4] though the later plays contain dreams which are less primitive, and more artfully integrated into the dramatic situation.

[*66–74*] Clarence's words to Brakenbury at the close of his narrative pick up the central theme of the second section of the

[1] Cf. *Troades*, Andromache's dream (433 ff.).

[2] Cf. B. T. Stewart, 'The Renaissance Interpretation of Dreams and their Use in Elizabethan Drama', in: *Summaries of Doctoral Dissertations, Northwestern University*, X (1942), pp. 33–36.

[3] Cf. *Selimus*, 2215 ff; *Leir*, 1479 ff.; *Woodstock* IV, ii, 6; *Alphonsus of Aragon*, 1355 ff. Cornelia's dream in Kyd's *Cornelia* (adapted from Garnier's play) in which the 'ghost of Pompey' appears to her (III, i, 67 ff.) belongs to a different category; cf. in this connection Seneca, *Troades*, 438 ff.

[4] Cf. *Richard III*, III, ii. Cf. also *Romeo and Juliet*, V, i, 1; *2 Henry VI*, I, ii, 22; III, ii, 31.

dream, the theme of conscience, and lead on to the prayer.[1] Clarence is not alone in invoking God in this play; almost every character calls upon, or at least names God, and this happens more frequently than in the other Histories.[2] Richard also addresses God, but in a hypocritically ironic tone, whereas what we have here is the true prayer of a man in mortal anguish. One way in which Shakespeare differentiated his characters was by presenting them with the same problems to solve, making them use the same key-words and expressions in different senses, and placing them in similar situations. Thus the way in which various characters in *Richard III* call upon God tells us something about their nature.[3]

Brakenbury's Monologue (76–83)

Brakenbury's altogether impersonal monologue consists of moral reflections – choric in nature, addressed to the audience, and having nothing to do with the preceding episode – on the hollow satisfactions of high station. This speech does nothing to make of Brakenbury a more important figure than his previous remarks had shown him to be (though here again, the soliloquy may be designed to illustrate Brakenbury's detached and uncomprehending attitude). Whatever Shakespeare may have intended, the monologue is without doubt the weakest part of the scene, lacking any real relation to the action or to the character who speaks it. Shakespeare was following a convention whereby such undramatic pieces of moral comment were introduced into both serious drama and romantic tragi-comic plays,[4] forming a kind of

[1] Howard Baker stresses the importance of this prayer: 'Now this scene is a series of manipulations of the theme of divine vengeance. Clarence's prayer is the foundational passage in it, the norm for the rhetoric' (*Induction to Tragedy. A Study in a Development of Form in Gorboduc, The Spanish Tragedy and Titus Andronicus*, 1939, p. 60).

[2] 73 times as compared to 5 in *King John*, 37 in *Richard II*, 19 in *3 Henry VI*, 25 in *1 Henry IV*, etc.

[3] Cf. for instance how God is invoked and named in I, iii by the three main characters: Richard, 59, 77, 140, 181, 315. Margaret, 111, 137, 212, 271, 288, 303. Elizabeth, 35, 76, 182. And cf. in connection with Clarence's prayer, Richmond's prayer at the end (V, v).

[4] Cf. W. Clemen, *English Tragedy before Shakespeare*, passim.

moralizing running commentary.[1] In Parts 2 and 3 of *Henry VI*
such moralizing passages occur,[2] but their relationship to both
situation and speaker is closer than here. Clarence, after all, has not
mentioned his 'princely lot' nor has it played any part in the
events of the play. This digression on princes and their 'titles'
disturbs rather than contributes to the total impression of a
scene which moves us by its human qualities.

The rather pompous morality of this speech[3] is couched in a
series of antitheses. The contrast between *outward* honour and
inward toil echoes the basic theme of appearance and reality. For
what raises princes above their fellows is after all illusory; the
glories which they possess are in fact intangible. Shakespeare
touches here upon a theme that constantly recurs in the Histories,
though one has only to read Henry IV's lines on sleep (*2 Henry IV*,
III, i, 5 ff.) and Henry V's great speech on ceremony and the lot of
a king (*Henry V*, IV, i, 229 ff.) to recognize the primitiveness of
this earlier passage. Even Henry VI's reflections on kingship and
the crown (*3 Henry VI*, II, v, 21 ff.; III, i) are profounder and more
personal.

The Murder-Scene (84–281)

The episode consists of two parts: first, a lengthy prose conversation in which the murderers discuss the subject of conscience;
then, after Clarence awakens, a verse dialogue between them and
Clarence. The noticeable break between these two parts raises the
question of the ways in which they are linked. For in the prose
dialogue the murderers show themselves to be jocose, clownish
ruffians, while in the scene with Clarence they are eloquent
accusers and, at the same time, solemn instruments of a divine

[1] Greene rarely misses an opportunity to insert moral observations. Cf.
for instance *James IV* and *Friar Bacon and Friar Bungay*.

[2] Cf. for instance *3 Henry VI*, V iv, 1 ff.

[3] Paraphrased by H. Spencer as follows: 'the only gratification princes can
have from their glories is the possession of their titles, and that amounts to
a merely superficial honor in return for a real and deepseated necessity of
constant exertion (*an inward toil*); while in return for such abstractions as
their titles (*imaginations*), which after all are intangible (*unfelt*) they often do
actually feel the weight of a whole world of cares that deny them any rest'
(p. 177).

fate, using language and scriptural references[1] quite out of character with the brutish murderers of the prose dialogue. The contrast is great enough to justify the suspicion that the two parts stem from different sources and were not conceived as a unit.[2] It is, of course, possible to argue that the rhetorical language and the rhyme of the second part is purposely adopted by the murderers, who feel themselves in some sense instruments of a higher will, of fate's decree. Indeed, the Second Murderer begins by exclaiming 'My voice is now the King's' (164). Or it may be argued that the murderers *must* speak in verse because – in keeping with the convention of pre-Shakespearian drama – they have to adapt themselves to Clarence's verse speeches. These arguments, however, do not satisfactorily explain the switch in style between the two parts.

If, on the other hand, we accept the assumption that the prose dialogue was a later insertion, this insertion was certainly worked into the scene in a very skilful way. Far from disturbing, it highlights the tragic element by means of contrast, and provides a counterpoint to the discussion of conscience in both the dream-episode and the latter part of the scene.

It also delays the forward movement of the action. Not only is the act of murder postponed, but once or twice the murderers even seem to waver, so that the audience is able to hope that the murder may not take place after all. The audience will have been expecting the murder to take place from the moment the murderers enter Clarence's cell; their suspense is fed instead with a semi-comic dialogue whose position between the two verse sections of the scene serves to emphasize its very different quality.

2 Henry VI contains several prose scenes, but this dialogue is the only thing of its kind in the present play. *Richard III* is, however – more so than *2 Henry VI* – a rhetorical tragedy, a

---

[1] 'Not only does Clarence argue for his life with an abundance of theological and Biblical learning, but, in outrageous defiance of decorum, the murderers are quite as learned in the Scriptures and the Prayer Book as he is' (V. K. Whitaker, *Shakespeare's Use of Learning*, 1953, p. 62).

[2] Cf. L. L. Schücking, *Über einige Nachbesserungen bei Shakespeare*, p. 26: 'It was surely not the author's intention to turn these talkative clowns into awe-inspiring Eumenides.'

verse drama in which we would hardly expect to find prose passages. This fact makes the contrast between the comic dialogue and the language of the rest of the play of particular interest.

The conventions governing the use of prose in pre-Shakespearian drama are sometimes contradictory and will not serve to explain the presence of all Shakespeare's prose passages,[1] for, although the old conventions continue to be followed, prose is also used for many new purposes. In the present scene Shakespeare follows the convention which put prose in the mouths of low and clownlike characters, particularly in comic scenes. Prose was also used, in Senecan tragedies and in the popular drama, for purposes of presenting realistic episodes – and the two were often associated.[2] But the prose of pre-Shakespearian drama was for the most part crude and unpolished, a vehicle for slapstick and abuse and possibly a few rough jokes, without a trace of wit or refinement of feeling. Lyly was the first to develop new possibilities in the use of prose passages in drama, making prose into an instrument for witty dialogue, irony, and subtle allusion. In *Love's Labour's Lost* Shakespeare, though still influenced by Lyly in his use of prose, is beginning to shed the artificiality of euphuism and draw nearer to the language of everday life. The prose in Scene iv of *Richard III* derives even more clearly from both the studied, literary tradition and from the more forthright everyday speech found in serious and popular pre-Shakespearian drama.[3] Thus the answers which the murderers give to Brakenbury's initial questions are certainly straightforward enough: but they reveal in addition a certain grim cunning, an insolence mixed with dry humour – a sophistication that played no part in the earlier prose passage.

Just as Brakenbury's moral soliloquy had formed a sorry contrast to the vitality of the First Murderer's opening 'Ho! Who's here?', so his flat, rather emotionless leavetaking casts the

---

[1] Cf. J. F. Macdonald, 'The Use of Prose in English Drama before Shakespeare' *UTQ*, II, 4 (1935); T. Eichhorn, 'Prosa und Vers im vorshakespeareschen Drama' *SJ*, 84/86 (1950) p. 140 ff.; R. David, *The Janus of Poets* (1935); Milton Crane, 'English Dramatic Prose before Shakespeare' in: *Shakespeare's Prose* (1951). For further references see Crane.

[2] Cf. for instance *Selimus*, Sc. xx, 1878–1987; *Wounds of Civil War*, IV, ii, 1750–1792.

[3] Cf. L. Borinski, 'Shakespeare's Comic Prose' *ShS*, VIII (1955), p. 57 ff.

ensuing comments of the murderers into sharp relief.[1] The words
that the First Murderer calls after him, 'You may, sir; 'tis a point
of wisdom' (99) are tinged with mockery, and make more evident
the weakness of Brakenbury, who so readily abandons his sleeping
charge.

From the very beginning the two murderers have distinct
characters – the First, rough, brutal, and loutish; the Second,
somewhat less callous and more intelligent.[2] It is the Second
Murderer who suffers more from conscience[3] and makes a witty
speech about it, and it is he who at the end is seized with pity for
Clarence, while the First Murderer strikes him down. The First
Murderer's objection to stabbing Clarence in his sleep (101–102)
is certainly meant to be crude and stupid;[4] it is the Second

[1] There are numerous differences in the two versions of the prose dialogue
which appear in Q1 and F. Everyday prose offered more temptation than
did the stricter language of verse for the actors to add short colloquial
phrases for emphasis, and Q, a 'reported text', has preserved these. For
instance, the First Murderer's line (148) 'I am strong-fram'd; he cannot prevail with me' had 'Tut' added at the beginning and 'I warrant thee' at the
end. In a number of cases, however, F offers improvements which correct
defective or unintelligible readings in the *Quartos*. For example, Q1's 'Back
to the Duke of Gloucester tell him so' (116) ought surely to read 'I'll back
to the Duke of Gloucester and tell him so' – as it does in F. And line 85
should also follow F and read 'What wouldst thou, fellow, and how cam'st
hither?' W. W. Greg (*The Editorial Problem in Shakespeare*, 1951, p. 83) has
given a convincing explanation of the alternative Q reading attributed to
Brakenbury – 'In God's name what are you and how came you hither?' – by
pointing out that 'the *Quarto* has anticipated Clarence's own words "In
God's name what art thou?" that occur in both texts some eighty lines further
on'. For further discussion of textual problems in connection with this scene,
cf. J.D.W., p. 140 f., p. 185 ff., and A. Walker, *Textual Problems of the First
Folio* (1953). And cf. observations by R. W. Babcock on over a dozen individual passages from this scene ('An Introduction to the Study of the Text
of *Richard III' SP*, XXIV, 1927, pp. 252–253).

[2] On the difference, see C. J. Sisson, *New Readings in Shakespeare* (1956), II,
p. 90: 'the First more of a dangerous clown, the Second more complicated in
thought and soul!'

[3] Though at one point they exchange rôles; for after the discussion on
conscience the First Murderer is troubled by scruples and the Second allays
them. Each is shown to have a troubled conscience and each bolsters the
other up. Nevertheless, the Second Murderer is clearly differentiated from his
partner.

[4] On this whole passage cf. the reading suggested by C. J. Sisson, a com-
promise between Q and F (*New Readings*, II, p. 90).

Murderer who assigns a meaning to *when he wakes* and whose mention of *judgment* (which he repeats at 107) provides the cue for the conversation about *conscience*.

The Conversation on Conscience

The themes of *judgement, conscience,* and *remorse,* of central importance in this play, had been touched upon more than once in the earlier part of the scene (43–63, 66–72); now they are taken up in another key. The Second Murderer's thoughts, like Clarence's, turn to everlasting perdition; indeed, his words ironically anticipate Clarence's later arguments (195, 250). The problem raised in these lines comes up more than once in the ensuing verse section – the dilemma of the man ordered to commit murder, who is responsible both to his earthly superior and to God. Here the problem is presented in compact form, and its inherently antithetical nature is stressed by echoing words and phrases (*kill – killing, a warrant – no warrant*). This is the only part of the prose dialogue where a figure of rhetoric is used in an obvious manner.

The discussion *about* conscience shows at the same time the power *of* conscience; the two companions try to argue away their pangs of conscience, to evade them, to lull themselves with trivial, comforting arguments. What we witness here, therefore, is a psychological process in which the ebb and flow of primitive yet cunning psychological reactions find their expression through humorous utterances. Even certain rather subtly worded phrases strike us as at once comical and psychologically revealing (*a kind of remorse,* 108; *this passionate humour,*[1] 118; *some certain dregs of conscience,* 121).

Conscience is repeatedly personified and treated as though it were alive – like a troublesome insect that comes buzzing back after being chased away. The First Murderer exclaims 'Zounds, 'tis even now at my elbow, persuading me not to kill the Duke', while the Second Murderer sees conscience as a devil to be

---

[1] Following *Q*1 ('my holy humor'), Sisson suggests: 'this holy humour of mine'. He gives as a reason: 'the Second Murderer has religious qualms (not emotional), connected with the *Judgment Day,* being *damned,* and *conscience.* There is a grim humour in being limited to a short duration of such moods (l. 122)' (*New Readings,* II, pp. 90–91).

seized and imprisoned.[1] This witty handling of the theme exactly catches the primitive concreteness of the murderers' way of thinking.

The personification of *conscience* reaches its climax in the Second Murderer's speech where, in a series of rapid sketches, he outlines the rôle of conscience in our lives: the short, pithy, parallel phrases (the language of proverbial and popular sayings) convincingly reflect the coarse, lively mind of the murderer; equally authentic is his ability to produce concrete, down-to-earth images with a minimum of words.

Shakespeare frequently subjected abstract ideas to this process of giving them a concrete form. The results are entertaining, illuminating,[2] and more evocative than had been similar attempts by Marlowe, Peele, and Greene. *Conscience*, too, takes shape before us elsewhere in Shakespeare,[3] notably in *The Merchant of Venice* where Launcelot's conscience and the diabolical tempter within him vie for control of his actions (II, ii). Shakespeare's contemporaries were accustomed to personifying attributes in this way, and enjoyed expressing abstract notions in significant images, using concrete examples of human behaviour to clarify the abstraction. Bacon's method of personifying abstractions such as *envy*, *ambition*, and *deformity* is not far removed from what Shakespeare does here. Even in the decades before Bacon we find a rich storehouse of this kind of 'definition' – Lyly's as well as Shakespeare's definition of *love* in their comedies provide further examples. The passage personifying conscience in the prose dialogue is, however, a very special case: what had been until then an ingenious and often merely ornamental literary exercise

[1] A. H. Thompson (*Arden*) interprets this line as follows: 'Take hold of, i.e. grapple with conscience, which is the devil in thy mind, and believe him not'; Wright and J.D.W. have similar readings; Warburton on the other hand interprets as follows: 'Take the devil into thy mind, and believe not conscience – the blushing shamefast spirit, for which the devil will be more than a match' (*Arden*). This explanation is preferable in that it seems improbable that 'conscience' is to be equated with 'the devil in thy mind'.

[2] e.g. Falstaff's speech about *honour* (*I Henry IV*, V, i, 131 ff.); and the Bastard's speech on *commodity* (*King John*, II, i, 573 ff.). Cf. also the lines on *rumour* (*2 Henry IV*, Ind., 15 ff.)

[3] Cf. for example *King John*, II, i, 564; *Henry VIII*, II, iii, 32; *The Tempest*, II, i, 275–278.

is here steeped in popular idiom, and so transfused with new life.

The fact that the digression is on conscience, prevents the brutal question: 'Come, shall we fall to work?' and the First Murderer's answering suggestion (containing the first mention of the famous *malmsey-butt*[1]) from striking us as too abrupt. But the murder is postponed once more ('we'll reason with him'), and this second delay at a moment of high tension contributes to the sense of time passing, which is a particular quality of this scene. The 'here-and-now' immediacy of the dialogue (cf. 'How dost thou feel thyself now?', 120; 'Where is thy conscience now?', 126; 'Zounds, 'tis even now at my elbow', 143) reinforces this sense of time, suggesting that each new moment may bring not only new situations, but new feelings as well (117–119). The treatment of the time-element in this scene is new to English drama.

The Dialogue with Clarence (157–266)

The first exchange between the murderers and Clarence is a blend of irony, spontaneity, and artifice. Clarence's simple request, 'Give me a cup of wine' (ironically anticipating the malmsey-butt), will be echoed in Richard's later commands on the eve of his death, 'Fill me a bowl of wine' and 'Give me a bowl of wine' (V, iii, 63, 72). Similarly, Clarence's comments on the appearance of the murderers, natural enough under the circumstances, are also camouflaged stage-directions of the type we have observed elsewhere in the first act.

The transition to verse is marked by two short lines:

> *Clar.*   But not as I am, royal.
> *2 Murd.* Nor you as we are, loyal.
> (161–162)

the second echoing the first in length, rhythm, and rhyme. The

---

[1] Shakespeare used this detail to unite a scene of his own invention with material taken from the source. On the historical validity of this version of Clarence's death, cf. J. W. Spargo, 'Clarence in the Malmsey-Butt' *MLN*, LI (1936), pp. 166–173, and H. Goldschmidt, 'Das Ertränken im Fass, eine alte Todesstrafe in den Niederlanden' *Zeitschrift für vergleichende Rechtswissenschaft*, XLI (1925), and XLII (1926).

verse, interrupted briefly by the murderers' stammered confession of their purpose (168), is characterized by parallelism and inter-locking lines. We realize that Clarence is indeed as *well-spoken* as Richard had claimed him to be (I, iii, 348).

In the ensuing discussion not only are the specific accusations of the dead in Clarence's dream (accusations mentioned earlier in I, iii, 135) again taken up, but more general questions of justice are looked at from various points of view.[1] Temporal and divine justice are contrasted, and obedience to an (unjust) order by a temporal superior set against absolute obedience to God's decree (189-196; cf. 110-112); the question is more than once raised of the degree to which man is justified in making himself an instru-ment of Divine Vengeance[2] and carrying out God's punishment (195 f., 212 ff.) and the degree to which a man who has himself sinned is justified in appealing to God's law (201 ff.). The con-versation is thus closely connected to the central themes of guilt and expiation, and both murderers as well as Clarence repeatedly cite the Bible and the Book of Common Prayer.[3] These large moral and religious issues are not, however, presented simply for their own sake; they are woven into the dramatic fabric as argu-ments and counter-arguments in Clarence's desperate struggle for his life.

Suspense is introduced into this final part of the scene by the fact that Clarence may be murdered before our eyes at any moment and by the Second Murderer's undecided, 'What shall we do?' (254) which provides an extra injection of suspense and a sudden moment of hope for Clarence almost at the close of the scene. In addition we are waiting for Clarence to realize who had com-missioned the murder. The Second Murderer's plain statement about Gloucester (229) leaves Clarence unconvinced. He retains his touching belief in his brother's friendship even in the face of the series of ironical comments on Richard's nature uttered by the murderers. It is only at the very last moment that he rids himself

---

[1] On the theme of justice in Shakespeare, cf. M. D. H. Parker, *The Slave of Life. A Study of Shakespeare and the Idea of Justice* (1955). *Richard III* is not, however, among the plays with which Parker deals.

[2] Cf. Mroz, *Divine Vengeance*; Lily B. Campbell, *Shakespeare's Tragic Heroes, Slaves of Passion* (1930), p. 24.

[3] Cf. R. Noble, *Shakespeare's Biblical Knowledge* (1935), pp. 133-135.

of his misconception. He is the first in a series of tragic figures in Shakespeare who shortly before their death realize that they have been blind victims of an illusion.

The arguments with which Clarence hopes to move the murderers range from abstract and theoretical points to the final appeal to human feeling. Clarence opens his argument with the plea – ironic in the light of all that is to come – that the law does not permit punishment without proper trial and sentence (178 ff.). He reminds the murderers that their salvation will be imperilled by the horrid deed they contemplate. Their argument that they are acting upon the King's command he counters by citing the Sixth Commandment of the 'King of kings', and warns them of what must happen if they break God's laws; but the murderers point out that Clarence himself must suffer God's vengeance for his sins.[1] Clarence's rejoinder that God uses no 'indirect or lawless course'[2] applies not only to the murderers, but to Richard as well. Richard, who, godless as he is, assumes a rôle suitable only to God himself.

Having vainly cited first Temporal, then Divine Justice, Clarence calls brotherly love to his aid, telling the murderers that Richard will reward them generously for sparing his life. Clarence's final appeal, a far cry from his initial invocation of abstract justice, is to the murderers' human feelings, to their pity and conscience (256 ff.). In his short speech, and particularly in its two closing lines of self-description with their play on the word *beg*, the reasoned argument of his earlier pleas is replaced by a desperate appeal to the murderers' sympathy. This, significantly, is the first appeal to have any effect, as Clarence's descriptive comment, 'My friend, I spy some pity in thy looks' (261) makes clear (in striking contrast to Clarence's initial statement 'Your eyes do menace me', 166). But since only one of the murderers responds, even this appeal is made in vain.

[1] Both sides echo passages from the Bible at this point. Cf. R. Noble, *Shakespeare's Biblical Knowledge*, p. 134: 'The argument of the assassins, with the Scriptural foundation, seems too shrewd to be in character.'

[2] The repeated refutation of the murderers' view of the matter ought not to be overlooked in a consideration of this passage. To cite isolated phrases as Shakespeare's own opinions (cf. Mroz, *Divine Vengeance*, pp. 123–124) is a dubious procedure.

It is impossible to find an answer to the vexed question of what the author himself felt about the various arguments on law and justice raised in this sequence, since, far from pursuing a particular line of argument, Shakespeare chooses here to present several points of view, examining the ethics of the situation from different angles. Whereas his contemporaries had embodied a clear moral position in their dramas and had usually identified themselves with it, Shakespeare remains anonymous and impartial. Clarence is both guilty and innocent; what is said for and against him in this scene mirrors this fact and tinges Clarence's death with tragedy.

In spite of the foreshadowing and preparatory nature of the dream, the dialogue, and the murderers' conversation with Clarence, the main 'event' in the scene – the murder of Clarence – is not the climax of the scene; it is simply the completion, on the level of external action, of a process which has been going on on a completely different level. It is no more than a foundation for the inner drama in which Clarence, the first victim of the doomed Richard, suffers for his earlier crimes. In this scene, as in hardly any other in Shakespeare's early plays, our consciousness is carried by the language beyond the obvious level of the external action into a sphere where death and destiny hold sway.

The theme of conscience, which in varying forms has pervaded the scene, now dominates the conclusion. Clarence's cry of *relent* (245 ff.) is answered in the Second Murderer's words of remorse and in his final admission: 'For I repent me that the Duke is slain' (276). The Second Murderer's comparison of his own situation with that of Pilate (270) underlines once more the strongly moral and religious bent of a scene abounding in references to Christian ideas and to the problem of conscience.

Murder-Scenes in Pre-Shakespearian Drama

Murder-scenes satisfied the Elizabethan love of the sensational, and became a frequent ingredient in sixteenth-century tragedy once the convention that deeds of violence might only be reported had been dispensed with. Almost all the murderers of pre-Shakespearian drama (Marlowe's are the sole exception) displayed comic and coarsely realistic characteristics. Sometimes a foreigner, often a Frenchman, was chosen, so that his jabbering might add to the impression of a character both grotesque and malicious.[1] Shakespeare was the first to introduce murderers capable of reflection, and capable, moreover, of expressing the fruits of their reflection wittily; his murderers were the first to assume the rôle of accusers, of instruments of a higher destiny.

Several elements in Shakespeare's treatment of the murder are found in earlier drama as well: for instance, other murderers felt pangs of conscience and remorse, either before or after the deed (*Leir*, Sc. xix; *True Tragedy*, 1295; *Woodstock*, V, i, 231; *Wounds of Civil War*, 1008; cf. also 2 *Henry VI*, III, ii); other victims were at first ignorant of the identity of the real instigator of the crime (*Edward II*, *Leir*); other murderers called upon their victims to offer up their last prayers and prepare themselves for death (*Massacre at Paris*, 1016; *Leir*); other victims seemed to read their fate in the murderer's face (*Edward II*, 2492; *Massacre*, 996; *True Tragedy*, 1281 f.); and other murderers recited their orders to the keeper who then let them in and gave up his keys (*Edward II*; *True Tragedy*, 1204). These, however, are similarities of detail which do not really matter.

The best scene for purposes of comparison is that where old Leir is to be murdered (*Leir*, Sc. xix, 1431 ff.).[2] Leir has a prophetic dream about the murder then being plotted against him – a murder actually attempted later in the same scene by the so-called 'messenger'. Like Clarence, Leir too grasps, after a long conversation with the murderers, who it is who wishes to have him slain; but, unlike Clarence, he succeeds (with the help of some cautionary thunder and lightning) in softening the murderer's heart. As in *Richard III*, an attempt is made (in this case by Perillus) to make the murderer realize that his deed will result in pangs of conscience and the torments of hell. Yet here again, despite some likenesses in detail, the naive, loquacious style of *King Leir* is a far cry from the tense and highly dramatic scene in *Richard III*.

---

[1] e.g. Jaques in Greene's *James IV* (III, ii; IV, iii).
[2] R. A. Law (*PMLA* XXVII, 1912, pp. 117–141) first drew attention to these parallels. Cf. also J.D.W., Introduction, p. xxxii.

A more genuinely tragic tone is struck in the scene of Wood-stock's murder from the play of that name (V, i). Woodstock's dream follows the conventions of the prophetic dream where a ghost utters a warning. The presentiment of disaster that weighs on Woodstock after his dream-vision is comparable to Clarence's emotions after his nightmare.[1] As in *Richard III*, the two murderers are clearly differentiated,[2] the second suffering from pangs of conscience – though not until the deed is done.[3] But the two murderers, who do not speak more than 33 lines between them, are experienced killers without a spark of intelligence or wit. Only Laporte[4] (commander of the fortress of Calais and inter-mediary between the murderers and their royal employer) suffers from pangs of conscience *before* the murder.

The most effective non-Shakespearian murder-scene is perhaps that of Edward II in Marlowe's play of the same name, where the victim's accurate presentiment is effectively contrasted with the murderer's hypocrisy. The scene, free from all ideological dis-cussion, depicts the situation of a man in the grip of a mortal terror who foresees his own terrible fate; psychologically it is more convincing than Shakespeare's scene, richer though that may be in ideas. These scenes provide interesting examples of two highly effective yet very different treatments of a similar situation.

[1]
> My state is fear-full, and my mind was troubled
> Even at thy entrance, with most fearful visions;
>
> (V, i, 197 f.)

[2] So are the two murderers Dent and Will in the *True Tragedy*: Dent feels remorse before the deed but is quickly talked round by Will and is then quite determined again – 'for now I am resolute' (1293–1302).

[3] 'Tis done ye damned slave . . . pull ye dog: and pull thy soul to hell in doing it . . . for thou hast killed the truest subject, that ever breathed in England' (V, i, 231 ff.).

[4]
> Horror of conscience, with the king's command
> Fights a fell combat in my fearful breast.
>
> (V, i, 35)

Act II

SCENE ONE

The opening scene of the second act with its court setting and large cast of characters resembles the third scene of the previous act, and is in marked contrast to the murder-scene, Scene iv. But the unhurried pace of the first act, where each scene presents a rounded-off incident, now gives way to a quicker-moving and more energetic mode of presentation[1] – a series of short scenes in which the links in the chain of plot follow more rapidly one upon the other. This increase in the pace at which the plot unfolds can be observed in most of the other Histories as well.

Yet though the scene is shorter than any that precedes it, in terms of thematic content it is rich and complex. The reconciliation between court enemies, brought about by the King (1–44) and carried further by Richard (46 ff.), is cut short by Richard's revelation of Clarence's death (79–94). Derby's petition (95–101) leads on to the King's speech of remorse in which he recalls the past (102–132). Richard's final comments, designed to exploit the new situation for his own ends, round off the scene (134–139).

---

[1] It is of course very doubtful whether the acts in a Shakespearian play do in fact represent structural units. But the contrast in method of composition between Acts I and II of *Richard III* and the different use of the sources that distinguishes the whole of Act I, suggest that in this case the act division may actually correspond to an organic division in the play itself. On this debatable point cf. the discussion between Sir M. Hunter (*RES*, II, 1926), who defends the division into five acts, and J. D. Wilson (*RES*, III, 1927), who rejects it. And cf. E. K. Chambers, *Elizabethan Stage* (1951), vol. III, pp. 50, 199, *Shakespeare* I, esp. pp. 199–201; W. W. Greg, *The Editorial Problem*, p. 35 ff. and *The Shakespeare First Folio*, p. 142 ff., 197, 121; T. W. Baldwin, *Shakspere's Five Act Structure* (1947).

King Edward, the only new character in the scene, appears on stage for the first and last time. Yet his entry has been foreshadowed by talk of his illness and plan of reconciliation (I, i, 136; I, iii, 33–35). In the earlier parts of *Henry VI* whole groups of characters suddenly appear on stage; but in *Richard III* new characters are introduced with greater care, and more sparingly.

Not only the King's illness and his project of reconciliation links the present action to the earlier scenes: the enmity between Hastings and the Queen's faction (I, i), the indirect reference to Buckingham's support of Richard (I, iii, 289 ff.), and the Queen's expressions of doubt and foreboding (I, iii) have all prepared us for what now takes place.

The Reconciliation-Scene (1–45)

Thus the reconciliation-scene is viewed by the audience in the knowledge that the forces of good which manifest themselves here are too feeble to prevail. In addition, the forces opposing Richard are actually shown to be insufficiently single-minded to be able to hold their own. For no sooner has King Edward brought about a general reconciliation than his own guilt is made apparent, and he leaves the stage a dispirited, indeed a broken man. The earlier references to the King as an enfeebled womanizer (I, i) also contribute to our lack of confidence in his ability to reconcile the court enemies.[1] The atmosphere of hopelessness, of 'too late', is such that this reconciliation-scene, which might at first seem to hold out hope of retarding the course of the tragedy, in fact seems unreal and illusory.

The colloquial turn of phrase in the King's opening line ('Why, so') indicates that he is in the middle or at the end of a speech. His hearers, already won over to the reconciliation, seal the new peace with handshakes and with high-minded speeches. But the exaggerated emphasis on the motif of the new-forged bond of peace

[1] The final scene of *3 Henry VI* also prepares the audience for the irony of King Edward's attempts at reconciliation. For there Edward exhorts his brothers: 'Clarence and Gloucester, love my lovely queen; | And kiss your princely nephew, brothers both' (26 f.), whereupon Gloucester makes his real attitude known in a cynical aside.

stamps the reconciliation as mere lip-service. The insistence on the theme of reconciliation may also serve the dramatic purpose of sharpening the contrast between all this professed love and the actual state of affairs.

Technique of Repetition

The reconciliation-scene is a mosaic of verbal repetitions and balanced antitheses, in which variations on key-words (*love, hate, peace, falsehood, heaven, treachery, friendship,* and *guile*) are particularly noticeable. The word *love* occurs 11 times in the first 70 lines, *hate* and *peace* 6 times each.[1] The technique of repeating certain key-words centred on a particular theme is a device common in the sonnet-cycles of the period, where, however (as in Lyly's comedies), it is largely an exercise of verbal skill. But in Shakespeare's Histories key-words are put to dramatic use and tend to occur in connection with particular characters. Used in this way, they help to portray aspects of their personalities. The repetition of words with similar or contrasting meanings may also help establish (as in the present case) dominant themes and ideas. The constant movement back and forth between *love* and *hate*, *peace* and *enmity* focuses our attention on themes of central importance in the play; and the stress on *love* and *peace* in particular makes us all the more aware that these are absent in the court-world.

During the ceremony of reconciliation the action stands still; the words spoken only underline what is being expressed in gesture and movement (7, 10, 21, 23, 25, 28, 40). At the same time this episode contains anticipations of future events: Buckingham's

---

[1] The *hate* (*hatred*)–*love* antithesis occurs at lines 8, 9–10, 24–26, 32–33, 35, 50, 61. Cf. also *hidden falsehood* 14 – *love* 16; *friend* 36, 37 – *treacherous, and full of guile* 38; *peace – enmity* 50, 59–60; *peace – grudge* 62–65; etc. In connection with this antithetical use of *love* and *hate* cf. also More's 'The oration of the king on his death-bed' (More, pp. 9–12, Hol., pp. 363–364), where *love* occurs nine times and where we find such sentences as 'For it sufficeth not that all you *love* them, if ech of you *hate* other', or '. . . ye never had so great cause of *hatred*, as ye have of *love*'. A little later we read (of Hastings and Buckingham) 'These two not bearing ech to other so muche *love*, as *hatred* both unto the queenes part . . .' (p. 366). Cf. also the use of *peace* and *charity* in More.

vow of loyalty towards the Queen takes the form of a conditional curse against himself, to come into effect should he prove untrue – and this curse (cf. V, i, 13 ff.), parallelling the curse called down by Anne upon herself (I, ii, 26 ff.), contains a prophetic description of Richard's subsequent behaviour.

Irony and Ambiguity

Not only the reconciliation-scene as a whole, but also the ambiguously worded individual utterances are ironic in tone. The King's reference to 'this united league' (2), for instance, inevitably strikes us as ironic, for we do not believe that the peace brought about by Edward can persist in the atmosphere of this court. The irony of the King's wish that Richard might be present 'to make the blessed period of this peace' (44) is emphasized by the strong alliteration.[1]

The similarities between Edward's words and those of Clarence in the previous scene make explicit certain similarities and differences in their respective situations. Clarence has had no time 'to make peace with God' (I, iv, 247, 249). Edward, however, is confident, at least at first, that his work of reconciliation will leave his soul 'more at peace' [2] (5) than it might otherwise have been. The audience, of course, views Edward's 'good day's work' (1) with certain reservations, and Edward himself at the close of the scene no longer possesses a peaceful soul. His reference to the King of kings (13), reminding us of Clarence's use of the same words in his admonition to the murderers, foreshadows Edward's death. Later in the scene a troubled conscience rouses painful memories of Tewkesbury in the King, as it does in Clarence in the previous scene.

---

[1] In *Q*1 this alliteration is even more marked: 'perfect period of this peace' – a version which has the advantage from the actors' point of view of being easy to memorize.

[2] F: 'more to peace', *Q*: 'now in peace'. Capell was the first to read 'more at peace'. J.D.W. (p. 191) rightly points out that stylistically this reading is a suitable counterpart to 'at peace on earth' (6).

Richard's Entry (46–94)

Richard, as usual, adjusts himself effortlessly to the situation with which he is confronted. His hypocritically friendly words contribute to the atmosphere of mutual apology and concord. Even his greeting, 'a happy time of day' (47, cf. I, i, 122), provides the King with a cue to elaborate on the new 'happiness' and the 'deeds of charity' (48 f.; cf. 1). Richard's protestations of his friendly feelings outdo everything that has so far been avowed. But the irony in this passage is somewhat overdone, as, for instance, in Richard's 'I thank my God for my humility' (72).[1] In any case, the involved logic and syntax (two parallel conditional clauses preceding the main clause, 53–58) mark Richard's speech as hypocritical – and its smooth conversational rhythm may add to this impression of dishonesty.

Richard slyly treats Elizabeth's plea on Clarence's behalf as flouting his vow of friendship: 'Who knows not that the gentle Duke is dead?' (79). His tidings represent the turning-point of the whole scene; the situation suddenly darkens and the speech pattern changes (short sentences, exclamations, questions). In a single line, the illusion so carefully built up is toppled to the ground; and the altered situation is reflected in the altered looks and gestures of the characters (cf. 82–85).[2]

Richard refers to the messenger carrying the order for Clarence's murder as a 'winged Mercury', but to the second messenger as some 'tardy cripple'; such physical images are a recurring characteristic of Richard's speech (cf. I, i, 12, 17).

[1] For an explanation of 'humility' cf. Furness (*Var.*) and J.D.W. Milton quotes this passage in his *Eikonoklastes* (*Prose Works*, ed. St John, I, 326), comparing the 'strain of piety and mortification' in Richard's expressions with the hypocritical wording of *Eikon Basilike*. Milton, using Richard III as an example, says: 'The poets . . have been . . so mindful of decorum as to put never more pious words in the mouth of any person, than of a tyrant.'

[2] Shakespeare frequently portrays the reaction that follows news of a death. Cf. the scene (earlier in date) where King Henry VI receives the news of Gloucester's death (*2 Henry VI*, III, ii).

The Derby-Episode as a 'Mirror-Scene' (95–110)

The 'petition-scene' [1] with Derby is not designed to advance the plot; rather Derby's plea for mercy is a mirror image of the King's failure to extend pardon, and emphasizes Edward's tragic guilt. Such symbolic episodes in *Henry VI* occur outside the normal framework of plot and character, and are peopled with special characters, as for instance in the scene in *3 Henry VI* demonstrating the futility of civil war (II, v), where a father appears with the corpse of the son he has slain, and then a son with his father's dead body. [2] Here, however, the symbolic function is less obvious, especially since Derby is not a character devised for this particular scene, but plays a minor part in the events of the play.

The Derby-episode also furnishes a concrete situation from which the King's speech of remorse and self-accusation with its recapitulation of past events naturally follows.

The King's Final Speech (103–133)

In pre-Shakespearian drama a character wishing to convey an emotion simply stated in abstract terms that he was moved by this emotion;[3] here, however, the speaker's feelings are revealed through images drawn up out of his own past. Indeed, stirrings of conscience in this play always involve recollections of earlier happenings. Clarence's conscience stirs up a dream-memory of his desertion of Warwick at Tewkesbury (I, iv, 50 ff.); and here Edward's conscience throws up a memory of the same event, viewed in a different light. Direct speech gives Edward's next memory – Clarence's rescue of Edward – a living quality (113; cf. the use of direct speech in narrative passages at I, iv, 50, 55; II, iv, 12). Of the three memories, the most vivid is that in which

[1] Cf. e.g. *Spanish Tragedy*, III, xiii, 1115 ff. (where the petition-episode also has a symbolic function); *1 Tamburlaine*, 1782 ff.; *Alphonsus*, V, iii; *Troublesome Reign*, I.

[2] Cf. H. T. Price, 'Mirror-Scenes in Shakespeare', *Joseph Quincy Adams Memorial Studies* (1946), p. 104. Price does not include the Derby episode among the mirror-scenes because it diverges from the usual scene of this type.

[3] Cf. Clemen, *English Tragedy before Shakespeare*, passim.

Clarence wraps his freezing brother in his own clothing ('. . . and did give himself, | All thin and naked, to the numb cold night?' 116 f.), an incident invented by Shakespeare himself. Just as Clarence holds his 'rage' partly responsible for his murder of Plantagenet (I, iv, 220),[1] so here Edward holds 'brutish wrath' (118) responsible for deleting these memories from his mind. Memories of the past, then, continue to serve an expository purpose, but they also help to delineate a state of mind.

The King's self-accusation is linked to a not altogether convincing indictment of his courtiers who seek pardon for the crimes of their drunken servants, yet find no word to say on Clarence's behalf. Thus the responsibility for Clarence's death seems to fall on several heads; the murder begins to take shape as the final event in a tragic sequence ruled by accident and neglect – and this despite the obvious fact that it is Richard who is the immediate cause of Clarence's death. The King, whose guilt is, in fact, rather minor, nevertheless feels himself to be guilty; but his attempts to plant some of this guilt on others has the ironic result of involving him once more in even greater burdens of guilt. His speech, while illuminating for us the circumstances leading to Clarence's death, makes it clear that at a court infected with inadequacy, cowardice, and selfishness, the forces of good can have little hope of prevailing. The fact that a loutish murderer is pardoned while a prince dies undefended is judged by the King as an irony of fate. But from another point of view these events reveal the weakness and the collective guilt of both King and court. Only in a society as mortally sick as this one is shown to be, could Richard's wickedness prosper.

The King's final words do, in fact, convey doubts about himself and his circle. Their hopeless tone (the shortness of the two concluding lines[2] as well as the altered metre of 'Ah, poor

---

[1] A large number of passages where *rage, wrath, fury* are mentioned show that Shakespeare regarded such emotions not so much as the demonstrations of feeling, but rather as the workings of evil, diabolical forces which render men blind and unjust, seduce them from what is good and from what their own conscience dictates, and lead them to do wrong. Cf. references in Bartlett, *Concordance*.

[2] Although most editors (Al. among them) follow *Q* here and print one lengthened line (133), similar constellations at an exit or at the end of an

Clarence!' help communicate Edward's distress) is in direct contrast to the buoyant confidence of his opening lines (1–6); the two contrasting speeches serve to frame the scene. The King's parting words are, in addition, prophetic, the kind of choric utterance that often rounds off a scene. The bodily collapse which follows (133), expresses in physical terms the spiritual breakdown.

Once again Richard exploits the new situation, throwing suspicion upon the Queen's faction by drawing attention to the involuntary pallor of that 'guilty kindred'. His ambiguous: 'God will revenge it' (138), and Edward's: 'O God, I fear thy justice will take hold . . .' (131), stand in ironic contrast to Edward's calm opening references to God as the 'Redeemer' (4).

The entire scene exemplifies Richard's indirect method of intrigue; remaining for the most part in the background, he nevertheless uses his announcement of Clarence's death to reverse the existing situation, and takes advantage of the general uncertainty to establish his own position still more firmly.

The exit of the broken and dying King has, in its context, a special significance: his death will leave the country kingless and in the gravest danger, a danger made more acute in that all hopes for a victory of the forces of good have been reposed in this departing figure. As the Queen herself declares, two scenes earlier, 'The loss of such a lord includes all harms' (I, iii, 8).

SCENE TWO

The first two-thirds of this scene concentrate on the reactions of relatives of King Edward and of Clarence to the events which have

---

episode (cf. I, iii, 322 f.) would seem to justify an adherence to the F reading of two short lines (cf. H. Spencer). It is possible that the line has been unduly lengthened by the erroneous insertion of Hastings' name, for it seems unlikely that a man just released from prison would be asked for help. J.D.W. notes, however (p. 193), that the matter concerns 'the duty of a Lord Chamberlain'.

taken place; only after Richard's entry does the action move forward. Whereas in *Henry VI* a large part of the dialogue serves to advance the plot, in *Richard III* a surprisingly large proportion of the play is devoted, as in English classical drama, to showing the effect of what has taken place, the reactions of those concerned. Yet this Senecan manner exists side by side with techniques taken over from the chronicle plays and these mixed influences are evident in the present scene.

The Opening: The Children (1–33)

Scene ii, like the one which precedes it, opens at the end of an episode which we do not see. What went before is made clear by the children's questions, which echo the prior words and gestures of their grandmother; moreover, the children actually make use of their grandmother's words and behaviour in their own arguments. This opening has the two-fold advantage of avoiding the possible tedium of an extended lamentation-passage, and of starting the scene in an especially dramatic fashion. It is, in any case, the way of children to repeat stubbornly what they have observed in order to ferret out the truth.

The conversation continues the exploration of a topic opened in the previous scene – the extent to which the King bears the guilt for Clarence's death. In both scenes the chief guilt is imputed to the King, but in both cases this imputation stems from Richard. The boy's echoing of Richard's words from the previous scene, 'God will revenge it' (14) reminds us of the rôle Richard has played in Clarence's death, and prepares us for the child's recollections of a meeting with Richard – recollections which keep us informed on Richard's intrigues at the same time as they illustrate Richard's persuasiveness and skill in deceiving a child. The boy's account of Richard's behaviour wrings from the Duchess a bitter generalization (ll. 27–30) – which is in fact a choric utterance – touching on the appearance and reality theme; aphoristic, decked out with alliteration and word play,[1] these lines stand out starkly from the surrounding dialogue.

[1] J.D.W. notes the word play in *shape – vizor – vice*; 'deep vice' (F) therefore seems preferable to 'foul guile' (Q).

The gullibility of the two children contrasts with York's critical attitude towards Richard two scenes later, and with that of young Prince Edward in III, i after he has begun to see through his uncle. Although a child's way of thinking is accurately captured in some passages of this dialogue, in lines 12–15 this childlike quality is relinquished, and in the ensuing dialogue of lamentation (34 ff.) the two children abandon entirely their earlier mode of expression and adapt themselves to the prevailing stylistic pattern·

Children in Elizabethan Drama

Shakespeare's children usually sound more childlike than do the over-adult creations of his contemporaries and predecessors. But Shakespeare, like other Elizabethan dramatists, was still under the influence of the idea, which originated with the pagan writers of late classical times,[1] that the children of kings and emperors possess a moral sense beyond their years. Thus children in Elizabethan drama are often prematurely wise, infant versions of the men they will later be.[2] The speech and bearing of such children is often formal and precocious; they live, not in a child's world with other children, but in a world of adults in which they share the fate of adults. In pre-Shakespearian drama children generally appear as peripheral figures, with no dramatic function to perform.[3] Yet even such relative neglect seems preferable to the unhappy alternative (cf. for instance the *Battle of Alcazar*, I ii) of entrusting to a child a thoroughly unchildlike dramatic task (in *Alcazar*, a circumstantial and flowery account of a battle). In Marlowe's *Edward II*, however, a child who plays an important part is really depicted as a child. The young Prince later develops from an innocent, docile child into a suspicious though still

---

[1] E. R. Curtius, *European Literature and the Latin Middle Ages* (1953), p. 98 ff.
[2] In *Edward II* we find Isabella saying of her son:

> A boye, this towardnes makes thy mother feare
> Thou art not markt to many daies on earth.
>
> (1387–1388)

Cf. *Richard III*, III, i, 79, 94. Cf. also King Henry VI's words concerning young Henry, Earl of Richmond, *3 Henry VI*, IV, iv, 71 ff.
[3] Cf. *Cambises*, 536 ff.; *2 Tamburlaine*, 3437; *Massacre at Paris*, 1057 ff.

powerless boy and then into a thoroughly alert young man, but
the earlier utterances of the Prince are appropriate to his tender
years.

   In the *True Tragedy*, in a scene similar to *Richard III*, II, i, Queen
Elizabeth's two children ask her why she is sad and try to comfort
her; but their speech, though prose, is unnatural and utterly un-
childlike (789 ff.). Little Elizabeth's 'Good mother | Expect the
living and forget the dead' (792) would more appropriately come
from an adult, and indeed in Shakespeare's scene this sentiment is
expressed by Rivers (99–100). By comparing Shakespeare's *King
John* with *The Troublesome Reign of King John* we see even more
clearly the ways in which Shakespeare has moved beyond earlier
writers in creating in young Arthur a believable child-character.
Yet despite the greater veracity of Shakespeare's young Arthur,
the child's speech still abounds in rhetorical figures and allegorical personifications.

The Lament[1] (34–100)

The rhetorical and melodramatic lamentation-scene opens with
the entry of the distraught Elizabeth, *her hair about her ears*.[2] The
passage seems rather like a preliminary study for the great scene
of lamentation in IV, iv; in style it may also be compared to the
central section of I, iii, where Margaret delivers her curses. Like
that earlier episode, this one too is static: the action seems to
stand still, there is no movement on the stage.

   The extreme formality and artificiality of this type of scene
creates difficulties for a modern audience. Such lamentation-
scenes do not depict, as we might expect, a grief *struggling* to
express itself in words; on the contrary, the sorrow is loudly and
insistently, indeed almost triumphantly displayed. Moreover, the

---

[1] For references to classical and pre-Shakespearian lament cf. Clemen,
English Tragedy before Shakespeare, ch. 14.

[2] This is one of those pictorial stage-directions which distinguish the text
of *F* from that of *Q*. There are similar stage-directions in Parts 2 and 3 of
Henry VI, but elsewhere in Shakespeare they are rare. Shakespeare himself
appears responsible for these directions. Cf. Greg, *The Editorial Problem*,
p. 87; E. K. Chambers, *Shakespeare I*, p. 300; A. Walker, *Textual Problems*,
p. 18.

sufferer, at a moment of overwhelming emotional distress, displays an enviable mastery of linguistic and stylistic devices: never is he at a loss for a word, his feelings are clothed in elaborate simile and metaphor, in involved sentences and ingenious parallels. Almost every lament in pre-Shakespearian tragedy partakes of this artificial character; individual emotion is replaced by generalized conventional maxims, and generous use is made of cliché and stock phrases. The spontaneous and personal expression of grief has no place here.

Thus in the present instance the Queen bursts in 'to make', as she herself says, 'an act of tragic violence' (38),[1] and her two questions (41–42), linked by anaphora and other rhetorical figures, are addressed, as we might expect in this context of rhetorical emotion, not so much to any conversational partner as to some unnamed and universal power.

Yet although this dialogue is not in fact a conversational interchange between two speakers, the individual lamentations nevertheless are linked to one another as, in an antiphonal choric chant, several voices in turn make effective use of refrains in word and sound, or, in operatic trios and quartets, a common theme is varied by different voices. Stichomythia (72–79), anaphora and epiphora, parallel constructions and parallel sound-patterns all help to bind together the several parts of this lament.

Laments constructed like a canon, where the contributions of the individual mourners form part of the pattern of the whole, occur in English Senecan drama, but in a more extended form involving numerous lengthy stanzas. Here, in spite of what strikes us today as excessive rhetorical embellishment, and in spite of the exaggerated terms in which grief is expressed, the lament has been very much shortened. What Shakespeare attempts here is in fact more than an academic attempt at a rhetorical lamentation-scene: these symmetrical, repetitive lines build up an impression of a solemn and ritualistic[2] ceremony of mourning for the dead. The repetitions and parallel phrases emphasize the com-

[1] On the conventional gestures appropriate to a lamentation-scene cf. A. I. Perry Wood. *The Stage History of Shakespeare's King Richard the Third* (1909), p. 39.
[2] Cf. A. P. Rossiter, 'The Structure of *Richard the Third*' DUJ (1938).

mon nature of the suffering of each participant and by an exaggeration of the rhetoric convey an impression of mounting grief,
while the reiteration of Edward's and Clarence's names (59, 71,
72, 73, 74, 75, 82, 83, 84, 85) chimes out like an incantation.
Such purposeful rather than merely decorative use of rhetoric
distinguishes this episode from pre-Shakespearian lamentation-
scenes, and so does the fact that here the laments deal only with
what has actually taken place; in earlier lamentation-scenes specific
happenings are simply the occasion for conventional generaliza-
tions.

One other characteristic of this lamentation-scene should be
mentioned. Those who utter these laments are engaged in vying
with one another, each trying to outdo the other in causes for
grief. The speakers seem less concerned with appropriately expressing their grief than with demonstrating (by means of a logic
no less clean-cut and rigorous than that applied to solving mathe-
matical equations) that their grief is the greater. The speaker's
share of suffering is defined and computed, measured against
other suffering, so that it can be shown to be deeper. At the conclusion, the Duchess summarizes each round of lamentation (ll.
81–88), gathering together for herself all the suffering claimed by
the others.[1] The competitive aspect of this episode[2] may owe a
debt to the earlier academic disputations[3] which themselves
derived from the *débat*, or *altercatio*.

Dorset's and Rivers's attempts to comfort the bereaved (89–100)
recall the similarly unavailing attempts at comfort at the beginning
of I, iii. Here again vain hopes and illusions are offered as consola-
tion; but this time their ineffectiveness is emphasized by the complete lack of response from the sufferers.

Rivers's advice to the Queen to consider the young prince 'like
a careful mother' contains, of course, elements of dramatic irony

---

[1] J. W. Cunliffe (*The Influence of Seneca on Elizabethan Tragedy*, 1925, p. 79)
compares 80 ff. with Seneca's *Troades*, 1060–1062 (Hecuba's Lament), a comparison which shows Shakespeare's lament to be much stiffer and more
contrived.

[2] On the *topos* of outdoing, cf. E. R. Curtius, *European Literature and the
Latin Middle Ages*, 1953, ch. 8, § 6, pp. 162 ff.

[3] Other plays had made use of these disputations; cf. for instance Hey-
wood's *Interludes* and *The Foure PP*.

('in him your comfort lives', 98); it also sounds an obscure note of warning. His two final lines of good counsel with their anti-thetical reference to 'dead Edward's grave' and 'living Edward's throne' (99–100) lead over to the next phase in the action, and also mark a turning-point within the scene. The *lamentatio* looks back into the past, but these lines include past and future within their compass; the words 'plant your joys in living Edward's throne' focus attention on what is to come and so give the action a fresh direction. At the same time Rivers's reference to 'living Edward's throne' draws attention to the next obstacle blocking Richard's path. These two rather conventional lines illustrate once more how past and future are linked in a few short lines of text.

Richard's Entry (101–111)

At this moment Richard steps on stage, creating one of those frequent ironic contrasts between the words just spoken and the character who then appears, almost as though the preceding words were his 'cue'.[1] Richard, no doubt knowing that his mother can see through him, seems deliberately to overlook her in order to offer counterfeit sympathy to the Queen who, appar-ently, is disarmed to the extent of finding no words to say against him. His subsequent ostentatious apology to his mother, besides putting his 'humility' on display, makes it impossible for the Duchess to do anything but provide the requested blessing. Richard's short speech (101–106) might almost seem to present a miniature 'conversion-situation' but for the fact that the Duchess's estimate of Richard's character obviously remains unchanged – her blessing is couched in the form of a *wish*, and with what we assume to be half-conscious irony she wishes for Richard exactly those qualities which he lacks: *meekness, love, charity, obedience, true duty*.

Richard's malicious aside (109–111) is both an explanatory com-ment directed at the audience and a spontaneous expression of cynical glee at his own success and of scorn at his mother's

---

[1] Cf. III, iv, 27.

blessing. Villains[1] in pre-Shakespearian drama make frequent use of asides to reveal both their intrigues and their duplicity to the audience, thus opening up a field of interplay between actor and audience in which the audience becomes the confidant of the villain. In Shakespeare the asides are put to new uses, expressing the speaker's own character and springing from psychological impulses: Richard simply cannot resist capping his mother's blessing with a flippant remark (cf. also p. 98). This aside, then, is less a clarification for the audience's sake – we are already sufficiently well informed about Richard's rôle in this scene – than an expression of his character.[2]

Buckingham's Speech (112–122)

Buckingham, introducing at line 100 the topic of the crowning of the Prince, shows himself to be a supporter of Richard; indeed, he assumes here the rôle of Richard's agent, while Richard himself remains in the background. Two details from earlier in the play illuminate the present situation: Richard's inclusion of Buckingham among the 'many simple gulls' (I, iii, 329), and Buckingham's own ominous words: 'God punish me | With hate in those where I expect most love!' (II, i, 34 f.).

Buckingham's oration is quite short compared to the same kind of speech in *Henry VI*.[3] Indeed, formal speeches in *Richard III* are frequently much shorter than their counterparts in *Henry VI* and tend to be better integrated into the dialogue without, however, losing their character as 'speeches'. The formal apostrophe and the frequent concessive clauses (*though* . . ., 115), which are both

---

[1] Cf. an early instance, Ambidexter in *Cambises*; also Kyd, *Spanish Tragedy*; Marlowe, *Jew of Malta*, *Massacre at Paris*. Cf. also C. V. Boyer, *The Villain as Hero in Elizabethan Tragedy* (1914).

[2] B. Spivack sees Richard's liking for asides as deriving mainly from his literary descent from the character *Vice*. Pointing to Richard's asides in the final scene of *3 Henry VI*, Spivack notes that 'Richard in this scene becomes a creature of asides, an histrionic homilist who puts on a show of love and honesty and turns away with a grin to share his jest and register his art with the audience' (*Shakespeare and the Allegory of Evil*, 1958, p. 306).

[3] e.g. *1 Henry VI*, III, iii, 44–77; IV, i, 134–173; V, v, 48–78; *2 Henry VI*, I, i, 175–201; *3 Henry VI*, II, ii, 9–42.

common in this genre, the circumlocutions, decorative epithets, and emphatic repetitions mark this speech as an 'oration deliberative', a speech of statesmanly deliberation and advice. Buckingham's involved and stilted diction calls attention to the dishonesty of what he is saying, yet at the same time the pomposity and profusion of his words diverts attention from the cleverly placed closing suggestion. His insistence on the need to foster unity[1] only reminds us of the weakness of the new-forged ties.

Richard has now prepared the situation;[2] what has been secured by psychological manœuvring must (as in I, ii, 210 ff.) be translated into reality. Quick action is part of Richard's strategy; and once action has replaced persuasion, Richard's speech becomes noticeably more concise and simple.

Richard remains on stage at the end of the scene as he does in I, i, I, ii, and I, iii, and now Buckingham stays with him. Buckingham, though clearly in league with Richard, appears ignorant of any designs on the young Prince's life. Richard's closing paean of praise for his partner, working up to a peak of hypocrisy and cynical perversion, provides a strikingly dramatic conclusion which reveals the nature of Richard's tactics: his partner (in fact a mere tool) is to believe himself the initiator of all decisions. Richard finds it convenient, therefore, to echo in the closing lines his earlier references to himself as a *child* (I, iii, 142 and II, i, 71).

[1] In fact the image used here – 'broken rancour . . . but lately splinter'd, knit . . .' – stresses former dissension rather than present unity. 'The image is that of an ulcerated wound swollen with the poison of hatred to bursting point, and recently dressed' (J.D.W., p. 195). Buckingham uses a similar image at 125.

[2] The final acquiescent 'with all our hearts' (145) spoken by the Queen and the Duchess is found in *Q* but not in *F* (Al. does not print it but J.D.W. does. Cf. J.D.W., p. 146). In its favour is the fact that Richard's question at 143–144 seems to call for, if not to require, an answer, and also that the phrase echoes Anne's final 'with all my heart' (I, ii, 219).

SCENE THREE

This scene, though it is inessential for the action, ought not (as is often the case) to be omitted in stage productions. The scene comes at the conclusion of the first major section of the action. Edward and Clarence are dead, but Richard has not yet resorted to open violence. II, iv will deal with Richard's first undisguised move in the direction of the throne – the imprisonment of Rivers and Grey. Meanwhile sorrow over the King's death combines with apprehension over the future of an England ruled by a child. The references to Prince Edward, both anxious and hopeful, recall Rivers's words to his mother in the previous scene (96 ff.).

The Time-Element in 'Richard III'

One function of this scene is simply to mark the passage of time. On the Elizabethan stage, which had no curtain, the need to bridge time often led to the insertion of scenes which do not advance the plot.[1] In plays containing a subplot or several strands of action, the problem is solved by presenting the various streams of action in a temporal sequence. But plays such as *Richard III* with a single plot require intermediary scenes. It would not do, for instance, for news of Rivers's and Grey's imprisonment (II, iv, 41) to follow immediately upon the scene where Rivers comes to terms with Buckingham. A short interposed scene must create the illusion of the passing of time. Shakespeare is, in fact, more keenly aware of the time-element than are either his contemporaries or his successors.[2] In *Richard III* the frequent specific references to time convey an impression of the swift passage of time. The technique of telescoping time, of bringing together events separated, in reality, by a period of time, is used again and

[1] On the bridging of intervals of time, cf. especially A. Sewell, 'Place and Time in Shakespeare's Plays' *SP*, XLII (1945).
[2] Cf. M. Buland, 'The Presentation of Time in the Elizabethan Drama' *YSE*, XLIV (1912).

again. Shakespeare condenses fourteen years into less than a month, of which eleven days are portrayed on the stage.[1] Transitional scenes such as II, iii contain, characteristically, no specific references to time.

II, iii as a Choric Scene

II, iii is to some extent a choric scene.[2] Not only are the events of the drama surveyed from a distance, but the specific case is seen as exemplifying a more general truth, and as standing, therefore, in some relationship to the great universal laws operative in other spheres as well (32 ff.). Behind the individual destinies of those involved we are made aware of the destiny of the whole country (11, 19, 30). Yet in spite of the choric function performed by the three unnamed citizens who play no further part in the events of the play, and in spite of the gnomic character of many of their utterances, they are not simply puppets manipulated by the dramatist; they seem in fact to be three ordinary men each of whom has observed the happenings at court and reacted to them in his own way. Their opening lines are informal, realistic, and therefore un-chorus-like; the opening and concluding play of question and answer suggests that they come from a workaday world to which they will return at the close of the scene. These citizens, then, occupy a place somewhere between impartial, choric figures and characters involved in the action.

Shakespeare never completely eliminated the choric element from his drama as realistic and naturalistic dramatists later considered it necessary to do. In *Richard III* the choric element is integrated into the dramatic structure in a way unattempted in English classical tragedy[3] and far superior, for example, to Greene's device in *Friar Bacon and Friar Bungay* or *James IV* of putting into the mouths of leading characters long choric or reflective utterances.[4]

---

[1] Cf. the time analysis of P. A. Daniel, *Var.*, p. 617.

[2] E. M. W. Tillyard regards it as such (*Shakespeare's History Plays*, p. 201).

[3] Cf. e.g. the chorus in *Gorboduc, Gismond of Salerne, Misfortunes of Arthur*, and Ate in *Locrine*, who serves as a chorus.

[4] Cf. Clemen, *English Tragedy before Shakespeare*, ch. 10.

II, iii as a Mirror-Scene

The scene also has certain of the characteristics of a mirror-scene.[1] Such scenes stand outside the plot and may contain characters invented *ad hoc*. Here, happenings at court are mirrored in the reactions of the artisans, and the uneasiness and apprehension at court are shown to have spread to the people.

The mirror technique used in this scene thus effectively widens the scope of the play, for we see that it is not simply particular members of England's aristocracy who are placed in peril by Richard's machinations, but England itself. Shakespeare's Histories differ from Marlowe's in always displaying a consciousness of national destiny, of the supra-personal aspect of kingship. The concerns of the play stretch well beyond the immediate province of the chief characters in the drama.

But this scene also summarizes in terms of atmosphere the events and actions of the previous scenes. Shakespeare seems to have been the first dramatist to make use of what might be called 'atmosphere-scenes'. A number of pre-Shakespearian plays, to be sure, contain episodes only very loosely connected with the main action, often of an anecdotal character, which amuse, instruct, and at times point a moral.[2] Peele's dramas in particular include a large number of scenes serving primarily decorative purposes.[3] But no one before Shakespeare includes scenes which, by looking backwards and forwards, create an atmosphere which prevails throughout the rest of the play. An imitation of this scene appears in *Edward III* (III, ii) – an indication, perhaps, of its striking originality.[4]

[1] Cf. H. T. Price, 'Mirror Scenes in Shakespeare', *Joseph Quincy Adams Memorial Studies*.

[2] e.g. *Friar Bacon and Friar Bungay*, II, iv; *James IV*, IV, iii; V, iv. Cf. also *1 Henry VI*, II, iii and *2 Henry VI*, I, iv. And see E. M. W. Tillyard, *Shakespeare's History Plays*, p. 158.

[3] Cf. A. M. Sampley, 'Plot Structure in Peele's Plays as a Test of Authorship' *PMLA*, LI (1936), pp. 689–701.

[4] III, iii in *Woodstock* may also be compared to this scene; the conversation between three ordinary men (a farmer, a butcher, and a grazier) shows how the measures taken by the King affect simple people. But then the intervention of Nimble and Master Ignorance links the scene with the main stream of events. For a discussion of this scene cf. the preface to A. P. Rossiter's edition of *Woodstock* (1946).

Though the three citizens clearly spring from the people, a number of details suggest that Shakespeare was not in this case attempting a 'populace scene'.[1] For one thing, prose is not used, nor is there any wryly satirical characterization of popular types to provide comic relief. Moreover, the device (already present in *Henry VI*) of linking such scenes to the main action by bringing into them characters from elsewhere in the play is not made use of here. In fact, none of the three Histories following *Henry VI* (*Richard III*, *Richard II*, and *King John*) include populace scenes of the earlier type. Only when Shakespeare came to write *Henry IV* did he return to the populace scene, and by that time he had developed a new way of handling it.

The scene from the Histories which most resembles the present one is the gardener scene in *Richard II* (III, iv), where humble characters standing outside the action also discuss past events and future prospects. But the Queen herself first listens to and then converses with the gardeners, whereas here in *Richard III* the citizens are quite alone.

Structure and Themes

These citizens, who appear to meet by chance, only gradually disclose their anxieties. At first they simply express their feelings ('I scarcely know myself') and only then – a convincing progression – do they give reasons for them.

Here, in this relatively informal dialogue, as everywhere in the play, echo and recapitulation are put to work:[2] twice we hear of the King's death, each time with a reference (5, 9) to the troubled future which lies ahead. But on the second occasion the differing attitudes of the citizens begin to emerge: the first is optimistic (but after the poetic and aphoristic speech of the third citizen, 'When clouds are seen . . .', 32, he has nothing more to say). The third and most important speaker is pessimistic and full of foreboding from the start. The second citizen stands between the

[1] Cf. Brent Sterling, *The Populace in Shakespeare* (1949).
[2] Cf., for instance, 'I fear, I fear' (5).

other two, not knowing quite what to think, willing to hope, yet doubtful.[1]

The conversation is at first dominated by the two central themes of the previous scene: Edward's death and the hopes centred on the Prince. Rivers's earlier, over-confident 'And plant your joys in living Edward's throne' (II, ii, 100) is now offset by the third citizen's sombre and prophetic 'Woe to that land that's govern'd by a child' (11) – words which, rooted both in the Bible[2] and in proverbial wisdom, carry great authority. These general observations are followed by a concrete discussion of the specific historico-political circumstances governing the present situation. The scene, as it progresses, alternates between these twin strands of its composition: on the one hand, a stress on the specific circumstances of the present situation, on the other, an emphasis on the darkly prophetic utterances, choric in nature, inspired by recent events.

The citizens are shown to be deeply, if involuntarily, involved in this conflict – a fact clearly recognized by the third citizen:

> For emulation who shall now be nearest
> Will touch us all too near, if God prevent not.
>
> (25–26)

This thought leads on quite naturally to the subsequent reference to Richard and to the Queen's relatives – following which the conversation reverts to the general forebodings concerning the future. The first citizen's reassuring: 'all will be well' (31) is answered by the third's more cautious: 'all may be well' (36) – and both echo Elizabeth's 'Would all were well! But that will never be' (I, iii, 40). The language of the scene reaches its climax in the rhetorical, resonant lines[3] of the third citizen: 'When clouds are seen . . .'

---

[1] These differences lead Furness to the (unwarranted) conclusion that Shakespeare saw the first citizen as a young man, the second as middle-aged, and the third as 'an old man full of wise saws and modern instances' (*Var.*, p. 177).

[2] Ecclesiastes x. 16; Holinshed and More quote the same biblical passage from the *Vulgate* (Hol., pp. 730–731; More, p. 71), but it appeares at a later point, in 'The duke of Buckingham's oration'. R. Noble (*Shakespeare's Biblical Knowledge*, p. 135) also cites *1 Henry VI*, IV, i, 192.

[3] And cf. 'By a divine instinct men's minds mistrust' (42).

(32-37). This and the following speech (41-45) contain the strongest statement of fear and foreboding.

Anticipation and Foreboding

Clouds, falling leaves, the setting sun, the approach of night, and storms are often in Shakespeare symbols of danger and impending disaster;[1] here, in lines 32 to 37, they are heaped one upon the other. This speech is among the few 'poetic' passages in the play, and carries forward the feeling of foreboding which permeates the play, particularly the earlier acts.[2] Accounts of dreams, expressions of anxious fear and vague foreboding, curses, warnings, and prophecies are all vehicles for conveying a sense of approaching danger; remarks tinged with dramatic irony are put to similar use.

If we look for a moment not at the anticipatory function of this passage but at what is actually said, we see that the approaching political storms possess the inevitability of a natural law: like the seasons, like night and day, they relentlessly advance, overwhelming the little man as well as the great.

The scene reflects at a socially undistinguished but none the less profound level the effects of what has happened at court. The second citizen's reference to all those not present (38-40) tells of a fear and dread extended now to embrace the whole populace. As the scene closes, the broadened scope of its concern is made explicit.

The Use of Proverbs

This scene, like the choric passages in Senecan drama, is especially rich in maxims and adages;[3] moreover, the gnomic statements

[1] On storm-metaphors cf. G. Wilson Knight, *The Shakespearian Tempest* (1932). On the image of the declining sun, cf. Caroline F. E. Spurgeon, *Shakespeare's Imagery and what it tells us* (1935), p. 63.

[2] Cf. W. Clemen, 'Anticipation and Foreboding in Shakespeare's Early Histories' *ShS*, VI (1953). For examples of foreboding in Seneca's plays cf. *Thyestes*, 419 ff. and 956 ff.; *Hercul. Oet.*, 725 ff.: *Hercul. Fur.*, 1147 ff.

[3] Cf. H. Weinstock, *Die Funktion elisabethanischer Sprichwörter und Pseudo-sprichwörter bei Shakespeare* (1966).

here have their counterparts in the gnomic *exempla* from various spheres of nature employed by Seneca to give his choric utterances the force of universal laws. But early Elizabethan dramatists (and even Shakespeare in *Henry VI*), though they follow the Senecan example, do not always choose *exempla* appropriate to the individual situation.[1] These three citizens, however, are burdened with no abstract phrases unsuited to simple men; instead they utter short popular proverbs derived from the realm of everyday experience (32–35; 44).

Recurrent Key-Words

In a scene so devoted to the creation of atmosphere the presence of recurrent key-words should hardly surprise. *Danger*, *fear*, and *dread* occur repeatedly (5, 31, 38; 40; 27, 43), as indeed throughout the play. *Fear* and *dread* in particular may remind us of Clarence's terrifying dream and of the Queen's words in I, iii, 41 and the King's in II, i, 131 f. *Heavily*, too, is related to the *fear–dread* constellation: in I, iv, 1 Clarence is asked: 'Why looks your Grace so heavily today?'; but now there is no one 'that looks not heavily and full of dread' (40).[2]

In this scene, as in the four preceding ones, there are frequent references to God (6, 8, 10, 26, 36, 45). Though the action of the play is predominantly concerned with the growing power of the forces of evil, the language repeatedly reminds us that there exists a higher, indeed a supreme instance.

So this scene, which has been unjustly belittled,[3] has important functions to fulfil: it serves, at the outset of a new phase in the action, to intensify the atmosphere of dread and foreboding, and at the same time it shows the intrigues at court to be vitally connected with the destiny of the nation.

[1] Cf. H. Weinstock, *Die Funktion elisabethanischer Sprichwörter und Pseudosprichwörter bei Shakespeare* (1966).

[2] Cf. also Clarence in I, iv, 74, 'My soul is heavy, and I fain would sleep' and the thrice-repeated 'Let me sit heavy on thy soul to-morrow!' (V, iii, 118; 131; 139) spoken by the ghosts of Richard's victims.

[3] e.g. H. Spencer: 'This tedious brief scene'.

SCENE FOUR

This scene, like II, ii, begins with a conversation in which a child takes part; it ends with an impassioned lament by the Queen and the Duchess. As in II, ii, the language passes from relatively informal dialogue to the high rhetoric of lament. Action takes second place here. Though the plot moves forward, it does so almost casually; the various important developments in the scene – the news of the Prince's expected arrival (1–3) and of the imprisonment of Rivers, Grey, and Vaughan (42–43), as well as the Queen's decision to seek sanctuary (66) – seem more like items of information than movements of plot. At the centre of the scene, however, there is neither action nor information, but conversation growing out of the new facts which have been reported.

Portrayal of Richard (10–36)

The young Duke of York's remarks concerning his uncle prepare us for the next scene in which Richard confronts another young prince, Prince Edward. At the same time, young York's words recall II, ii: there, the unsuspecting children tell of a harmless and friendly Richard; but here York's witty, less innocent comments suggest a lesser susceptibility to Richard's wiles.

The indirect portrayal of Richard through young York's account of a table conversation with him continues that constant probing of Richard's character which occurs in almost every scene[1] – even in those in which Richard himself does not appear. A few well-chosen words, and Richard stands there before us. Thus the half-jesting and half-ironical proverbial utterance, attributed to Richard, with which he masks his real thoughts: 'Small herbs have grace; great weeds do grow apace' (13), is quite characteristic of his manner.[2] Similarly, the Duchess's reference to Richard's childhood succeeds in reminding us of his physical deficiencies: the theme of

---

[1] e.g. II, iii, 27.   [2] Cf. Richard's use of proverbs in III, i.

Richard's deformity, already touched upon at I, i, 20 and I, iii, 228 ff., is here continued.

References to Time and Place

II, iii is a 'timeless' scene (cf. p. 108), but the beginning of II, iv deliberately draws us once more into the stream of time. The scene opens with the Archbishop's summary of the previous day's happenings, and the plans for the coming evening and morrow. The Duchess's optimistic rejoinder heightens the audience's concern about what is going to happen.

Places are mentioned by name in this scene, but the exact location of the action remains somewhat unclear. The editors' designation *London. The palace* is probable, but not suggested by the text itself. This same vagueness characterizes the majority of scene-locations in the play. Location is not as yet used to convey atmosphere. Only the scenes that take place by the Tower or outside Pomfret Castle (V, iii, for instance) begin to make use of the dramatic possibilities of particular locations. The art of suggesting a definite locality by means of 'word-scenery' [1] is first evidenced in *Richard II*.

Dialogue-Technique

Striking is the new ease and lightness with which this conversation is handled. In the latter parts of *Henry VI*, conversation either takes the form of threats, demands, provocations or of question-and-answer dialogue communicating inquiries, instructions, or reports.[2] Conversation sometimes also consists of stylized speeches (A. P. Rossiter's *ritual style*), found in scenes of lament or wooing, in which contrapuntal allusions, parallel phrases, antitheses employing stichomythia and echo effects create a patterned dialogue.[3] The stylized wooing-scene between King Edward and

---

[1] Cf. R. Stamm, *Shakespeare's Word-Scenery* (1954).
[2] A. P. Rossiter (influenced by C. Leech's 'Document and Ritual' *DUJ*, 1937) used the term 'documentary' to describe this sort of report. Cf. 'The Structure of *Richard the Third*' *DUJ* (1938).
[3] Cf. for instance *3 Henry VI*, II, v.

Lady Grey in *3 Henry VI* (III, ii) is a case in point: everything that is said there is directed towards a specific end-result. The same clarity of purpose shapes the dialogue in *Richard III*, I, ii. Here, however, we have something quite different – a talk in which various topics are touched upon, a conversation which is not dominated from the outset by the particular goals of any one speaker. One topic leads to another, the talk ambles first in one direction, then in another. Thus what we hear of Richard's congenital deformity is told us indirectly and with interruptions ('his nurse . . .'; 'I cannot tell who told me'). The language, notwithstanding the occasional literary devices, is lively and spontaneous, with frequent colloquial turns of phrase, ejaculations,[1] and skilfully varied words of address.[2]

The Messenger (38–48)

The Queen's angry and fearful reaction to young York's 'biting jest' at his uncle's expense and her warning proverb: 'Pitchers have ears' (37),[3] closes the dialogue on a note of general disquiet to which the tidings of the messenger give definite direction.

The entrance of this messenger brings a rather static scene once more into contact with the central stream of action. Messengers and messages are frequently and variedly used in Shakespeare;[4] here, as in most of the Histories, the messenger's report is short and precise, and, moreover, broken up into dialogue. But the messenger's news does not immediately result in further action (the sequel to the news comes later in III, iii); rather it provides an impetus for the two closely related speeches of the Queen and the Duchess, who are suddenly conscious of what is going to happen. The atmosphere of foreboding conveyed in symbolic images in the previous scene now thickens into anticipation of predictable evils. Step by step, the sense of approaching evil has been

---

[1] Cf. *Ay*, 8; *Why*, 9; *Ay*, 12; *methinks*, 14; *Good faith, good faith*, 16; *no doubt*, 21; *Now, by my troth*, 23; *How, . . . I prithee*, 26; *Marry*, 27; *Go to*, 35.

[2] *mother*, 8; *my good cousin*, 9; *Grandam*, 10, 30, 32; *my gracious madam*, 21; *my young York*, 26; *pretty York*, 31; *Good madam*, 36.

[3] For an explanation cf. J.D.W., Wright, etc.

[4] Cf. Clemen, *Wandlung des Botenberichts bei Shakespeare* (1952).

heightened, and each phase has been given its adequate expression through the language.

These successive speeches by the Queen and the Duchess are juxtaposed recitatives rather than parts of a normal conversation. They are melodramatic monologues on the Senecan model, addressed to no particular person, containing some general reflection, and not directly affecting the course of the action.

Language and Style of the Passionate Rhetorical Speech (49-65)

The language now takes on the characteristics of the passionate rhetorical speech: piled-up personifications (51, 53, 63); apostrophes (53, 55, 63); balanced antitheses (e.g. 'to joy and weep their gain and loss', 59); parallels ('brother to brother, | Blood to blood, self against self', 62 f.); slow-moving sequences of weighty nouns ('Welcome, destruction, blood, and massacre!', 53); and doubling of qualifying adjectives ('innocent and aweless throne', 52; 'accursed and unquiet wrangling days', 55; 'preposterous and frantic outrage', 64 f.). The total effect is one of ponderous, measured formality. It is in keeping with the prophetic quality of these speeches that reality is described in symbolic images. An animal image is once again applied to Richard ('The tiger . . .');[1] and tyranny itself is pictured as a beast of prey bearing down[2] upon the throne (51 f.).

This prophetic vision is accompanied, as so often in Shakespeare, by memories of the past which provide further nourishment for fears concerning the future. The Duchess sees the approaching evil as a prolongation of the bloodshed and the confusion, the 'domestic broils' (60) which have plagued her own life, and at the same time a prolongation of the activity of suprapersonal forces of retribution. Thus her cry, 'O, preposterous | And frantic outrage, end thy damned spleen' (63 f.) is not simply

[1] Cf. Clemen, *Development of Shakespeare's Imagery*, p. 51; A. Yoder, *Animal Analogy in Shakespeare's Character Portrayal* (1947).

[2] A. Schmidt: *jet* = 'to stalk', 'to strut'; here 'to insult over', 'to treat with insolence'. J.D.W.: 'to encroach'.

poetic phraseology. Her whole speech is a powerful allusion to the concept of a fate which passes from generation to generation; it also reminds us that *Richard III* stands at the *end* of the tetralogy.

The Queen's words, 'Come, come, my boy' (66) once more bring the scene back to the central thread of action, and the general departure to seek sanctuary closes the scene in a manner typical of the Elizabethan theatre.[1]

[1] Cf. the manner in which most scenes in the play are concluded by setting out, departing, being dismissed, etc.

Act III

SCENE ONE

Various seeds planted earlier in the play are developed in this
scene. The young Prince, whose coming is announced in II, iv,
1–8, actually arrives. We have already heard mention of his
physical growth (II, iv, 5), and now we can examine him in
person. From the common people we have heard both hopeful
(II, iii, 10, 12) and troubled (II, iii, 11, 18) comments about his
future reign. Buckingham has cunningly suggested that he be
fetched by only a small band of retainers (II, ii, 120 ff.), and in
the same scene Rivers's lines 'Let him be crown'd; in him your
comfort lives' (98) as well as 'And plant your joys in living Edward's throne' (100) indicate for the first time the office which
Edward is expected to fill. Finally, the Queen's decision in II, iv to
seek sanctuary leads directly to the events of the present scene,
and young York's first words to his uncle (102 ff.) refer to
Richard's earlier pronouncements on growth (II, iv, 12).

The Prince's rôle in the play is more important than his single
appearance in this particular scene would indicate. Although he
remains in the background, attracting our attention more through
his relationship to Richard than through his personal qualities,
he is nevertheless clearly and forcefully depicted, particularly
when he comments on the Tower and Julius Caesar, and furthermore by contrast with his brother, the Duke of York. Nine
scenes later, when we hear of the murder of the two boys (IV, iii),
the memory of the Prince as he appears in this scene is still alive
in our minds.

Structure of the Scene

The dramatic necessity of clearly depicting Richard's two young
victims helps to explain the somewhat unusual construction of the
scene: while some sections are directly related to the action, others
consist simply of conversations which have little connection with
the action but serve rather to reveal character. In each of the two
conversations – between Richard and Prince Edward, and between
Richard and York – the concentration is on the character of one of
the two princes.

The scene is so constructed that although eight characters
appear in it the conversations take place between not more than
two or three of them at a time. The rest have not yet come on, or
have already left the stage, or else they are only drawn into the
dialogue at its close. No attempt is made to include five or six
people in a conversation, as in I, iii and II, i, possibly because such
group discourse would have diverted attention away from the
two young princes. The comings and goings of the different
figures, though successful in conveying a feeling of activity, are
otherwise not altogether happily handled: the Lord Mayor, for
instance, speaks only one line, and we cannot be sure whether he
remains on stage until line 150 or leaves at some earlier point.
Similarly, Hastings and the Cardinal return (at line 95) and leave
again (at line 150) without having uttered a word.

The Arrival in London (1–23)

Missing here is the magnificent pageantry which the audience
would naturally expect upon the arrival in London of the heir to
the throne and to which there are allusions in the source.[1] The
conventional addresses of welcome[2] are conspicuously absent, and
even the Lord Mayor's greeting is confined to a single line, so that

---

[1] The Lord Mayor's train is described in Hol. (p. 369): 'all the other
aldermen in scarlet, with five hundred horses of the citizens, in violet'. The
reason put forward in the source for the Prince's sparse following is, however, not the reason given in the present play.

[2] Cf. e.g. *Edward I*, I, ii; *2 Tamburlaine* IV, iii; *Wounds of Civil War*, III;
A Looking Glass for London, I, i.

the sparse welcome contrasts with the one expected.[1] The 'small train' for which Buckingham has astutely and successfully argued thus fulfils a specific dramatic purpose.

Richard follows his ambiguous 'Welcome, dear cousin, my thoughts' sovereign'[2] with another of the many indirect stage-directions scattered through the play: 'The weary way hath made you melancholy' (3). Richard evidently hopes to prevent the Prince, who has not yet spoken, from stating the real reason for his depressed state. But the Prince's first words, 'No, uncle' make clear that he will not accept Richard's explanation. His description of the journey to London as 'tedious, wearisome, and heavy' and his mention of 'crosses[3] on the way', at once indicate the prevailing mood of troubled dejection which will deepen perceptibly just before the two princes leave the stage. The anxiety underlying everything the Prince says lends a tragic note to his reflections about Caesar, fame, and his own future deeds, and provides a dark background for his brother's flashes of wit.

Richard's reference at this particular moment to 'the world's deceit' (8) brings once more to the surface the theme of appearance and reality, which is at the root of the whole tragic irony in the play;[4] the other uncles, whose greetings the Prince misses, are 'dangerous' and 'false friends' speaking 'sug'red words' which, however, conceal 'the poison of their hearts' (12–15).

Richard accuses others of being what he himself is; and he obviously derives a malicious pleasure from uttering this disguised warning against himself. The Prince's response, 'God keep me from false friends!' (16) expresses his own premonition, and at the same time illustrates the tragic irony implicit in much of what both princes say. The irony of the Lord Mayor's 'God bless your

[1] 'Here, as in his imagery, Shakespeare achieves an artistic contrast between the somberness of the particular entry he depicts and the joy which is usually associated with such occasions' (A. S. Venezky, *Pageantry on the Shakespearean Stage*, 1951, p. 42).

[2] The final phrase carries the suggestion that Richard's thoughts are much occupied with plans for the boy's death; and he is doubtless 'welcome', because now Richard has him in his power.

[3] = 'troubles'. He means in particular the arrest of Rivers and the others, which he had witnessed. Cf. H. Spencer and *Warwick*.

[4] Cf. the Duchess at II, ii, 27; Margaret at I, iii, 289 ff.; and Richard's soliloquies, in which this theme repeatedly appears.

Grace with health and happy days!' (18) is a little different; for although this Lord Mayor later acclaims Richard as king, it hardly seems likely that he is being hypocritical here. One should note, incidentally, Richard's adroitness in drawing the Prince's attention to the Lord Mayor at the very moment when his own conversation with the boy is becoming dangerous.

The Discussion of Sanctuary (24-60)

During the thirty lines which follow Hastings' entry, the spotlight shifts from the Prince to Buckingham and the Cardinal. Their discussion on the Duke of York's right to sanctuary is cast in the dramatic mould of a short conversion-scene: the Cardinal, at first opposed to the idea of fetching the boy out by force, yields when Buckingham argues his case a second time. Buckingham's speech, with its wealth of rhetoric, its identical rhymes, and its arguments, is a typical conversion-speech. The abruptness with which the Cardinal reverses his original vigorous protests, declaring himself to be won over, is altogether in the tradition of the pre-Shakespearian conversion-scene.[1] The surprising rapidity of this reversal may also be intended to show the Cardinal's weakness of character, which is also evident in the source.

In More–Holinshed the question of sanctuary is discussed at some length. Yet Shakespeare was no slavish follower of his source; his decision, therefore, to retain this particular episode probably rested on better grounds than mere historical validity. In Shakespeare's version the ethical rather than legal aspects of the infringement of sanctuary are clearly of central interest. Buckingham, addressing the Cardinal, uses specious arguments to persuade him to ignore a hallowed and traditional right. Such behaviour he justifies by a reference (not present in the source) to the 'grossness of this age' (46). Buckingham is suggesting that by the admittedly depraved standards of the time[2] the Cardinal would be guilty of no injustice in using force to fetch the Prince from sanctuary. This argument, and the reproach that the Cardinal is 'too ceremonious

[1] Cf. *James IV*, IV, v; *1 Tamburlaine*, 348 ff.

[2] Wright, citing Johnson's paraphrase of this passage, draws attention to the second meaning that *weigh it* (46) can have here (Wright, p. 173).

and traditional' (45) is characteristic of the fashionable contemporary morality for which Richard repeatedly stands model, and which displays certain affinities with English Machiavellism. Richard is not only a tyrant, a villain, and an instrument of the devil; he also represents a political creed emergent in Shakespeare's own century, a creed which would justify the means by the end, and regarded as old-fashioned not only consideration for established and inherited rights, but also conscientious inquiry into what constitutes morally acceptable behaviour.[1]

The dialogue also shows Buckingham occupied in moulding others to Richard's will. His various speeches,[2] ceremonious and verbose, seem exaggeratedly rhetorical, burdened with an overabundance of antitheses and parallel phrases. In three places monosyllabic words are rhymed with themselves (*place, it, there*), thus lending an exaggerated conviction to the argument. This spurious rhetoric serves to heighten the impression of insincerity and deception.

The Discussion about Caesar (69–94)

Richard's conversation with Prince Edward covers the span of time needed for the Cardinal to fetch young York from sanctuary; it also places before us a regal young prince whose reign – now never to be – might well have been an honourable one. The main theme of the conversation is posthumous fame, how a man's deeds are passed on by word of mouth or in writing after his death – a subject which aroused great interest during the Renaissance.[3] This discussion of enduring fame is deeply ironic: for Richard has made up his mind to get rid of both of his nephews (his description of the Tower as 'most fit | For your best health and recreation', 66–67,[4] is consciously ironical). Our knowledge

[1] On the influence of Machiavelli see in particular Mario Praz, *Machiavelli and the Elizabethans* (1928); W. A. Armstrong, 'The Influence of Seneca and Machiavelli on the Elizabethan Tyrant' *RES*, XXIV (1948); N. Orsini, *Le traduzioni elisabettiane inedite di Machiavelli* (1937).
[2] Cf. II, ii, 112 ff.; III, vii, 71 ff.; III, vii, 117 ff.
[3] Cf. E. M. W. Tillyard, *Shakespeare's History Plays*, p. 203.
[4] Cf. the ironic phrases used in speaking of the impending deaths of other victims: I, i, 49; I, i, 119; I, i, 151; I, ii, 107.

K

of the Prince's approaching fate makes his references to Caesar ('Death makes no conquest of this conqueror', 87) and to the manner in which truth persists down through the ages (75–78) particularly moving. Richard's name will also live on – and this too contributes ironic undertones to the passage; just as the truth about Caesar persists, so in Richard's case a true account will be passed on 'even to the general all-ending day' (78).

The irony of this dialogue is underlined by two proverbs[1] uttered by Richard as asides (79, 94) which strike a particularly cynical note, for by adopting the proverbial, general form (*they say*) the Prince's early death is treated as though it were in some way lawful and natural, whereas in fact Richard himself bears the responsibility for the murder. Thus the two proverbs are also an ironical foreshadowing of the tragic events to come.

Richard's skill in the use of proverbs, maxims, and proverbial expressions,[2] evident from the first scene onwards, is a particular facet of his verbal ability, and one of the weapons with which he carries his intrigues forward. Whereas in *Henry VI* maxims and proverbs seem like interruptions, decorative additions rather self-consciously employed by the speaker, Richard's proverbs flow forth quite naturally and are put to a variety of uses. Sometimes he masks his real intention with wise generalities; sometimes his proverbial sayings furnish him with a potent weapon in a verbal engagement (I, ii). But above all he uses proverbs to show himself and others in an ironic light, to put forward a distorted or downright false version of a situation, or to present some circumstance for which he alone is responsible as if it were a well-known general rule.[3] Some of the short, pithy, workaday proverbs coined by Richard have become an accepted part of the English lan-

[1] Cf. M. P. Tilley, *Dictionary of Proverbs*, L 384; 'Too soon wise to live long'. The second proverb is not identical with the then current proverb 'sharp frosts bite foreward springs'; it is Shakespeare's own invention (cf. R. Jente: 'used apparently as a proverb', 304, *The Proverbs of Shakespeare*, Washington University Studies XIII, 1926). Cf. also H. Weinstock, *Die Funktion elisabethanischer Sprichwörter*, p. 105 f.

[2] Cf. K. Lever, 'Proverbs and Sententiae in the Plays of Shakespeare' *The Shakespeare Association Bulletin*, 13 (1938), Nos. 3 and 4 (esp. p. 231). Cf. also H. Weinstock, *Die Funktion elisabethanischer Sprichwörter*, p. 103 ff.

[3] Cf. I, i, 62, 160; I, iii, 71; IV, iv, 217, 291.

guage.[1] They are a natural outgrowth of his prosaic, colloquial, often bluntly laconic conversational style.

Richard and the Figure of Vice

The fact that the Prince half overhears Richard's first aside (80) introduces a new element into dramatic dialogue, lessening the artificiality of the aside and tying it more closely into the conversation.[2] Richard is obliged to incorporate the last two words of his original proverb into an innocuous remark; this remark he then proceeds to comment upon in a characteristic explanatory aside in which he compares himself to 'the formal vice, Iniquity'.[3] *Vice* is the Devil's accomplice or follower in the morality plays, which still retained their popularity in Shakespeare's time.[4] *Vice*, a master at twisting the meaning of words and at the art of double entendre, intersperses his diabolical tricks with coarse jests and wordplay designed to entertain the audience.[5] Richard's gift for verbal irony may well have stemmed from this source. Not, of course, that Richard is a comic figure; nevertheless, the triumphant glee with which he applauds his own skill at disguise and deception and his ability to cause trouble may, in fact, be inherited from the allegorical *Vice*. Richard's aside, directed at the audience, seems to invite them to honour his skill in dissembling and in the use of words: in the same way *Vice* too always invites applause.

[1] V, iii, 193; V, iv, 13. Cf. H. Weinstock, op. cit.

[2] There is an overheard aside – though without the present ambiguity – in *2 Henry VI* (II, i, 36–48).

[3] On *Vice*, cf. D. C. Boughner, 'Vice, Braggart and Falstaff' *Anglia*, LXXII (1954), pp. 35–61. B. Spivack (*Shakespeare and the Allegory of Evil*) sees Richard's character and rôle as growing out of the allegorical *Vice*. The same writer also points to other cases where *Vice* is equated with 'Iniquity' (Dekker, *Old Fortunatus*; Jonson, *The Devil is an Ass*, I, i, 115; and *1 Henry IV*, II, iv, 439: 'that reverend vice, that grey iniquity . . .'). And cf. *Arden*, p. 91; Wright, p. 175; H. Spencer, pp. 190–191.

[4] On this point cf. also A. P. Rossiter, *English Drama from Early Times to the Elizabethans* (1950).

[5] B. Spivack sees this, too, as stemming directly from the *Vice* and therefore appropriate to Richard, whom he regards as a reincarnation of the *Vice*: 'The historical figure who ruled England dissolves into the theatrical figure who ruled the English stage' (*Shakespeare and the Allegory of Evil*, p. 395).

But Richard is not the only character in the play to parade his
own person in this manner. A similar type of behaviour can be
detected in the lamentation-scenes, for the explicitness at which the
early drama always aimed probably accounts for the occurrence of
such behaviour in the present play.

The Talk with York (95–145)

Richard's conversation with young York demonstrates how very
different young York is from his older brother. York has more
assurance, his wit is bolder and more nimble, and his fearless
verbal attacks on his uncle bring down upon him Prince Edward's
displeasure (126–127). York openly objects to spending the night
at the Tower, whereas Prince Edward speaks only of his 'heavy
heart' (149) as he goes off in that direction. Richard recognizes
York's unusual qualities: 'a perilous boy; | Bold, quick, ingenious,
forward, capable' [1] (154 f.). Richard has found in York what he
rarely meets with – his rhetorical equal. York openly scorns and
mocks at his uncle, twisting words to make of them piercing
weapons which he directs against Richard.[2]

York's brilliance necessarily gives the conversation a very different flavour from that of his brother's measured and reflective
exchange with Richard. The younger brother's conversation with
Richard is characterized by a rapid interchange of single and half-
lines (112, 124, 145), by repartee and adroit verbal skirmishing.
The irregularity in the metre, especially where short and half-
lines, pauses and sudden starts in the conversation occur, contributes to the flexible, impromptu quality of the passage.

Each of these two conversations forms in its own way a background to the deaths of the two princes. Prince Edward's talk of
his future deeds as king and of his fame contains a patent tragic
irony, the more so since every member of Shakespeare's audience
was aware of the approaching assassination. In the exchange
between Richard and York, the witty, jesting tone and airy tossing

---

[1] Cf. the explanation of this word given by Wright, *Arden*, and A. Schmidt
(= 'quick of apprehension', 'intelligent').
[2] On two occasions Buckingham explicitly calls attention to York's attacks on Richard (133, 153).

of words to and fro forms a bitter and ironic contrast to the horror of the situation. The comic relief of pre-Shakespearian drama here assumes a different and more subtle form: it is much more closely connected with the central themes of the drama.

Forms of Irony

The dialogue-technique used here, like that in I, ii, derives from comedy, and serves to emphasize the irony of events.[1] This scene, however, contains more than situational irony. York's manner of addressing Richard ('gentle uncle' 102, 'my kind uncle' 113) provides obvious examples of intentional verbal irony, and so does the way in which the boy picks up and reapplies such words as *lightly* (121), *little* (125), and *bear* (128). Richard's ironic promise to York ('A greater gift than that I'll give my cousin', 115) is another example, though somewhat subtler, of the same sort of consciously ambiguous statement. The unexpressed thought in this line is emphasized by Richard's subsequent comment, 'It is too heavy for your Grace to wear' (120). But the ironic undertones to York's side of this exchange – to his 'O, that's the sword to it!' (116) and to his pert statement that he will thank his uncle 'little' for the promised gift – are not, of course, felt by York himself. Even so York's conversational style is often consciously ironic, as Buckingham makes clear in his shrewd comment at the end of this exchange; Richard waits until York has left the stage to deliver his judgement of the boy's character (154–155); with York on stage, he chooses to employ familiar tactics, diverting attention from the embarrassing situation produced by his nephew's words by reverting to facts and urging that his nephews make their way to the Tower.

The second mention of the Tower brings with it changed associations; instead of thoughts of Caesar,[2] mention of the Tower now summons up memories of Clarence's murder. Growing fear and foreboding cloud the princes' departure. Whether the princes

[1] York asks Richard for his dagger (or his sword) as a 'toy'. But he himself will later fall victim, though only indirectly, to Richard's sword.

[2] On the origin of the fallacy that Caesar built the Tower (69 f.), cf. J. A. K. Thomson, *Shakespeare and the Classics* (1952), p. 97.

are aware of the exact nature of the danger threatening them is never made clear; precisely this lack of clarity, however, nourishes the pervading atmosphere of foreboding.

Versification

Certain lines in the later sections of this scene are given a special emphasis through changes in the pattern of verse. At line 143 the altered cadence and the shortened line emphasize Richard's diabolical question, 'Why, what should you fear?'; similarly, lines 146–147 stand out not only because of the importance of their content but because of the sudden brevity of line. The inversion of the Prince's last line, besides resulting in a special stress on the pronouns *them* and *I*, places the pregnant 'Thinking on them' at the outset of the line.

Final Section (151–200)

The conspirators, as so often in Elizabethan drama,[1] are finally left on the stage together, where they proceed to sum up York's behaviour. Though the audience may well benefit from this analysis of York's likeness to his mother, neither Buckingham's description of Elizabeth as 'subtle' nor Richard's comparison of young York with Elizabeth can really be considered objective reflection on the former queen, for elsewhere Shakespeare takes pains to represent her as not particularly intelligent.[2] With a hasty: 'No doubt, no doubt' (154) Richard appears to dismiss Buckingham's question concerning York's taunts. Buckingham's concluding: 'Well, let them rest' (157) may be an ironic allusion[3] to the fate, known to both speakers, awaiting the young princes.

It is, of course, Buckingham and not Richard who gives Catesby the commission to sound out Hastings; Richard intervenes only to

[1] Cf. *James IV*, *Jew of Malta*, *Massacre at Paris*; cf. also the present commentary on II, ii, p. 106.

[2] Cf. H. Spencer's note to line 152 on p. 192 of his edition. Neither Elizabeth nor any of the other female characters in this play, however, are depicted with any degree of consistency.

[3] J.D.W.; i.e. 'they're safe'.

give the most essential instructions, so that Buckingham is strengthened in the illusion that it is he who is taking the initiative (cf. II, ii, 112 ff., 151 ff.). Buckingham's reference to Richard's accession to the throne (164 f.) is the first explicit mention of the contemplated usurpation.

Catesby is markedly more astute than Buckingham. He knows that Hastings and Stanley are not to be won over to Richard's side (165 f., 168). Buckingham, however, with characteristic, excessive zeal, is not deterred from giving precise instructions on how Hastings should be treated. Richard, in sharp contrast to his subordinate, cuts through all petty detail and – in total command of the situation – orders Catesby to convey not simply the news that Rivers and Grey have been beheaded, but an additional insulting reference to the relationship between Hastings and Mistress Shore (184–185). Richard has already named this lady in his earlier mocking comments on the King (I, i); here she is mentioned again in the same jocular rather than condemnatory manner. Richard later alludes with hypocritical anger and sorrow to this relationship between Hastings and Jane Shore in his final judgement of Hastings (III, iv, 76; III, v, 31).

Catesby's exit brings out still more sharply the contrast between the two remaining conspirators. Richard answers Buckingham's anxious question as to what should be done should Hastings prove unyielding (191 f.) with a curtly laconic 'Chop off his head – something we will determine',[1] which effectively checks Buckingham's efforts to gain more of Richard's confidence. Richard's promise to Buckingham of the earldom of Hereford (194 f.) prepares us for IV, ii; his special admonition: 'And look to have it yielded with all kindness' (198) catches our attention. His cynical suggestion that further discussion may be preceded by a meal is echoed in his later suggestion that Tyrrel make his report after supper (IV, iii, 31), and it is echoed in reverse in Richard's pronouncement (III, iv, 79) that he cannot dine until Hastings has been beheaded.

The final thirty lines of dialogue abound in references to what is

---

[1] On the _Q_ reading here, cf. notes by H. Spencer, p. 193. On the vague _something_ cf. J.D.W., p. 205: 'He has not yet invented an excuse. Thus Shakespeare prepares us for the flagrantly trumped-up charge in More, which he uses in III, iv.'

expected, planned, or imminent (172, 179, 183, 188, 190, 191, 194); all these references to the future – to a *to-morrow*, to a *this evening*,[1] to a *when* or *if* – combine to rouse expectations and create the impression of a sudden sweeping forward of events.

SCENE TWO

III, ii and III, iv carry the Hastings episode to its grim conclusion. This subplot is, as Moulton[2] first pointed out, part of the symmetrical sub-structure, one of the minor Nemesis Actions leading up to the more comprehensive Nemesis Action centred on Richard himself. Like most subsidiary episodes in the play, it points beyond its own specific limits, demonstrating the fall of a man from the heights of happiness and confidence. The speedy disposal of Hastings also shows Richard's efficiency in removing any obstacle barring his way.

In the Hastings episode its predominantly illustrative and explanatory nature leaves little room for the independent development and depiction of Hastings' character. Only in later plays does Shakespeare succeed in creating subsidiary characters who, in addition to fulfilling their dramatic function, also emerge as complete human beings.

The Hastings episode is built into the drama almost as if it were an *exemplum*; the over-obvious and primitive serial technique is, indeed, reminiscent of the morality play. Each of Hastings' five successive encounters conveys an indirect or explicit warning. The sixth and last encounter (with Buckingham) has a special significance: here Hastings unknowingly faces a man who is an

---

[1] Once, indeed, *this evening* is used when the event does not in fact take place till the next day. For Catesby, who promises to converse with Hastings 'ere we sleep' (188), does so the following morning. But, as H. Spencer rightly observes, 'the present line is a short-term hint intended to convince the audience that events are moving rapidly' (H. Spencer, p. 193).

[2] R. G. Moulton, *Shakespeare as a Dramatic Artist*, p. 109.

accomplice in planning his downfall and who, in a final aside, reveals his designs to the audience.

It is not in the structure of the scene alone that there is evidence of over-emphasis. The scattered ironical hints and allusions are also too numerous and too obtrusive – reminiscent, in fact, of Shakespeare's early style. The point made at the outset – that Hastings trusts his enemies too unreservedly and is deaf to every warning – is made rather too often.

The Messenger's Entry (1–8)

The scene opens with the entry of a messenger. Only after Hastings' ambiguous question, 'Cannot my Lord Stanley sleep these tedious nights?' (6) – the word *tedious* recalling the opening of the previous scene, 'tedious, wearisome, and heavy' (5) – does the messenger explain his errand. This fluid, realistic opening with its gradual approach to the heart of the matter (reflected also in the prose beginning which is then followed by verse, 4/5) contrasts sharply with the compact, direct presentation of such messenger-scenes in English classical drama; though in *Henry VI* there is in fact some attempt to weave the messenger's report into the scene.[1]

Stanley's Dream (10–34)

The poetic form of Clarence's dream-narrative, its wealth of imagery and richness of meaning, result in a closer approximation to the dream experience than anything earlier dramatists had been able to achieve. But Stanley's more conventional warning-dream[2] is summarized in a single line devoid of all detail.[3]

Hastings' own boastful and patronizing interpretation of the dream amounts to no more than a far-fetched play upon the word *boar*; 'the boar will use us kindly' (3) is one of the many ironic

[1] Cf. Clemen, *Wandlung des Botenberichts bei Shakespeare*, p. 13.

[2] Cf. *Selimus*, 2210 ff.; *Woodstock*, IV, ii, 4 ff.; *King Leir and his Three Daughters*, 1479 ff.; *Spanish Tragedy*, I, iii, 364.

[3] On the heraldic significance of the imagery here cf. C. W. Scott-Giles, *Shakespeare's Heraldry* (1950), p. 175.

ambiguities contained in the scene.[1] Even the opening words of his speech: 'Go, fellow, go . . .' are contemptuously superior in tone. But the audience – for all these denials of the truth of dreams – remembers how the truth of Clarence's dream was proved within a single scene.

The Catesby-Episode: Ironic Contrast (35–73)

The impartial messenger is followed by the hostile Catesby, whom Hastings has just described (22) as his trustworthy servant. Hastings' repetition, 'What news, what news . . . ' (37) displays a light-heartedness (cf. also 74 and 92) which contrasts with the two expressions 'this our tott'ring state' (37) and 'It is a reeling world indeed' (38), which carry more meaning for the audience than for the speakers.

Catesby, ignoring Buckingham's instructions, follows his scarcely veiled intimation of Richard's accession plans with the blunt announcement that Richard hopes Hastings will join his party (46 f.). Catesby's directness may be designed to illuminate the extent of Hastings' delusion, which remains firm even in the face of so unmistakable a warning. Hastings protests vehemently on hearing of Richard's proposed accession, but seems to forget all about it when Catesby tells him that Rivers, Vaughan, and Grey are to die. This 'tragedy',[2] as Hastings calls it, is repeatedly alluded to and stands in ironic contrast to Hastings' naive sense of his own security. Moreover, the constant references to the forthcoming executions (50, 66 f., 85 ff., 93 f., 105, 115, 118) prepare us for the following scene where we see the condemned men actually on their way to the scaffold.

The *unconscious* irony in Hastings' words (43–44,[3] 55, 68, 73) contrasts with Catesby's *conscious* irony (56, 64–65, 71), which is made especially explicit in his final aside (72). In Hastings' threat

[1] kindly = 1. 'gently', 2. 'after his boarish nature or kind' (*Arden*).

[2] Hastings uses *tragedy* here (59) as it had been used in the *Mirror*, in the sense of 'a fall from on high'. Cf. Lily B. Campbell, *Tudor Conceptions of History and Tragedy in A Mirror for Magistrates* (1936).

[3] Hastings' pun on the word *crown* contains both conscious irony and unconscious, tragic irony.

to his enemies: 'I'll send some packing . . . ' (61), we detect an
ironic echo of Richard's earlier use of the same colloquial idiom in
I, i, 146, where he speaks of his plans for Clarence.

[*74–96*] In the meeting with Stanley, Hastings' confidence
swells to scornful triumph, reflected in Stanley's answer: 'You
may jest on' (77). And again we have an explicit comparison with
the over-confident and carefree 'lords at Pomfret' (85 f.); the
word *sure* applied to the lords (86) matches Hastings' *secure* (83),
and both recall the *safe* in line 68 (cf. also I, i, 70, 71 and the echo
at III, iv, 93).

In later plays Shakespeare often deals with the proud confidence
of those about to fall. Hecate in *Macbeth* says: 'And you all know
security | Is mortals' chiefest enemy' (III, v, 32 f.). But this theme
also occurs in pre-Shakespearian literature – occupies for instance,
a central place in the *Mirror*,[1] and is in fact essential to the medieval concept of 'tragedye'.

[*97–113*] The next two encounters with a Pursuivant[2] and a
Priest follow the morality-play pattern of symbolic meetings with
representatives of different social orders or with anonymous
persons. The Pursuivant merely provides an opportunity for
Hastings to repeat his self-confident assertions. The irony of their
present meeting is underlined by Hastings' recollection of a previous one ('Then was I going prisoner to the Tower', 102).

The technique of Buckingham's final aside is similar to Catesby's in line 72; it too adds a postscript which is intended to make

---

[1] Cf. *Mirror* ('Duke of Buckingham'):

> When least I fearde, then nerest was my fall,
>   (411)

and

> For such is Fortune when she lyst to frowne,
> Who seemes most sure, him soonest whurles she down.
>   (419 f.)

[2] In *Q* and in Holinshed and Hall the Pursuivant has the same name as
Hastings. Stage-directions in *Q* read: 'Enter Hastin a Pursuant'. No attempt
is made here to discuss this textual problem, which is of no great interpreta-
tive significance; see, however, J.D.W., p. 154; P. Alexander, *Shakespeare's
Henry VI and Richard III* (1929), p. 160; A. Walker, *Textual Problems of the
First Folio*, p. 30.

the cruel irony of the conversation clear to the audience. There is additional irony in the fact that yet another scene is rounded off with talk of supper (cf. III, i, 199).

The Tower as a Scene of Action

In this scene, as in the previous one, several characters are on their way to the Tower (91, 102, 119). Hastings' proposed visit necessarily calls to mind the identical destination of the young princes in the previous scene. Although *Richard III* contains little direct or indirect description of locality,[1] the Tower, at least, is vividly present in the play. It is, in fact, more than a mere locality;[2] the associations which cling to it – associations systematically intensified during the play – make it an appropriate setting for Richard's bloody deeds.

SCENE THREE

The short scene that concludes the Rivers–Grey subplot not only has its place in the total design of the play, but necessarily occurs at precisely this point. The repeated references in earlier scenes to the impending execution of Rivers, Grey, and Vaughan (see p. 132) link the Hastings episode to this similar chain of events occurring *simultaneously* with it. From this linkage arises an element of ironic augury: Hastings feels an increased confidence upon hearing the fate of the 'lords of Pomfret'; for the audience, however, it carries a completely different meaning. This scene, therefore, showing the final destiny of the three men, forms a prelude and a parallel to the next, where Hastings falls victim to his fate.

[1] Cf. R. Stamm, *Shakespeare's Word-Scenery* (1954).

[2] It is mentioned 27 times – far more frequently than in the other History plays. (The Tower is mentioned four times in *Richard II*, three times in *King John*, and nine times in *1 Henry VI*.)

But this simultaneous handling of two or more threads of action also serves a more prosaic purpose – that of camouflaging gaps in the passage of time. In fact the various actions are so skilfully interwoven that the effect is that of a steady and simultaneous progression. In the third act the careful reader can see how breaks in the continuity of a particular subplot (A) caused by a shift to another subplot (B) are made use of to suggest that actions necessary to the continuation of subplot A have, in the meantime, been carried out.[1]

Treatment of a Minor Episode

The manner in which the Rivers–Grey subplot is developed reveals the care with which even a minor episode is woven into the action of the play. The 'Queen's kindred' are first mentioned in I, i, and appear on the stage in I, iii. Rivers himself appears only in I, iii; II, i; and II, ii; but in all three scenes the situation presented is related to later events. In I, iii Rivers opens the scene with false hopes of the King's recovery; in the same scene he attempts to defend the Queen against Richard's attacks, and is included in Margaret's prophetic curses. In II, i he is ceremoniously reconciled with Hastings and in II, ii he supports Buckingham's proposal to conduct the Prince 'with some little train' (II, ii, 138 f.). The subsequent scenes carry increasingly specific references to the arrest and pending executions of the 'lords of Pomfret', and now, in III, iii, we witness their final hour. The same event is presented in different ways: first in a short objective report by a messenger (II, iv, 41 f.); next in a message from Richard, the man responsible for these executions, to the man who is to be his next victim (III, i, 183); and then by Stanley in a warning to Hastings (III, ii, 85 ff.), and by Hastings in a foolhardy allusion to his own security (III, ii, 105 f.); and finally by Buckingham in his ironic greeting to Hastings (III, ii, 115 f.).

---

[1] Thus Catesby is ordered to sound Hastings in III, i, and actually does so (III, ii, 35 ff.) after the conversation between Richard and Buckingham and the conversation between Hastings and the messenger. The present scene serves to fill in the time required for Hastings to get from his house to the Tower (III, iv) – and so on.

Indeed, in none of the *Henry VI* plays can we find a scene so thoroughly prepared for in such a variety of ways. In pre-Shakespearian drama the only means of introducing an off-stage action into the play is to have someone report it. Here a far greater ingenuity is exercised in keeping a particular happening before the audience's eye in the absence of the persons involved. The action proceeds upon the 'inner stage', carried forward through reflection, through the making of plans, and through the expression of emotional involvement, until, finally, it takes shape before us.

The Spectacle and the Text

Once more, what we actually *see* on the stage makes plain what the scene in its entirety seeks to express. Tension, development, contrast – all these are missing. Instead, what we have is a spectacle, reminiscent of morality-play pageant-technique. The spoken words usher in no action; they are like titles under a dumb-show, although after all the preceding hints even titles would be unnecessary. Shakespeare is utilizing here an earlier dramatic convention – one which attempts no individual characterization, displaying instead marked choric features. The scene resembles a choric lament divided up among several speakers whose rôles are interchangeable.[1] The usual exchanges between the condemned prisoners on their way to execution and those who have condemned them[2] are missing, and so, consequently, are the pleas for pity, the self-defence and the accusation. The very fact that only the prisoners' point of view is presented greatly limits the possibilities for dramatic development.

The function of this scene, then, is to recapitulate past events and to foreshadow future ones. The short pause afforded the condemned men is devoted to retrospection (12, 15 ff.), prophecy (7), prayer (18 f.), and also to a formal apostrophe addressed to the

[1] Cf. Peele, *David and Bethsabe*, VIII (1–43); for an interpretation cf. Clemen, *English Tragedy before Shakespeare*, p. 262 ff. J.D.W. also comments on the likeness to Peele (p. 209).

[2] As, for example, in *1 Tamburlaine*, IV, iv; V, ii; *Edward II*, 2413 ff.; *Spanish Tragedy*, III, vi; *Promos and Cassandra*, II, vii.

castle of Pomfret (9).[1] This is an instance of Shakespeare's more
concrete use of the apostrophe, which in Senecan drama is usually
addressed to abstractions and persons but rarely to localities. In
IV, i, 99 the walls of the Tower are apostrophized in a similar
manner.

Turning-Point in the Action

In this scene for the first time, Margaret's curses are recalled
(15–18).[2] Here, about half-way through the drama, the fulfilment
of at least part of the prophetic curse in I, iii is depicted. What the
earlier scenes had carefully led up to we are now to witness step by
step – how fate overtakes not only Rivers, Grey, and Vaughan,
but Hastings, Buckingham, and the rest. Indeed, Rivers' detailed
references to Margaret's curse (17–20) prepare us for the death of
the others, while the prayer for the safety of the two princes draws
them into the circle of those threatened by an inimical fate. Rivers'
words, 'Then curs'd she Richard' (18) indicates – and for the first
time – that Richard's own death will follow upon those of his
victims. With this scene, then, a turning-point has been reached in
the flow of the action.

SCENE FOUR

This scene, unlike the two previous ones, is thoroughly dramatic.
One of the reasons for this may be the fact that Richard is present:

---

[1] This address has been carefully prepared for: Pomfret Castle was mentioned once in II, iv, six times in III, ii. Cf. A. Müller-Bellinghausen, 'Die
Wortkulisse bei Shakespeare' *SJ*, 91 (1955), pp. 182–95.

[2] Daniel notes that Margaret curses Rivers, Dorset, and Hastings, but not
Grey; Wright and Furness comment that Buckingham is *not* cursed but
simply warned and included 'in a general malediction with the rest' (*Var.*
p. 229).

no scene in which he has played a part hitherto has been without
dramatic tension.

The dramatic effect is achieved in various ways: at the beginning, for instance, Hastings is still supremely confident; at the
end he is a condemned and broken man. Richard, too, appears in a
double rôle: at first he adopts a jovial manner, but in his savage
onslaught on Hastings we see the real man. Finally, the constant
coming and going on the stage contributes both to the liveliness
of the scene and to its dramatic impact.

Hastings' Rôle and Dramatic Irony (1–21)

Once again the scene revolves around Hastings. He utters the
opening and closing words, and on him is centred all Richard's
and Buckingham's concern. As in III, ii, Hastings' naive sense of
security is emphasized by dramatic irony. It can even be detected
in the way Hastings accelerates his own end when he insists that
the coronation should take place without delay. His presumption
in speaking on behalf of Richard on the question of the coronation date ('I know he loves me well', 15) oversteps all bounds.
Buckingham's warning that the face is no guide to the heart (11)[1]
has passed Hastings by, so much so that using the same words
(*face*, *heart*) he says precisely the opposite (55). But Buckingham's
warning is applicable to himself as well, for he too fails to see
through Richard in time.

Richard's Entry (22–43)

Like a puppet on a wire, Richard appears on stage just as the
others are discussing him. Attention is even drawn to the exact
timing of this entry when Buckingham observes that Richard has
come upon his 'cue' (27). Richard's buoyant spirits are of course in
ironic contrast to his plans and to what is to follow. The casual
words which mask his purpose: 'I have been long a sleeper' (24)
are taken over from the source; here they underline Richard's
grim irony.

[1] Cf. *Macbeth*, I, iv, 12.

Richard's response to the account of Hastings' presumptuous behaviour offers a unique opportunity for any actor. His words lull Hastings in his false security and show how complete is Richard's self-command. Moreover, his skill in sizing up a situation is evident in the request to Ely to fetch strawberries from the garden – another detail taken from the source.[1] The unexpectedness and indeed frivolity of this interruption (which Richard uses to divert attention from his aside to Buckingham) deepens the grotesqueness of the situation. At this moment, all that matters happens below the surface and remains unspoken. At a critical point in the development of the play new dramatic techniques have been put to work.

Derby's advice to postpone the coronation date (44–47) contains a warning which in this meaningless council goes unheeded. The assurance of the Bishop of Ely that the strawberries are being fetched (49) rings out in the circumstances like a mockery of the whole proceedings. Meanwhile Hastings talks calmly on, oblivious of the warning contained in Derby's question (56); in his absurd inversion of Buckingham's earlier warning not to judge by appearances (III, iv, 11 ff.) he actually denies the split between appearance and reality. At the same time his words (50–55) constitute an ironic preparation both for Richard's reappearance and for the speaker's own downfall.

The Reversal of the Situation (61–81)

With Richard's return the whole tone of the scene changes: his black and accusatory mood is reflected in his speech ('my death', 'devilish plots', 'damned witchcraft', 'hellish charms'). A similar reversal occurred in II, i and – though here in a different context – in I, iii; there too the initiative came from Richard.

What follows is a short, though many-levelled, scene of the utmost concentration. Thanks to Richard's brutality[2] and also to

---

[1] Cf. J.D.W., 'A Note on *Richard III*: The Bishop of Ely's Strawberries' *MLR*, LII (1957), pp. 563–564; L. J. Ross, 'The Meaning of Strawberries in Shakespeare' *SRen*, VII (1960), pp. 225–240.

[2] Cf. King Edward's remark about Richard in *3 Henry VI*: 'He's sudden, if a thing comes in his head' (V, v, 86).

his undoubted histrionic skill (witness the gesture with which he bares his crippled and allegedly bewitched arm), Hastings' removal is accomplished with quite incredible speed. Hastings, who has unwittingly pronounced his own death sentence (68), is not allowed to defend himself. Richard shows the same brazen impatience as in I, iii, where he breaks in upon Rivers (92); here he twists Hastings' opening *if* into an annihilating charge against him, orders his execution, and, uttering his usual oath 'by Saint Paul',[1] sweeps off.

This summary and rash judgement of Hastings is no act of passion on Richard's part, but a further demonstration of his craftiness. Through his precipitate action he cuts off any discussion of Hastings' guilt, and indeed not one of the bystanders questions what has been done. Richard's speedy withdrawal serves to put the seal on a completed act.

Hastings' Epilogue (82–109)

Hastings' speeches, taken together, form his epilogue. The interruptions by Ratcliff and Lovell, urging haste ('the Duke would be at dinner . . . ') contrast in their rough brevity with Hastings' impassioned and eloquent lament. These interruptions prevent us from losing sight of the grim realities of the situation.

Nevertheless, Hastings' epilogue is much more a choric utterance than a speech in character. The fact that he begins and ends with a lament for England (the supra-personal hero of the Histories) forms a point of resemblance with the choric lines in II, iii, and his reflections on the 'momentary grace of mortal men' (98) are quite obviously choric.

Moreover, the speech contains Biblical echoes[2] as well as echoes from the *Mirror*, which had constantly reminded its readers of the unreliability of man's favour. The medieval Christian warning against putting one's faith in worldly success rather than divine

[1] In the chronicle Richard uses the same oath at this point. Shakespeare makes it a recurrent, characteristic feature of Richard's speech (cf. I, ii, 36; I, ii, 41; I, iii, 45; V, iii, 216). For the signification of this oath cf. G. Carnall, 'Shakespeare's Richard III and St Paul' *SQ*, XIV (1963), pp. 186–188.

[2] Noble cites Proverbs xxiii, 34; Jer. xvii, 5; and Psalm cxlvi, 2.

grace finds expression through the image associated with *tragedye* – the fall from high estate.[1] Margaret had already used the image of a fall to destruction in the first act (I, iii, 259). The phrase: 'tumble down into the fatal bowels of the deep' also recalls Clarence's dream. Clarence too is destroyed because he naively trusts his enemy.

The Hastings episode closely resembles the 'punishment tragedy' in Lydgate's *Fall of Princes*[2] and in the *Mirror*.[3] It is made quite clear how Hastings himself incurs guilt; he, more than all the rest, is blind and obsessed with the conviction of his own security. That he should enlarge on his own fate as an *exemplum*, that he should assume the chorus's rôle as commentator is, therefore, altogether fitting.

The words of a dying person were usually imbued with a special significance in Elizabethan drama,[4] and frequently expressed observations of a general, choric nature. The dying man became a prophet – just as Hastings does here (106). *Henry VI* contains further examples,[5] and in this play Edward IV's final words before his collapse (II, i, 131 f.) fit the pattern. Gaunt in *Richard II* (II, i) delivers the most striking of all prophetic death-speeches. Comparing Hastings' speech with similar ones in *Henry VI* (Part 1, IV, vii, 1–32; Part 3, V, vi, 35–56), we find this later speech to be much more complex, more intimately bound up with the action of the play. And comparing Hastings' speech to pre-Shakespearian death-speeches, we note that the general formulas (apostrophizing Fortuna, the heavens, etc.) and mythological names and parallels have been replaced here by language of a far more concrete nature.[6]

[1] Cf. Lily B. Campbell, *Tudor Conceptions of History and Tragedy in A Mirror for Magistrates* (1936); R. Chapman, 'The Wheel of Fortune in Shakespeare's Historical Plays' *RES*, I (1950); Paul Reyher, *Les idées dans l'œuvre de Shakespeare*, p. 245 ff.

[2] Cf. W. F. Schirmer, *John Lydgate* (1961), p. 206 ff.

[3] Cf. W. F. Schirmer, 'The Importance of the 15th Century for the Study of the English Renaissance' *English Studies To-day*, ed. C. L. Wrenn and G. Bullough (1951).

[4] Cf. e.g. dying speeches in *Selimus*, 1301 ff., 1839 ff.; *Locrine*, I, ii; II, vi; IV, v; V, vi; *Tamburlaine*, 1051, 2067, 4617 ff.

[5] e.g. York in *3 Henry VI*, I, iv.

[6] Cf. Clemen, *English Tragedy before Shakespeare*, ch. 12.

Before speaking the prophetic words which close the scene and direct our minds to the future, Hastings recapitulates all the warnings he has failed to heed, including one that is new (his horse has stumbled, 86). All the themes contained in the foregoing action are now gathered together and made explicit at this climactic moment. An apostrophe to Margaret, for instance (94), refers to her earlier curse (I, iii, 211 ff.) – a curse which was also recalled in III, iii, 16. The interlocking pattern formed by such references to earlier utterances reflects the 'chain of destiny' which binds together the fates of the individual characters in *Richard III*.

Scene-Endings in 'Richard III'

Once again the final lines of the scene bring movement after a static passage.[1] Both the rhyme (frequent in the closing lines of a scene[2]) and the regular metre lend emphasis to the final prophecy uttered by Hastings. These terse, axiomatic phrases follow a dramatic convention of the 1580's, whereby the scene-ending was rounded off in a rhyming couplet, either an epigram summing up the past or an adage pointing to the future. The plays of Shakespeare's early and middle periods contain many such conclusions. In contrast, most scenes open in a freer, more casual way, as, for instance, do those scenes in which we are taken right into the middle of a conversation that has started off-stage.

SCENE FIVE

This scene forms an epilogue to the Hastings episode in that the sudden execution must now be justified before the Lord Mayor

[1] Cf. for instance I, iv; II, ii; II, iii; II, iv.
[2] Cf. for instance I, i; I, ii; I, iv; IV, i; IV, ii; IV, iii; V, i; a total of 11 scenes end with a rhyme. On this function of rhyme, cf. F. W. Ness, 'The Use of Rhyme in Shakespeare's Plays' *YSE*, XCV (1941), p. 79 ff.

and the citizens. When Hastings' head is brought in, we are again
reminded of the preceding scenes. At the same time, however,
Richard's instructions to Buckingham and the arrangement to
meet at Baynard's Castle prepare us for the events of III, vii; and
Richard's final words (106–109) lead on to IV, i.

Acts I and II and the earlier scenes of Act III contain various
strands of action, and these individual strands are frequently
interrupted. But Scenes III, iv to III, vii show a marked continuity in the handling of both characters and action (III, vi is an
exception, but it consists of nothing but a fourteen-line monologue). All these scenes are dominated by Richard and Buckingham jointly. Richard's first open act of violence (against Hastings)
is now followed by a spurt of activity. Indeed, in Scenes III, iv to
III, vii Richard is pressing vigorously forward, aided by luck and
by his native shrewdness. Richard's subsequent difficulties will
later form a contrast with the present smooth passage of his
intrigues.

Here, as elsewhere in this play, the technique of gradual
intensification is used. Just as Richard's overt move against
Hastings oversteps the bounds of his earlier, largely underground,
tactics, so in the coming scenes Richard reaches new heights of
hypocrisy.

Contrast as a Structural Element

The scene is built up on a pattern of contrast; rapid dialogue
which furthers the action alternates with longer speeches. After
their opening speeches, Richard and Buckingham engage in a
dialogue made up of short lines, calling for much gesture and
movement. Then comes a section with longer speeches; after the
Mayor's exit, Richard delivers the longest speech we have yet
heard from him. The end of the scene consists of shorter speeches
as the characters are one by one dismissed by Richard.

Richard assumes various rôles in the course of the scene; once
again we see him both as he wishes to be seen and as he really is.
For similarly as in I, i the middle passage (in this case the passage
with the Mayor) is flanked on either side by passages in which the

conspirators show themselves without disguise. Here, this technique of contrast is more subtly applied than in the explanatory
monologue at the end of I, i. For the exchange between Richard
and Buckingham at the close of III, v is above all part of the
unfolding action in the course of which Richard's true purpose
quite naturally reveals itself.

Richard's and Buckingham's Opening Speeches (1–13)

The fairly extensive stage-directions at the beginning of the scene
(unusual, on the whole, in Shakespeare) show how Shakespeare
occasionally supports the spoken word by direct instructions as
to costume and use of stage. Since the source also mentions 'rotten
armour',[1] it seems likely that the stage-direction really does stem
from Shakespeare himself and not simply from the prompt-book.[2]

In this opening conversation between Richard and Buckingham
skill in dissembling is compared with the art of acting. The actor
is obliged to pretend, to live in a world split between appearance
and reality,[3] where his chosen task consists in making believable
what is only make-believe. In addition, these lines cast a retrospective light on what has gone before. Thus, as in the first two
scenes of the play, the spiteful relish with which Richard regards
his dramatic talents is once again brought to light.[4] His hypocrisy
gains in effect by being quite consciously 'staged'.

Furthermore, these lines lay down the rôle of both performers
and their appropriate behaviour in what is to follow. The various
emotions to be counterfeited are enumerated with obvious

[1] More, p. 78: 'harnesed' (Var., p. 242).
[2] Cf. A. Walker (Textual Problems of the First Folio, p. 18): 'These suggest
an author thinking of production rather than a book-keeper concerned in
regulating a performance.' For an overall survey of scholarly discussion
about the frequent and detailed stage-directions in the F text of Richard III
cf. W. W. Greg, The Editorial Problem, p. 171 and also p. 87; E. K. Chambers,
Shakespeare I, p. 300. And cf. W. W. Greg, The Shakespeare First Folio (1955),
p. 193 ff.
[3] On the significance of the appearance–reality opposition in Shakespeare,
cf. Th. Spencer, Shakespeare and the Nature of Man (1942/1949); Clemen,
Schein und Sein bei Shakespeare (1959).
[4] On the conception of Richard as an actor and as a 'mocking comedian'
see A. P. Rossiter, Angel with Horns (1961), p. 15 f.

pleasure, and a particular emphasis (supported by the metre) falls on the verbs (*quake, change, murder, begin, stop, counterfeit, speak, look back, pry, tremble, start*), which thus indicate the appropriate gestures.[1] The actor's art, then, as Buckingham explicitly states, is to be used to further the basest of undertakings ('to grace my stratagems', 11).

Dissimulation is so common in Elizabethan drama that it is no exaggeration to claim for it a particular affinity with that age. There are very few plays of Shakespeare's in which there is no dissimulation, and in the case of some of Shakespeare's best-known characters (e.g. Iago, Hamlet, Macbeth) it plays a decisive part. The importance of the theme of dissimulation in the works of Kyd, Greene, Marlowe, Ben Jonson, and many others would certainly justify a careful examination of its origins and the intellectual climate in which it flourished. Interest in the villain[2] goes only part of the way towards accounting for the amount of dissimulation in the sixteenth-century theatre. Far more, this concern is a sign of new experience, of a new way of looking at the world, which springs from the contemporary evolution in political and social thinking. The name of Machiavelli, mentioned by Richard himself in *3 Henry VI* (III, ii, 193), is but one of the clues to a whole set of relationships.[3]

The Scene with the Mayor (14–71)

The eight lines that follow the Mayor's entry are a fine example of 'word-scenery'.[4] Incomplete phrases, cries, commands, warning shouts and sound-effects off stage ('Hark! a drum') create with maximum economy an impression of lurking danger – an impression heightened by the audience's uncertainty as to what is happening. Only after the arrival of Ratcliff and Lovell, which

[1] On the relationship between declamation and gesture, cf. B. L. Joseph, *Elizabethan Acting* (1951).

[2] Cf. C. V. Boyer, *The Villain as Hero in Elizabethan Drama* (1914). For a more recent study cf. C. N. Coe, *Shakespeare's Villains* (1957).

[3] On Richard as the archetype of Machiavellism in Elizabethan eyes cf. Lily B. Campbell, *Shakespeare's 'Histories'. Mirrors of Elizabethan Policy*, p. 321 ff. And see notes on pp. 62 and 123 *supra*.

[4] Cf. R. Stamm, *Shakespeare's Word-Scenery*.

Richard shrewdly makes use of in his conversion of the Mayor, does the mist begin to clear.

Henry VI contains no passage so packed with indirect stage-directions,[1] producing so powerful an illusion of movement with so few words. What we have here is the drama of action, where much happens though little is said. 'Rhetorical drama', of which the play contains a variety of examples, and 'action drama', blend in this scene.

Hastings' severed head[2] reminds us of Richard's oath in III, iv, 79, 'I will not dine until I see the same'; consequently his tears and protestations of love[3] strike a particularly grotesque note. Ironic too is Lovell's reference to Hastings as *unsuspected* (23) when *unsuspecting* would be more appropriate. Richard has supposed him to be 'the plainest harmless creature' (25) and that, of course, is exactly what he was. In the line: 'So smooth he daub'd his vice with show of virtue' (29) Richard is in fact describing himself, and similarly Buckingham's character-sketch of Hastings (33–34) applies to both Richard and himself.

These speeches by Richard and Buckingham are 'dissembling-speeches' (cf. II, ii, 112 ff.). Richard favours a rather forced and formal mode of expression (cf. 29, 32) with elaborate and carefully balanced lines (29). Buckingham's speech, on the other hand, is characterized by interpolations (35, 36 f, 54 f.) and an involved order of clauses (35–39), and he borrows Richard's trick of reinforcing an adjective with a superlative (*plainest harmless*, 25; *covert'st shelt'red*, 33). The drawing-out of a sentence by the addition of fresh clauses and phrases (52–60) and the almost pedantic-ally digressive style ('speak, and timorously confess | The manner and the purpose . . .', 57 f.) suggest that his eagerness to carry out his hypocritical task also conceals his embarrassment.

[1] Here – and two scenes later – the upper stage or 'balcony' would have been used, an arrangement which offered certain advantages for the staging of this episode. Cf. A. I. P. Wood, *The Stage History of Richard the Third* (1909), p. 42.

[2] The displaying of Hastings' head runs counter to the classical rule whereby no deed of violence was shown on stage; but there had been other similar instances in pre-Shakespearian drama (in particular in the more popular plays). Cf. *Promos and Cassandra* (Andrugio's head), *Selimus* (Aga's hands).

[3] Cf. *3 Henry VI*, V, vi, 81 ff.

The Mayor

The Mayor is represented as a particularly feeble and gullible person. His diffidently interpolated question at line 40 (in which the shortness of the line and the resulting pause emphasize his hesitancy) betrays his doubt and apprehension, which Richard at once hurries over with his indignant: 'What! think you . . .' But after this one cautious question,[1] the Mayor becomes completely subservient;[2] indeed, neither the Mayor nor Hastings can be taken quite seriously as opponents of Richard's; rather they are both feeble victims of his duplicity. It may seem a weakness in the play that Richard's superiority is established through clashes with weaker opponents, particularly children and helpless women. (Margaret, an exception to this statement, is seldom seen and takes no part in the action, and Richmond, another, does not appear until Act V.) Such confrontations, however, may serve to show that precisely where men are weak and over-confident, evil and violence can easily prevail. The weak rather than the down-right evil gives free passage to the powers of darkness.

Richard's Instruction-Speech (72–109)

Richard, in the longest speech which he has yet made, for the first time gives detailed instructions as to what he wants Buckingham to do. He does not instruct Buckingham to *act*, but simply to deliver a speech. How and in what order Buckingham is to put forward the arguments, how far he may go, what is to be stressed and what merely hinted at ('as 'twere far off', 93) – instructions of this sort underline Buckingham's dependent position as Richard's instrument, even though Richard has successfully persuaded him that he is his 'oracle' and 'prophet' (II, ii, 152). The impression we form of Buckingham's dependency is strengthened by the fact that the scene rehearsed here is never played out before us but simply reported to Richard by Buckingham (III, vii).

   This speech of Richard's is much more compact than the earlier

---

[1] Cf. Hastings' fateful line at III, iv, 75: 'If they have done this deed . . .'
[2] Al. follows *Q* in assigning lines 50/51 to the Mayor, who thus takes up Richard's suggestion of line 31. Cf. Sisson, *New Readings*, II, p. 93.

dissembling-speech to the Mayor; the language is simple, clear, and matter-of-fact, dealing with many separate points in comparatively little space. The doubling of descriptive phrases (for example those that describe Edward's excesses: 'hateful luxury | And bestial appetite . . .', 80 f.; 'raging eye or savage heart', 83) are not, in fact, mere rhetoric; they make more precise the exact nuance that Buckingham is meant to catch.[1]

Buckingham's 'I'll play the orator' shows how the orator's art (like the actor's) is in this context thought of as the art of dissembling, of representing something not as it really is but as one wants it to appear to be.[2] Rhetoric, the orator's most important tool, is here shown to be used in the service of hypocrisy and deceit.

The plans which Richard, after the departure of Buckingham, Catesby, and Lovell, reveals to the audience in a final soliloquy are not identical with those which he has shared with Buckingham. Thus we are made aware of an area of reserve in Richard's relationship with Buckingham, and of the many levels on which his convoluted plans are carried out.

SCENE SIX

A One-Man Scene

This short passage spoken by the Scrivener has not always been regarded as a separate scene.[3] Pope, for instance, in his edition, incorporated it in the one before. But the empty stage before the Scrivener's entry and the Scrivener's mention of time makes it

[1] It may be that the stress thus obtained is intended to emphasize Richard's pleasure in drawing attention to these particular weaknesses of the King's (cf. his earlier remarks on them at I, i, 12 and I, i, 90 ff.).

[2] On the orator and the art of the actor, cf. B. L. Joseph, *Elizabethan Acting* (1951). For a different interpretation cf. M. Rosenberg in *PMLA*, LXIX (1954), p. 915 ff.

[3] It is one of the seven scenes not designated as such in F (III, v–vii; IV, iii; V, iii–v). Cf. W. W. Greg, *The Shakespeare First Folio*, p. 197.

inadvisable to append the passage to III, v; the modern editorial practice of treating it as a separate scene[1] is a better solution. In any case, the point of view expressed by the Scrivener is quite foreign to the concerns of Richard and Buckingham in III, v and III, vii.

In *Henry VI* there are no one-man scenes; there, the short scenes are for the most part brief interludes in the tumult of the fighting, involving several characters – scenes which resemble V, iv in the present play. In pre-Shakespearian drama, however (if we accept the way in which the plays were subsequently divided into acts and scenes), this type of one-man scene does occur.[2]

The Scrivener as a Man of the People

In *Richard III* the voice of the people is rarely heard. But the Scrivener, like the citizens in II, ii, is an anonymous figure and speaks for the citizens of London. Interrupting the flow of scenes depicting Richard's and Buckingham's intrigues, he lets us know that the people are after all not so blind to Richard's iniquities as the Mayor's behaviour might have led one to suppose, nor do they share the guilt of those drawn by Richard into his sphere of influence. The silent disapproval with which they later greet Buckingham's speech (see III, vii, 24 ff.) further illustrates their critical attitude.

The scene is thus more than a 'mere time-filler' (H. Spencer) and ought not to be omitted from performances. It is true that it gives no impetus to the rapid advance of plot (serving rather to mirror it[3]), but it does provide a pause and a moment of relaxed tension shortly before the conclusion of the second wave of action.

The various times which the Scrivener mentions[4] in order to

[1] On the question of division into acts and scenes, cf. the literature cited under II, i, p. 91 *supra*.
[2] e.g. *The Spanish Tragedy*, III, v; *Edward I*, xi, xviii; *Locrine*, IV, iii. Cf. Clemen, *English Tragedy before Shakespeare*, p. 77 ff., on longer one-man scenes.
[3] Hence H. T. Price classes it with the 'mirror-scenes' ('Mirror-Scenes in Shakespeare' *Joseph Quincy Adams Memorial Studies*, p. 105).
[4] 'to-day', 'eleven hours', 'yesternight', 'the precedent was full as long a-doing', 'within these five hours'.

prove that the indictment of Hastings was composed *before* his arrest, make us aware of the passage of time,[1] and draw attention to the careful planning that preceded the arrest.

The Lament on the State of the World (10–14)

The Scrivener, who employs the primitive technique of addressing himself to the audience ('And mark how well the sequel hangs together', 4),[2] concludes his speech with a general choric lament for the present times. The lament 'Bad is the world' (introducing the epigrammatic rhyming couplet that rounds off the speech) occurs frequently in pre-Shakespearian drama, where it is used as a choric commentary on whatever errors, crimes, and evils are being portrayed.[3] Here it is linked to the general prediction that 'all will come to nought . . .' (13), and takes its place, therefore, with similar laments in II, iii. However unimportant the speaker, such a choric utterance must be taken seriously. What we hear is the voice of an impartial observer, whereas the two flanking scenes deal exclusively with Richard's own sphere of influence.

SCENE SEVEN

The second great curve of action which started with Act II is at the end of this scene complete.[4] For Richard has achieved his goal,

[1] These indications of time are, however, somewhat confusing. The Scrivener has taken a total of twenty-four hours to copy the indictment, though he received the paper only the day before from Catesby. Hastings was still alive four hours earlier, though Catesby visited him to sound him on the morning of the previous day.

[2] T. W. Baldwin draws parallels between this mode of expression and Aphtonius's list of 'signs of confirmation' – the relevant sign here being *coherence*. These parallels, however, do not fully convince (*William Shakspere's Small Latine and Lesse Greeke*, 1943, II, p. 143).

[3] Cf. e.g. *Misfortunes of Arthur*, III, i, 11–14; *James IV*, IV, iii; IV, v; V, iv.

[4] For a different subdivision of the play into five movements see A. P. Rossiter, *Angel with Horns* (1961), p. 7 ff.

the crown of England, and the close collaboration between Richard and Buckingham documented in the preceding scenes now reaches its climax and conclusion. When next we see these two (IV, ii), dissension has broken out between them; with Act IV the obstacles in Richard's way begin to loom large, his downfall draws nearer.

Dramatic Techniques

In this important scene – the longest in Acts II and III – many of the techniques used in former scenes are employed in a greater concentration. The grotesquely reversed images (of Richard, of Edward, of Buckingham) arising out of the intrigants' public performance produce irony more biting than any in the earlier scenes, and this irony is subtly combined with the verbal irony permeating the scene. Nowhere else is the 'rhetoric of dissembling' so consistently sustained; nowhere else does Richard give such a dazzling display of acting in a scene of his own arranging; nowhere else is the 'great speech' so fully exploited. And no other 'spectacle' carries the impact of this one, where Richard, prayer-book in hand, appears between two bishops.

This scene is certainly one of the dramatic climaxes of the play. Yet the dramatic impact is not the result of exciting or violent actions on the stage, but of the inner tension springing from the triumph of Richard's intellect, and from the gap between what the audience knows of him and what is being acted out on the stage.

Shakespeare enables us in this scene to see through Richard's eyes, even to relish the brilliant staging and successful outcome of this inspired piece of trickery; yet at the same time we identify ourselves with Richard's victims in this scene. In pre-Shake-spearian drama the audience identified itself with only one of the parties, but here we are involved with both sides at once – quite apart from the moral implications which may continue to occupy us all the while.

The entire scene is built upon the same system of structural balance which governs both the whole play and the individual scenes. Buckingham's report of his vain attempt to talk the

citizens over (which of course arouses our interest in the outcome
of the second attempt) is balanced by his 'success' in 'converting'
Richard. Superimposed on this first ironical contrast is a second:
the early failure to win the people's support for Richard is
directly followed by the successful conversion of the 'people' in
the person of the Mayor and a few silent citizens. The familiar
conversion pattern adds both tension and suspense to this
sequence.

Buckingham's Report (1–41)

Richard's impatient question and Buckingham's negative reply
(1–3) immediately reveal the failure of the first attempt to win over
the populace, so that we listen to the ensuing report with no great
excitement. The points Buckingham says he touched upon in his
speech keep more or less to the order which Richard laid down for
them. The report is given hastily, with conjunctions omitted and
participial parentheses thrown in ('as being got', 10; 'being not
like the Duke', 11; 'Being the right idea . . .', 13), the whole
gathered into one unwieldy sentence (5–19). The report is unadorned and dry in tone, but with a hint here and there that
rhetoric has not been ignored in the actual delivery.[1] A few items
of information about the princes' and Edward's origins and about
the latter's 'contract with Lady Lucy' etc. are conveyed in the
course of the speech.

After Richard's interpolated question (23) Buckingham launches
out into a complete account of what happened at the Guildhall.
This passage, an important example of the use of narrative in the
play, is (unlike I, ii, 156 ff. or II, i, 109 ff.) not a recapitulation of
some episode which occurred long ago, *before* the beginning of the
present action. In plays on the Senecan model a good deal of
space is devoted to reports, often of an epic nature;[2] naturally
pre-Shakespearian drama is similarly full of long epic passages.
Shakespeare's movement away from this sort of report, his increasing attempts to use narrative for dramatic purposes is, there-

[1] Cf. the antithesis: 'Your discipline in war, wisdom in peace' (16); and
the climax: 'Your bounty, virtue, fair humility' (17).
[2] Cf. Clemen, *English Tragedy before Shakespeare*, passim.

fore, one of the most important factors in his development as a dramatist.[1] A comparison of this narrative with similar passages in *Henry VI*[2] shows that it is the narrator's subjective attitude which here forms the dramatic impulse. By substituting an account for a dramatized version of the event, Shakespeare is able to convey information about the speaker – a scene on the stage could not have done this so compactly. Buckingham's irritation at the citizens, those 'dumb statues or breathing stones' (25), his obvious desire to prove that he has done everything possible to elicit the people's approval, and finally the cynicism with which he admits having called his ten followers' feeble response 'general applause and cheerful shout' (38–40) – all this is included in a comparatively short account. Richard's angry reaction, his phrase *tongueless blocks* (42), is even stronger than Buckingham's *dumb statues*. His reluctance to accept Buckingham's failure is evident in his reformulating (42) his earlier question about the audience's reaction; Buckingham has, after all, twice repeated that they 'say not a word' (3), 'they spake not a word' (24).

Irony and Stagecraft in the Scene with the Mayor (45–220)

In his next lines (45–51), Buckingham suggests some final arrangements for the coming hoax. Buckingham's order: 'And stand between two churchmen' (48) appears to be his own contribution, though it must have been part of Richard's plan (see III, v, 99–100). Just as a hypocritical speech is often expressly described as such, so here a spectacle designed to deceive is announced in advance. The dubious nature of the whole situation is further emphasized by the ironic use of musical terminology,[3] and by the ironic dubbing of Richard's rôle as a 'maid's part' (51).[4]

What now follows is almost a 'play within a play'. The parts have been carefully assigned: Catesby plays the messenger sent to fetch the reluctant Richard, Buckingham is the spokesman of the people, and Richard the pious, unworldly soul yielding unwillingly

[1] Cf. K. Schlüter, *Shakespeares dramatische Erzählkunst* (1958).
[2] e.g. *1 Henry VI*, I, iv, 27 ff.; IV, vi, 10 ff.; *2 Henry VI*, III, ii, 82 ff.; *3 Henry VI*, I, iv, 1 ff.
[3] Cf. notes by H. Spencer and Wright.
[4] Cf. notes by Wright, *Arden*, J.D.W.

to pressure from outside. Moreover, the audience is carefully prepared for the entry of the principal actor by Catesby's running to and fro, his description of Richard's pious meditation (61–64) and doubts and fears (84–87), and Buckingham's eloquent portrayal of him (71–80).

Characterization and self-characterization are in this interlude ironically turned upon their heads (a reversal undergone by most dramatic devices in the course of this drama). Richard's upside-down portrait of himself and the deliberately distorted image Buckingham gives of both Richard and Edward are designed to further the work of persuasion. Supplementing Richard's words about himself (106, 154 ff., 205, 224, 230, 236) is the visual image which he puts before us as he appears between the two bishops, prayer-book in hand. The sight moves Buckingham to interpret its ethical significance (98–99) – he takes his cue from the Mayor's exclamation at 95. The grotesque image of Richard[1] is emphasized not only by numerous statements from Buckingham and Catesby, but also by repeated comparison between him and Edward.[2] Some of Richard's arguments that Buckingham used at the Guildhall are taken up again. Moreover, virtues which Richard has already attributed to himself are again put forward as characterizing him (cf. I, iii, 142 and III, vii, 210–211; II, i, 60–61 and III, vii, 224 etc.).

Buckingham's talk of 'our country's good' (124) is another instance of the ironic reversal of facts, while in lines 125–129 the truth is spoken about the state of England, but in a misleading manner (the facts about England are given correctly a short time before this in III, iv, 82 and 105). A similar ironic statement of the truth occurs when Richard, with assumed humility, says 'So mighty and so many my defects' (160), and when, referring to Prince Edward, he says:

> The right and fortune of his happy stars,
> Which God defend that I should wring from him.
>
> (172 f.)

---

[1] Noble (*Shakespeare's Biblical Knowledge*, p. 137) sees a connection between *sleeping, praying, watchful* at 76–77 and Matt. xxvi, 40, 41, which, if accepted, adds further irony to this image of Richard.

[2] Cf. also the earlier I, i, 36; I, ii, 90 ff.; III, v, 76 ff.

God and the Christian virtues are repeatedly invoked[1] with something like the same ironic cynicism, even (though obviously unwittingly) by the Mayor (81). The only word spoken by the
citizens, their *Amen* (241), comes as an ironic finale in this series.
Even the theme of conscience appears in an ironic setting in both
Buckingham's and Richard's words (174, 226). Moreover, conscious and unconscious (tragic) irony are once again coupled in
a single statement: though Richard's claim that he takes the
crown 'against my conscience and my soul' (226) is at the time
patently false, his own conscience does indeed later rise up to
plague him with 'a thousand several tongues' (V, iii, 193).

Buckingham's delay in answering Richard's question 'What is
your Grace's pleasure' (108) is made use of by Richard for a
further display of hypocritical virtue, and gives Buckingham a
chance to utter a fulsome preamble. Richard's wily logic protects
him against the misunderstanding which may ensue whichever
way he acts, disposing in advance of every objection.

Rhetoric as a Vehicle of Dissembling

The striking agglomeration of rhetorical devices lends Buckingham's first comparison between Richard and Edward (71–80) a
stilted, pompous, artificial air. Lines 72–77 include three couplets
with the same construction, each of them a variant of a single
antithesis;[2] alliteration[3] reinforces the effect. Moreover, the couplets at 74–75 and 76–77 follow the euphuistic pattern involving
corresponding phrases. The language of both speakers abounds
in synonyms and *variatio*, as in lines 117–122, in which synonyms
are linked by parallel phrasing and anaphora. Language so rich in
synonyms and periphrases tends to a rhetorical doubling of
phrases, particularly in Richard's speeches.[4] *Figura etymologica*

---

[1] 92, 106, 109, 165, 173, 226, 235, 237. The word *God* occurs seven times
in this scene alone. Cf. also *Christian prince*, 96; *Christian zeal*, 103; *Christian
land*, 116; *holy*, 92, 99, 246.

[2] Further examples of antithesis occur at 123–124 (*sleepy – waken*), 127
(*royal stock – ignoble plants*), 151–152, 154–155, 158–159.

[3] Further examples of alliteration: *deserves – desert* (154), *mighty and so many*
(160), *bark – brook* (162), *prize – purchase* (187), *disgrace – downfall* (217).

[4] 163–164, 158. For Buckingham, cf. 129, 131–132, 186–187.

M

(126, 154), *climax* (133–134, 136), *polyptoton* (165–166, 238), *mesophonia* (167), and *chiasmus* (171) all occur, and the speeches – as indeed the whole play – contain many ponderous epithets.[1] As we might expect, Richard's imagery[2] is more forceful and poetic than that of Buckingham; indeed, Richard's language here is almost Biblical[3] – a not unimportant factor in the context of a conversion scene.

Structure and Syntax of the Speeches

The speeches follow the recommendations on rhetorical structure found in treatises on poetics. In Buckingham's speech one can distinguish an *introductio* with *captatio benevolentiae* (100–109) and preamble, next a *narratio* (117 ff.) with six-fold *variatio* and finally a *conclusio* (137–140). Richard's speech begins with a *dubitatio* or *aporia*,[4] followed by a *narratio* combined with a *confutatio*.

The syntax, like the rhetoric, is of great importance in giving these speeches their particular tone. Richard and Buckingham both use long sentences and favour relative clauses (124, 130), appositional or participial phrases, and conditional constructions. The intricate style, clause within clause, is particularly marked in Richard's speech (141 ff.) with its frequent *if, whether – or, rather – than, but* and *yet* sentences.[5] Richard's avoidance of a definite answer[6] (for despite his clearly negative conclusion, he cunningly keeps in reserve the possibility of saying *Yes*) finds syntactic expression in the constant alternatives and in conditional and antithetical clauses. His final *No* which nevertheless expresses

---

[1] Some examples: *blemish'd stock, noble isle, proper limbs, ignoble plants, swallowing gulf of dark forgetfulness and deep oblivion, tongue-tied ambition, beauty-waning and distressed widow, base declension and loath'd bigamy, black scandal or foul-fac'd reproach.*

[2] 145–146, 162, 164, 168.

[3] Noble compares 166: 'The royal tree hath left us royal fruit' with Matt. xii, 33 and comments: 'The whole of Richard's speech reeks of Scripture but without particular reference except this' (*Shakespeare's Biblical Knowledge*, p. 137).

[4] Cf. Sister Miriam Joseph, *Shakespeare's Use of the Arts of Language* (1949), p. 214.

[5] 141–142, 143, 148, 152, 154, 156, 159, 161, 163, 166.

[6] In spite of his promise: 'Definitively thus I answer you' (153).

doubt and his wily provision of points of departure for counter-
arguments are very much indebted to syntactical devices, to, for
instance, the interpolation of such phrases as 'God be thank'd'
(165), 'were there need' (166, where *need* is repeated), and 'no
doubt' (170). Buckingham, a diligent student of his master, takes
over the *but*, *yet*, and *if* forms. Richard answers the triple appeal
by Buckingham, the Mayor, and Catesby – each more urgent than
the last – with triple anaphora (*I am* . . ., *I do* . . ., *I cannot* . . .,
205-7), following which Buckingham begins a new *if*-sentence
containing a double interpolation of such length that he forgets
the opening and carries on with a *yet* construction (214).

Act IV

SCENE ONE

Whereas in III, vii the realization of a deliberately laid plan had carried the action an important step forward, in this scene attention is centred on the after-effects of action, the emotional reactions of the characters, their memories of the past and fears for the future. Like most of the later scenes which show us the party opposing Richard, this scene comes near to being a lament. Richard's calculating will and sense of theatre provided the impetus in the previous scene, but here the characters seem to react to impulses from outside, so that the entries of Brakenbury and Stanley (12, 29) constitute the dramatic turning-point in a scene which began on a neutral level. The situation becomes increasingly black; the pathos of the rhetorically phrased closing lament, which carries with it a note of finality, is widely divergent from the opening conversational exchange of conventional greetings. The Tower, merely mentioned at the outset, becomes the object of an impassioned address at the end. Thus, not only is the setting of the action fixed, but the leit-motif of the Tower is once again sounded.

Here for the first time a united front against Richard is apparent. Resistance to him has become so strong that earlier internal dissensions have been put aside and active opposition begins to take shape. The scene suggests that Richard stands alone, that his position is less than secure – preparing us for the next scene where Richard's inner insecurity is revealed. The first mention of Richmond occurs in this scene, and in a context which marks him as a possible future opponent of Richard's (43, 92); moreover, Dorset's flight is decided upon. He is the first of several to take refuge,

acting upon the advice of his friends, in contrast to Hastings
(III, ii, 17) who, fatally to himself, chooses not to do so.

The Initial Meeting (1–11)

The meeting with which the scene opens seems a little contrived
if we compare it with similar meetings in Shakespeare's later plays.[1]
The rather too obvious technique of pre-Shakespearian drama also
obtrudes in the way the Duchess of York describes, as though she
herself were not present, what is happening (1–4). The word *joyful*
in Anne's greeting echoes Buckingham's farewell words ('most
joyfully, we take our leave', 245) at the end of the scene before,
which is possibly an ironic touch. Her words recall earlier greetings which stood in similarly unhappy contrast to what had followed them (I, i, 122; II, i, 47).

The Brakenbury Episode (12–28)

Brakenbury, who is made to appear 'in good time',[2] plays the
same part as in I, i: he follows instructions. In I, i he had carried
out King Edward's command in preventing Gloucester from
conversing with Clarence; here he obeys Gloucester's orders in
denying King Edward's wife access to the princes. The reversal
may or may not be intentional, but the parallel nature of the two
episodes is suggested by similarities in the wording.[3] Brakenbury's slip of the tongue (17)[4] brings to life the exchange between
himself and the Queen. The Queen's amazement at the word *King*
is also evident in the shortened line (Brakenbury's reply directly

---

[1] e.g. *Caesar*, I, i; I, iii; *Lear*, IV, ii.

[2] Cf. p. 8 *supra*.

[3] Cf. 'His Majesty hath straitly given in charge', I, i, 85; 'The King hath
strictly charg'd the contrary', IV, i, 17. The *Q* reading at IV, i, 17, 'hath
straitly (straightlie) charged . . .', makes the parallel even stronger.

[4] The same slip also occurs – though in a different context – in the *True
Tragedy* (cf. *Var.*). J.D.W. cites this parallel among others as a proof that at
many stages in *Richard III* Shakespeare was borrowing either from the *True
Tragedy* or from an earlier drama which he postulates as a common source
for both the *True Tragedy* and *Richard III* (*SQ*, III, 1952). Cf. also G. B.
Churchill, p. 509.

completing the pentameter). The bitterness which sweeps over her as Brakenbury instantly corrects himself ('I mean the Lord Protector') leads to the scene's only word play ('The Lord protect . . .'), which reveals the mockery of labelling Richard *Protector*.

The echo effect, present here in the Duchess's and Anne's adaptation of the Queen's: 'I am their mother' (22), is, as we have already seen, a recurring pattern in the lamentation-scene, and is also used in the great lament of the women in IV, iv.

Lament and Imprecation

The sonorous, ceremonious lines[1] in which Stanley now announces Anne's (and, by implication, Richard's) coronation are in sharp contrast with the Queen's woeful cry. As so often in Shakespeare, grief is expressed in concrete terms ('Ah, cut my lace asunder | That my pent heart may have some scope to beat' 34 f.).

From now on almost every line spoken by the three women reflects the mortal danger which surrounds them;[2] warnings, entreaties, protestations, and apostrophes break up the pattern of the conversation. In II, iv, 53 Elizabeth had called out 'Welcome, destruction, blood, and massacre'; now she is more specific and speaks of England under Richard as a 'slaughterhouse' and warns Dorset: 'Death and destruction dogs thee at thy heels' (40). She too now remembers Margaret's curse (I, iii, 209). The recurring theme of Richard's unnatural birth[3] appears in the curse which the Duchess utters on her own womb. Richard is likened to yet another loathsome animal,[4] this time a cockatrice. Anne, cursing herself, uses a highly concrete image referring specifically to the forthcoming coronation – a very different matter from Marlowe's extravagant imprecations which lack all connection with the events of the play.

[1] Cf. also the accenting of stem syllables of a word and the alliteration in 33.

[2] Cf. for instance *dead-killing*, 36; *death*, 40; *death*, 42; *dead*, 45, *death*, 54; *murderous*, 56; *deadly*, 62; *death*, 77; *die*, 46; *die*, 63.

[3] Cf. I, iii, 231; I, i, 19.

[4] Cf. p. 52, note 4.

Retrospection and Anticipation in Anne's Speech (66–87)

Anne's speech (over twenty lines long) is the only extended piece
in this scene. Like other characters making their last appearance
in the play, Anne takes a final look backwards and forwards,
surveying her destiny in a moment of vision. Her memories of her
earlier curse[1] and of her subsequent yielding to Richard underline
the ill-starred chain of events started in I, ii and ending with her
own death. For she clearly foresees her end (87); her death-wish
of line 62 will be fulfilled, though not in the way she describes
there.

Anne's part seems more extensive than it in fact is. She has
actually appeared only once (I, ii), though in a major rôle. But in
Shakespeare such a scene is not left as an isolated episode; the
threads of action are carried to their conclusion.

There are almost no plays in pre-Shakespearian drama[2] where
scenes occurring earlier in the play are recollected in such a way
as to be imbued with new life. For the repetition of a scene by
means of a report is altogether different from this deliberate
revival of a scene, which helps knit together the inner fabric of
the episodes in the play.

Anne's speech contains the first mention of Richard's 'timorous
dreams', and the first hint that broken sleep is the outward sign
of a mind not at ease.[3] Margaret's curse 'No sleep close up that
deadly eye of thine' (I, iii, 225) is fulfilled, and we are unobtru-
sively prepared for what the next scene is to show us more clearly
– that the King has grown unsure of himself, admitting (though
he lies about the cause) to broken sleep (IV, ii, 75); in V, iii
Richard's fear-induced dreams will give fullest expression to this
motif.

[1] Two explanations are possible for the variations in wording between
I, ii, 14–28 and the recollected curse here. Either Shakespeare deliberately
makes Anne a little imprecise over something far back in her memory; or,
writing at speed, he himself neglected to refer back.
[2] With the exception of the *Spanish Tragedy*.
[3] Cf. for instance the part played by sleep in *Macbeth*.

Stylized Farewell (87–97)

A stylized farewell-scene rounds off IV, i. Queen Elizabeth, Anne, and Dorset address one another with similarly worded phrases of farewell, and the Duchess bestows an appropriate parting blessing upon each.[1] Like the curses and the laments, these lines of farewell are symmetrically balanced, in the 'ritual style' of lament and imprecation. The Duchess assumes here the rôle of Margaret in I, iii, that of destiny's mouthpiece, pointing out to each his future path and indicating also her own coming end (95). The similarity in the wording used by these different characters is a measure of their new concord and of their unspoken alliance against Richard.

The Tower Apostrophized (98–104)

Elizabeth's call to pause and look back at the Tower is an indirect stage-direction that compels those leaving the stage to look round, thus providing a dramatically realistic preliminary to the unrealistic address to the Tower (which is personified, not described as is Pomfret Castle in III, iii). The conventional, pre-Shakespearian apostrophe rounding off a farewell-scene of this type would have appealed to Fortuna or some higher power. But what Shakespeare addresses here is in fact part of the actual, visible setting of the scene. Moreover, this apostrophe to the walls of the Tower reminds us of the princes[2] and of their imminent danger, preparing us for the events of Scene iii. The reference to the princes and their unenviable situation awakens our foreboding, especially when in the last line the mother bids farewell to these lifeless stones. For the symbolism of this passage is patent: the farewell to the stones stands for the thwarted farewell to the princes, and now their mother takes leave of them for

[1] V. K. Whitaker (*Shakespeare's Use of Learning*, 1953, p. 58) points to the difference between the wishes for Dorset ('good fortune guide thee') and for Anne ('good angels tend thee'). Only God and his angels (not merely Fortuna) can avail against Richard.

[2] Here – as in the mysteries – the mother visualizes her threatened children as *small* children ('tender babes', 'babies'). Cf. *York Plays*, No. 36: 'Mortificatio Christi'; *Corpus Christi Plays*: 'The Resurrection'.

ever. The triple description of the Tower (*rough cradle, rude ragged nurse, old sullen playfellow*)[1] is in keeping with the style of the whole play, abounding as it does in names and periphrases. We may also note that these names reflect the attitude and preoccupations of a mother.

Thus in spite of the predominance of negative forces in this play the corresponding positive qualities are also referred to: the tenderness and pity of a mother, and the Duchess's farewell blessing, 'pure heart's love' (4),[2] 'good fortune', 'good angels' and 'good thoughts' (92–94).

Its markedly stylized form gives particular emphasis to the conclusion of this scene. The double rhyming couplet spoken by the Duchess has already suggested a conclusion, but the apostrophe of the Queen is rounded off with a further rhyming couplet.

The Implicit and Explicit Progress of the Plot

Once more we see how the action in *Richard III* is carried forward by a variety of methods. For the plot advances not simply when action is taking place on the stage, but also in passages where plans are being laid, themes are being developed, in passages of reflection and retrospect, in mirror-passages and passages which portray action by means of a report. English classical drama, modelled on Seneca, had included scenes in which the entire action was conveyed through its after-effects or by means of a report. In the earlier chronicle plays, on the other hand, the action is usually shown as it occurs; rarely is it reported or its aftermath reflected. Shakespeare hardly ever gives us scenes that are *pure* reflection or *pure* action; by uniting various approaches, he achieves a unique density.

---

[1] For a criticism of these epithets by Dr Johnson and a defence by Malone, Rolfe, *et al.*, cf. *Var.* and *Arden.*

[2] Cf. also *love* at 21, 24.

SCENE TWO

The animation and realism of Scene ii is very different from the static, summing-up quality of the scene which preceded it. In Scene ii the rapid movement forward of plot brings with it changed intentions and changed human relationships; various threads of action are artfully woven together, and delay and suspense contribute to the dramatic effect. In the previous scene all the participants had been of one mind, united in their hostility to Richard; but here a dramatic conflict develops in the earlier part of the scene and breaks into the open at the end. There is a restless urgency about IV, ii, a quickening of tempo; one is conscious of the approaching catastrophe. The rise must now be followed by the fall.[1]

General Structure

The action involving Buckingham at the beginning and end of this scene frames Richard's preparations for the murder of the princes, which in turn is interrupted by the short episode in which Stanley brings news of Dorset's flight and Richard tells Catesby to spread the news of the Queen's mortal illness. This intricate structure (a scene within a scene, and another scene within that) helps make comprehensible Buckingham's final decision to flee, and underlines, moreover, the contrast between the beginning and end of the Buckingham episode; for Buckingham's uncomprehending response to Richard's demands is matched by Richard's subsequent deafness towards Buckingham's request.

Omission of the Coronation Ceremony

A magnificent coronation sequence would probably have marked the climax of Richard's career in a pre-Shakespearian drama, and

[1] On rise and fall as a structural principle common in Elizabethan tragedy, cf. M. Doran, *Endeavors of Art. A Study of Form in Elizabethan Drama* (1954), pp. 288, 337.

would certainly have catered to the contemporary taste for pageantry.[1] But the pageantry of a coronation could only have slowed down the increased tempo of this scene and conflicted with its mood. Moreover, since neither ambition nor the attempt to gain the crown provide adequate motives for Richard's actions,[2] a spectacle stressing these very things would not have been appropriate.[3] In any case, a coronation-scene in IV, ii would demand the presence of the entire court, whereas Richard has to be shown as isolated from his fellows. It could also be said that an earlier scene (III, vii) was as an anticipation of the pomp of the coronation-scene, though the dramatic excitement that it generates stems from the particular circumstances under which it occurs rather than from any pomp and ceremony in the scene itself.

The Dialogue between Richard and Buckingham (1–26)

With his first words Richard orders his followers to stand back,[4] so that the 'state scene' develops into a confidential dialogue between Richard and Buckingham which sets them apart from the others. Richard's gesture of taking Buckingham's hand to ascend the throne sums up the relationship that has existed between the two men, and also – with deliberate irony – places this symbolic action at the outset of a scene which depicts the growing dissension between them.

Following immediately upon the mere line-and-a-half which Richard devotes to proclaiming his success is his ambiguous two-

[1] Cf. A. S. Venezky, *Pageantry on the Shakespearean Stage* (1951), p. 20 ff.; and cf. the coronation scenes in *Tamburlaine, Alphonsus of Aragon, Troublesome Reign, Dido, Locrine.*

[2] Coleridge had stated: 'In *Richard III* the pride of intellect makes use of ambition as its means' (*Letters on Shakespeare and Milton, The Twelfth Lecture*). John Palmer's view is much the same: 'Richard, in acquiring the crown, was seeking an outlet for the exercise of his genius' (*Political Characters*, p. 103); and B. Spivack goes further: 'The side of Richard that inherits this formula is not on the stage to gain a crown but to offer another brilliant demonstration of "deep vice" masquerading under "a virtuous visor" ' (*Shakespeare and the Allegory of Evil*, p. 399).

[3] Cf. also III, i.

[4] Cf. A. I. P. Wood, *The Stage History of Richard the Third* (1909).

fold inquiry, which not only questions the permanence of this success but also reveals a lack of security, a fear for the future.

Up till now Richard has referred (though not very convincingly) to the attainment of the crown as the final goal towards which he is striving. Yet as if impelled by some inner compulsion, he now continues his attacks, not against obvious enemies but against those who do not even seriously threaten him. Heedless of what he has taken such trouble to obtain, he turns to fresh murders, revealing that all he has done thus far stems less from the desire to achieve some ultimate end than from inborn drives of the kind he had confessed to in his first soliloquy (I, i, 30).

This psychologically acute dialogue between Richard and Buckingham employs a new technique deriving ultimately from comedy (Lyly) and so far hardly ever taken up in serious drama. A does not understand (or does not want to understand) what B cautiously hints at, and B tries, without committing himself, to put the words (and the thought behind them) into A's mouth. In this scene, this game of understanding and misunderstanding is used to express irony. But Richard, as we might expect, soon abandons his cautious manner and switches abruptly over to the opposite extreme of over-explicitness (18). Buckingham's hesitation is conveyed by the shortened lines and ensuing pauses (11–14), and through the gradation of polite titles with which he chooses to address Richard.[1] Richard's mounting irritation and impatience betray themselves in his mimicry of Buckingham's 'True, noble prince' and in his triple prod, 'What say'st thou now? Speak suddenly, be brief.'

For the first time Richard has lost control of a conversation. He fails to get the answer he wants, and Buckingham leaves him without waiting to be dismissed. Richard is no longer able, as he had been in III, iv, to hide his annoyance and Catesby notes the King's angry gesture (an indirect stage-direction). What follows must be taken as an aside not intended to be heard by those present. Richard's growing isolation is underlined by his repeated monologue-like remarks (cf. 42–45, 62–67). This is a new type of

[1] 'my gracious sovereign', 2; 'my loving lord', 11; 'my thrice-renowned lord', 13; 'noble Prince', 14; 'your Grace', 21; 'dear lord', 24; compare this with 'my lord' repeated six times (85–113).

aside, neither an explanatory hint to the audience nor a sarcastic, high-spirited observation to himself (cf. pp. 105, 125).

However, Richard's uncontrolled annoyance does not prevent him from carrying forward his plan without delay.[1]

Richard's Reaction to Stanley's News (46–67)

Stanley's sudden and unexpected news of Dorset's flight discloses a new treatment of the messenger-scene in Shakespeare.[2] For the news is at first apparently disregarded, and does not register until later in the scene. Up till now, a statement or question demanding a response has as a rule immediately received one; yet this deliberate disregard of an important piece of news is an ingenious dramatic device.

Richard comments on the news forty lines after it is told to him, and after he has arranged the murder of the princes. Yet his real reaction is not contained in this later remark, but rather in the swift succession of orders with which he sets forth his countermeasures ('To stop all hopes . . .'). He rapidly arrives at the combination of murder and marriage by which he means to secure his position; this recalls his concluding soliloquy in I, ii and is intended to communicate his plan to the audience. The plan itself (52–64) exhibits a villainy so extreme as to seem almost grotesque. The concluding three lines of his speech (65–67), however, are not so much an explanation to the audience as a sudden self-revelation. The effect is surprising, for so far Richard has abstained from spontaneously revealing his inmost feelings, tending rather to explain his purpose. Disclosures of this kind point the way to character-tragedy, although this passage is not altogether successful.[3] It is in the last two acts that indications of character-development are to be found (cf. p. 223). But if we compare this passage with similar utterances in, for instance, *Macbeth* (especially in III, iv, 136), we see how in the later play

[1] The servant's description of a murderer who might be willing to do the job may be compared with a similar passage in Greene's *James IV*, II, ii (Ateukin and King of Scots).

[2] Cf. Clemen, *Wandlung des Botenberichts bei Shakespeare* (1952).

[3] For a fuller treatment of this (not quite successful) transition to character-tragedy, cf. H. B. Charlton, *Shakespearian Tragedy* (1949), p. 35 ff.

self-revelatory utterances of the hero are well prepared for and spring from the total personality developed in the course of the play.

In this passage Richard for the first time uses the word *sin* to describe his own actions;[1] up till now it has been used only by his accusers (I, iii, 219, 293). Richard's earlier assessments of his situation (cf. I, i, 162) have been quite confident, but now he sees his gain as 'uncertain'. The final line in the passage may be set side by side with Richard's earlier assertion that he has never shed tears (I, ii, 155), and with his declaration at the end of *3 Henry VI* (V, vi, 68): 'I, that have neither pity, love, nor fear'. Noteworthy, too, is the way in which Richard's inner agitation is reflected in language[2] and verse.

The Tyrrel Episode (67–84)

Agitation runs through the ensuing conversation with Tyrrel, in the course of which Richard confesses to uneasy spirits and disturbed sleep (75). This Tyrrel episode introduces a new variant of the familiar situation where a murderer receives his commission. For here Shakespeare makes Richard whisper his instructions instead of speak them. Silence[3] has joined gesture (the handing over of a 'token', 80) in becoming part of the dramatic structure.

[1] The significance of this passage is by no means impaired by the fact that it represents a variant of a Senecan maxim 'per scelera semper sceleribus tutum est iter' (*Agamemnon*, 115); cf. also *Agam.*, 235–236. As F. R. Johnson shows, this maxim recurs in a similar form in the *Spanish Tragedy* (III, xiii, 1066) and in *The Misfortunes of Arthur* (I, iv, 77); and in Shakespeare later (and still more appositely) in *Macbeth*, III, iv, 136–138 ('Shakespearian Imagery and Senecan Imitation' *Joseph Quincy Adams Memorial Studies*, 1948).

[2] Note the broken rhythm in 60–61 and 65–66, the marked inversion at 65–66 and the absence of a verb at 65. For passages like this where a murder was being planned, pre-Shakespearian drama always uses regular lines; cf. a similar passage in Greene:

> What, murther of my Queene?
> Yet to enjoy my loue, what is my Queene?
> Oh put my vowe and promise to my Queene:
> I but my hope to gaine a fairer Queene, . . .
> (*James IV*, II, ii, ll. 1140–44)

[3] On *silence* with reference to his other plays, cf. A. Thaler, *Shakespeare's Silences* (1920).

The Buckingham Episode (86–127)

The methods used to convey the developing conflict between
Richard and Buckingham suggest comparison with those used in
similar situations by Shakespeare's predecessors. In pre-Shakespearian drama arguments always proceed by means of open pro-
vocation and clear, often exaggerated threats and accusations. But
here the conflict is carried on below the surface; the opponents
avoid open statement, carrying on a disconnected dialogue in
which they talk around each other. This technique is often used
in earlier comedy, but not, as in this case, with intent to wound the
opponent. Richard skilfully employs a number of other techniques for diverting Buckingham from his theme and himself
avoiding the issue: he addresses a third party instead of answering
Buckingham (91 ff.), he talks of matters quite unconnected with
Buckingham's concerns (107 ff.), and he interpolates unintelligible
questions which confuse his hearer (116). Richard's digressive
tactics are not, however, merely strategic: thoughts now rise to
the surface which have previously been suppressed – the news of
Dorset, for instance, and the ominous memories that the name
Richmond stirs in him – so that what Richard says at this point may
be regarded as a kind of soliloquy.

Again and again in pre-Shakespearian drama one is struck by
the inadequate contact between two partners in a dialogue, the
awkwardness of their relationship, the fact that they are speaking
at instead of *to* one another. Here, however, a phenomenon that
had formerly been the result of an undeveloped dramatic technique
is consciously put to psychological-dramatic use.

Richard's recollection of two different prophecies in connection
with Richmond, and his further admission that he had 'started'
(109) at the name *Rougemont* mark the onset of his downfall. This
sudden seriousness about prophecies – in ironic contrast to his
earlier contemptuous scorn at the 'drunken prophecies' in Scene i
(I, i, 33), organized by himself – betrays his anxious state of mind,
and his five-fold repetition of Richmond's name prepares us for
the final act.

The play of words and meaning on the subject of the clock and the Jack (the clapper of the bell) rounds off this rapidly moving scene with an image that reminds us of the time-element. Not only does it express Richard's impatience, but it also warns us that for Richard, as for Buckingham, the 'hour will soon strike'.[1]

The inner estrangement that has taken place between Buckingham and Richard is now reflected in their speech. Not only are the two partners in the conversation out of touch with one another, but the lines which they exchange either fail to complement one another or do so very imperfectly (90, 103, 106, 112); in earlier scenes such irregularity did not occur. The fact that Richard's initial *we* (including Buckingham) is replaced at the end by the *I* of both parties (120, 122, 125) may serve to suggest that the break is now final.

---

[1] For an explanation of this passage cf. *Var.*, p. 302. For the double meaning in 'keep the stroke' cf. J.D.W., *Glossary*, p. 269.

103–120, the so-called *clock passage* occurs only in *Q* and not in *F*, which is as a rule the more complete text. Various theories have been advanced to explain the omission of this dramatically effective passage. While earlier editors and scholars (A. Schmidt in *SJ*, 15, 1880, Spedding in *New Shakespeare-Society Transactions*, 1875, P. A. Daniel in Griggs' Facsimile Edition of *Richard III*, etc., and more recently H. Spencer in Heath's Arden edition of *Richard III*) explain it as an actor's addition, a 'bit of fat', most editors accept it as authentic. N. Delius (*SJ*, 7, 1872) puts its absence in *F* down to 'pure carelessness on the part of the copyist or compositor'; W. D. Moriarty (*MP*, X, 1913, p. 451 ff.) thinks it unnecessary from the point of view of the action and also inappropriate in the light of Buckingham's character up to this point; O. J. Campbell (*MLN*, XXXI, 1916) thinks the passage effective, but feels that it diverts attention from the vastly more important dramatic impact of the foregoing lines. There, Richard's recollection of the prophecy concerning Richmond for the first time shakes his conviction of security, and alerts the audience to the change which is to usher in the Nemesis. W. J. Griffin (*RES*, XIII, 1937, pp. 329–332) supposes that the passage was subsequently suppressed by the censor since it might have been taken to refer to the man who was Duke of Buckingham at the time, who was also known to be ambitious and covetous. R. B. McKerrow (*RES*, XIII, 1937) also considers it likely that the censor had been at work, but more probably in connection with the previous prophecy about Richmond (cf. also W. W. Greg, *The Shakespeare First Folio*, 1955, p. 191). None of these theories seems quite convincing and each is open to counter-argument. Furthermore, the passage might have been omitted from *F* because the complex image with the clock and the clapper was no longer understood or was considered too difficult for the audience (L. L. Schücking). It seems unlikely at this late stage that any definitive explanation will be arrived at.

SCENE THREE

Telescoping of Time

This scene arises directly out of the preceding one: there Tyrrel receives his instructions and here he delivers his report on the double murder, which must have taken place between Scenes ii and iii. A more unusual degree of telescoping is noticeable in connection with Anne's death (announced by Richard in this scene), for in the previous scene Catesby had received orders simply to spread the rumour that she was ill. Similarly, Clarence's daughter (Margaret Plantagenet), for whom 'some mean poor gentleman' (IV, ii, 55) was to be sought out, is already married (37); and Buckingham, who had announced his departure for Brecknock at the end of Scene ii, is already 'in the field', leading his troops in open rebellion (48).[1]

The audience is hardly aware of the various instances of temporal foreshortening;[2] yet the sense which we gain from this scene of one event following fast upon the heels of another is at least in part due to the piled-up instances of telescoped time.

But even here there are repeated pauses in the action. Whereas news of the latest developments and of Richard's further plans occupy only the last third of this scene, the earlier part is devoted to an extended description of one single event – the murder of the princes.

Tyrrel's Report (1–22)

Contrasts of style and matter within this scene are supplemented by a further contrast between its first section and the closing

---

[1] Cf. M. Buland, 'The Presentation of Time in the Elizabethan Drama' *YSE*, XLIV (1912), p. 99; A. Sewell, 'Place and Time in Shakespeare's Plays' *SP*, XLII (1945).

[2] Cf. *Var.*: ed.'s notes to l. 181 (l. 39), and notes by R. G. White to l. 192 (l. 48), *Var.* pp. 312 and 314.

section of the previous scene. Tyrrel's lyrical and melodramatic report of the princes' murder contrasts strikingly with the terse dialogue between Richard and Buckingham that has preceded it. Tyrrel's report follows along conventional Senecan lines, with the exception that it is a 'report of a report'. Yet the impact of this speech is in no way diminished by the reporter's own distance from the events he recounts: his use of direct speech and his account of how the murderers reacted bring the whole incident to life for us – though what is actually described is not so much the event itself as the emotions it arouses in the murderers.[1]

Tyrrel's report is a monologue addressed to the audience. Yet Tyrrel is no mere conveyer of information. This hired cut-throat is so overwhelmed with horror at the deed (which he did not himself carry out) that he has to express his agonized feelings before providing Richard with a factual report – an attitude hardly consonant with his subservient eagerness in the previous scene.

Tyrrel does not express his own feelings directly; yet his moving description of the event conveys his own emotions quite as clearly as if he had voiced them. In *Macbeth*, however, the description of the emotions and reactions of the characters will replace any actual account of Duncan's murder. Tyrrel's report is technically primitive and undramatic compared to Macbeth's; yet even here our attention is focused on what goes on in the *minds* of the murderers.

Here, as in I, iv, Shakespeare's decisions as to whether acts of violence should be performed on or off the stage cannot be accounted for in terms of his observance or disregard of the conventions governing Senecan drama,[2] for both are to be found in

---

[1] On Tyrrel's monologue as narrative and report, cf. K. Schlüter, *Shakespeares dramatische Erzählkunst* (1958), and Clemen, *Wandlung des Botenberichts bei Shakespeare*.

[2] Cf. Horace, *Ars Poetica*, 182. – On-stage murders were frequent in pre-Shakespearian drama. Only in the early works of the English classical period when Senecan influence was dominant were they banished from the stage. The mystery plays too had included murder scenes; the Massacre of the Innocents by Herod's decree is fully and brutally enacted in all four great Mystery-Cycles. For scenes of murder or attempted murder on the stage, cf. *Cambises, King Leir, Battle of Alcazar, Selimus, James IV, Spanish Tragedy, Edward II, Massacre at Paris, Arden, Woodstock, Troublesome Reign*.

his plays; in each case these decisions are in fact determined by the structure of the drama itself.

Reappearance of the Conscience-Theme

The conscience-theme occurs at this point with a significant modification; *both* murderers (not simply one as in I, iv, 270) are overwhelmed[1] by 'conscience and remorse' (20) once the deed is done. We must, moreover, look to the wider context of this passage: for these two 'flesh'd villains, bloody dogs' (6) are susceptible to pangs of conscience, whereas Richard, as we see in the lines which follow Tyrrel's monologue, displays only cynical indifference – the report of the murder is to be served up with his evening meal (31).[2] The contrast between the two is thus emphasized. Tyrrel's speech also helps to prepare us for Act V; for what the murderers learn in this act – that pricking of conscience can be suppressed before the deed but will afterwards inevitably make itself felt – Richard will learn in the next.

Style and Language of the Tyrrel Monologue

The melodramatic and rhetorical tone of Tyrrel's speech cannot be satisfactorily accounted for by reference to the diction adopted by Seneca for similar speeches; for here the lyric pathos and poetic language are motivated from within. Not only is the murder of the two innocent princes Richard's cruellest, most devilish undertaking, but it is also the first which does not form part of the chain of Nemesis Actions.[3] Richard has rid himself not of enemies,

---

[1] *gone with* = 'completely overwhelmed by'; cf. A. Schmidt (cited in *Var.*, p. 308) and J.D.W., *Glossary*.

[2] More recent editors (also Al. and J.D.W.) follow *Q*'s 'soon at after supper' (= towards late supper), whereas *F* has 'soone, and after supper'.

[3] J. Palmer, however, views the boys' murder as a political one in keeping with customary practice: 'All down the ages the successful politician has shown little or no effective reluctance to out-Herod Herod in his slaughter of the innocents. The crime of Richard is the secular crime of the power politician in every age and there is a sense in which every political leader is a wicked uncle who kills little children in their beds' (*Political Characters of Shakespeare*, 1945, p. 101).

but of defenceless, innocent children – an action which seals his own doom.

The agglomeration of descriptive adjectives and epithets[1] serves both to express horror at the crime (1–3) and to paint a poetic picture of the two murdered princes (9–14). The lines 'Their lips were four red roses on a stalk | Which in their summer beauty kiss'd each other' (12–13) contain one of the very few images in this play to recall Elizabethan lyric poetry. The contrast of these lines to 'this piece of ruthful butchery' (5) could hardly be sharper. Edward (Anne's murdered husband) was said to have been 'fram'd in the prodigality of nature' (I, ii, 243); and now the princes are called, with greater emphasis,

> The most replenished sweet work of nature
> That from the prime creation e'er she framed.
>
> (18–19)

Their nature is the direct opposite of Richard's, that 'slave of nature', 'son of hell' (I, iii, 230).

Although Tyrrel's imaginative and dignified language is markedly poetic, it also contains dramatic and realistic features – the use of direct speech, the rapid sequence of gestures ('O, thus', 9; 'Thus, thus', 10), and the interpolation of what is almost everyday speech ('But, O, the devil –', 16).

Tyrrel's monologue provides the background against which his subsequent brief report to the King takes place, so that the irony of Tyrrel's answer to Richard's 'Am I happy in thy news?' (24–27) will be immediately apparent to the audience.

Richard's Monologue (36–43)

Richard's monologue belongs to the summarizing speeches, so familiar a feature of pre-Shakespearian drama. The way in which Richard, devoting a single line to each, counts up (and ticks off) his 'successes'[2] emphasizes his extreme cold-bloodedness. Whereas the first four lines deal with the past, the next (and concluding)

---

[1] Cf. e.g. *Tyrannous, bloody, piteous, ruthless, mild, sad, gentle, sweet.*

[2] Each linked with some previous statement or hint; for 36 cf. III, v, 107 and IV, ii, 57; for 37 cf. IV, ii, 56; for 39 cf. IV, ii, 53, 59.

four announce future plans; for the last time Richard can describe his own rôle as that of a 'jolly thriving wooer' (43).

[*44–57*] A further increase in pace accompanies Ratcliff's blunt announcement of Morton's flight and Buckingham's insurrection. The King's rapid assessment of the situation and vigorous action is in deliberate contrast to his nervous restlessness in the scene before, and even to his own behaviour earlier in this scene when his staccato questions to Tyrrel (27–28) betray his own fear. Richard's decline seems to be held up for the moment, for with his old heartless decisiveness he defends himself against the forces seeking to undermine him.

Richard prefaces his decision to act promptly with proverb-like axioms, which, like others elsewhere in the play,[1] have a direct bearing on what is happening at the time they are spoken. Here, as the scene ends, they emphasize the telescoping of time, the awareness that time is pressing urgently on; 'dull delay' and 'snail-pac'd beggary' are juxtaposed to 'fiery expedition' and 'we must be brief'. The mention of 'fearful commenting' (51) provides an ironic prelude to the next scene.

[1] Cf. e.g. II, ii, 103; III, vii, 145 f.; V, i, 29; V, ii, 23; V, iii, 309.

SCENE FOUR

This scene, the longest in the play, is also one of the most important in Shakespeare's early work. For the passages of lament and imprecation represent the climax in Shakespeare's development of the highly formal 'ritual' style – a style noticeable in *Henry VI*, but one to which Shakespeare, typically, did not choose to return after having brought it, in this scene, to its peak.

Three Types of Scene Combined

Combined in this single scene we find a section of lament and imprecation, a wooing and persuasion-scene, and a messenger-scene; three entirely different methods of composition stand side by side. The lamentation-scene – static, polyphonic, and hardly concerned with action, its speech strictly patterned, its language almost choric – is followed by a dialogue which moves steadily forward towards a goal, a genuine conversation in which both speakers exert an influence on each other. Finally, in the messenger-scene we have action, movement, a rapid tempo, and many references to what is happening off-stage – in sharpest contrast to the first section. The three parts of this scene are, as we shall see, interlinked by thematic repetitions, by contrasts set up between the parts, and by the transition passages which join the parts together.

A number of themes and situations introduced in earlier scenes are again taken up, answered, completed, various strands of action are concluded. Once more, past and future are brought into symbolic confrontation; Margaret, the figure from the past, now departs and is replaced by Richmond, the man of the future. His approach (promising both rescue and danger) is the subject of several reports at the close of the scene.

This scene, embracing the central themes of the play, carries us beyond the play itself: for Margaret's words conjure up not only the violence perpetrated by Richard but also the distant horrors

of the earlier civil wars; to a greater degree than in I, iii, what
happens in the play is seen as part of a larger pattern of historical
events and human destinies.[1]

Margaret's Opening Soliloquy (1–8)

In a prologue-like soliloquy Margaret objectively describes her
own place in recent events, and her present intentions. The concluding words addressed to herself (8), the account of what she
has been doing (3–4), the announcement of her plans (6–7), and
the advice she gives herself to withdraw (8) – all these stamp the
soliloquy as belonging to the primitive prologue-like speeches of
self-introduction common in pre-Shakespearian drama and especially in the morality plays. Yet the speech contains some points of
interest. Margaret describes her own rôle as that of an observer
('to watch', 4), which suggests her function as a choric figure
standing outside the action. Her hope that the sequel to what she
has witnessed will be 'bitter, black, and tragical' (6–7) points
prophetically to the future. *Tragical* is used here as in *A Mirror
for Magistrates*[2] and Lydgate's *Fall of Princes*, to refer to a fall from
high estate rather than to any inner tragedy.[3]

Margaret, in the strange opening image (1–2), describes herself
as though she were the spokesman of a confident, waiting destiny.
Her words summarize what is yet to come, and it is, of course,
appropriate that *she* should speak them. These two lines contain
a new kind of metaphorical language – clearly discernible for the
first time in *Richard III*[4] – which, instead of personifying or

---

[1] Any criticism, therefore, which describes the scene as 'tedious' and finds
fault with the repetition of earlier themes (H. Spencer, p. 213) fails to grasp
the particular structural principle that governs the play, in the design of
which this scene represents a main support.

[2] *Induction*, possibly a reminiscence of the *Mirror*, in this context may mean
'dramatic prologue', 'preparation'; cf. J.D.W., p. 269 (*Glossary*). It is possible,
however, that what we have here is a bitter ironic echo of Richard's first
pronouncement 'Plots have I laid, inductions dangerous' (I, i, 32). The word
induction occurs in only one other place in Shakespeare (*1 Henry IV*, III, i, 2).

[3] Cf. Lily B. Campbell, *Tudor Conceptions of History and Tragedy in A Mirror
for Magistrates* (1936); E. M. W. Tillyard, *Shakespeare's History Plays*. And cf.
how at line 68 Margaret calls Hastings, Rivers etc. 'beholders of this *tragic
(Q) play*'.   [4] Cf. Clemen, *The Development of Shakespeare's Imagery*, p. 50.

allegorizing abstract entities or ideas in the ordinary way, expresses them with the help of some concrete image. The result is a blend of what can be visualized and what is quite unimaginable – a fusion very frequently found in Shakespeare's imagery.

Margaret's Rôle in IV, iv

Margaret was last seen in I, iii. Her reappearance after so long an interval and the finality of her departure near the close of the episode contribute to the strange, unearthly impression which she conveys. Her isolation is given visible form when she remains in the background even after the entry of Queen Elizabeth and the Duchess (she says of herself in the soliloquy 'Here in these confines slily have I lurk'd', 3). Not until line 35 does she step forward to join the other sufferers. As in I, iii, where she also lurks in the background, her first remarks (15, 20, 25) are in the nature of asides; unheard by the others, she agrees or disagrees with what has been said, or interposes her own comments. Her asides gain in prominence through the use of rhyme, which stresses their general validity, their choric function.[1] From the beginning, then, a dramatic contrapuntal element plays a part in this choric lament. In what follows it is Margaret who sets or alters the theme: from counting up and comparing the griefs which afflict her and the other two she passes on to painting a black picture of Richard (48 ff.); her bitter and scornful triumph over his mother (57 f.) is followed, finally, by an all-embracing survey of the chain of guilt, ending in the contrast between *then* and *now* (82 ff.). Though this whole section (up to Richard's entry at 136) certainly strikes us as a lamentation-scene, in fact only a small part of it is confined to real lament. Again, in contrast to the lamentation-scenes of pre-Shakespearian drama, Shakespeare makes his lament *concrete*, using it as an opportunity to give contemporary meaning to events of the past. Thus the lament develops into an analysis and contributes to Margaret's understanding both of herself and of the workings of fate.

From Margaret, the aged prophetess and choric figure, we

---

[1] Cf. F. W. Ness, *The Use of Rhyme*, p. 58.

expect to hear summarizing speeches and objective judgements; nevertheless, some personal and human touches find their way into her speeches (cf. also I, iii). Thirst for revenge, scorn and triumph, the claim to be the first to lament (36) and to exceed all the others in what she has suffered (e.g. 66) – all this makes her no purely choric figure but one passionately and personally involved.

The Lament (9–135)

The most powerful impact made by this impressive scene results from the image of the three queenly figures, uttering lament and accusation, goddesses of revenge uniting to oppose the murderous tyrant; it is this dramatic image (containing in itself the essence of the whole drama) rather than the individual speech that lingers on in the memory. This total impression ought not to be allowed to sink under the mass of detailed observations resulting from an analysis of the scene.

Queen Elizabeth's and the Duchess's opening laments (interrupted by Margaret) contain the conventional themes of the lament:[1] the appeal to the dead (9, 19), the demand that the lament be listened to (19), and the question addressed to God, asking how he could permit such a deed (22). Elizabeth's first lament (9–14) contains the same abundance of epithets as had her appeal to the walls of the Tower at the end of IV, i. The words *tender babes* used in that speech (IV, i, 99) are repeated here and the souls of the dead children are thought of as being still close by – a common belief in Shakespeare's day.[2] The passage, then, does not simply convey a metaphorical image, but expresses a conviction of the time. The Duchess's declaration that excess of grief has silenced her is yet another element in the *topos* of lament. Her subsequent address to herself, in which eight different images describing her state are packed within three consecutive lines, represents a first climax in the patterned and concentrated diction

[1] For the pre-Shakespearian lament, cf. Clemen, *English Tragedy before Shakespeare*, ch. 14.
[2] Cf. A. Ackermann, *Der Seelenglaube bei Shakespeare*, 1914.

of this lamentation-scene.[1] The oxymora used by the Duchess may be a rhetorical equivalent of the paradoxical feelings of a woman who, still living, feels herself dead. Yet the extreme artificiality of these lines prevents us from accepting them as the language of genuine feeling.[2]

Indeed, all three participants in this antiphonal lament hardly seem to be individuals at all, but simply voices in a chorus. The mourners address not each other but the more keenly felt presence of the departed soul or God. The lament is like a canon: the theme is shared by several voices, now in counterpoint, now in unison.[3] Only in the later sections, after Margaret joins the other two, is a specific partner addressed (59, 61, 79). Here, although the Duchess and Elizabeth do not address themselves to one another, the rhyme and recapitulation of certain expressions connect what they say with Margaret's interposed remarks; thus these interruptions, heard only by the audience and used to contradict or correct the preceding lines, create a weird echo-like effect, distorting what the two other speakers say. Moreover, the effect of the rhyme is to link jarring (rather than to blend harmonizing) statements together (19–20, 24–25).

Gesture and movement reinforce the stylized pathos of the language in the subsequent sequence in which the women (after each one has spoken four lines) one by one seat themselves on the ground. This tableau of the three mourning figures on the ground is the focal point round which the three voices weave their intricate pattern. The linking of several lines by means of assonance, parallel construction, repetition, and rhyme brings to a peak the stylistic pattern which has already been employed in the *Spanish Tragedy*.[4]

[1] Lines 26 and 27 each contain two word-pairs (two of which are oxymora) of equal length which carry the line's first two stresses, and then follow single attributive phrases which take the three remaining stresses. The lament in *Romeo and Juliet* (III, ii, 75 ff.) is similarly well supplied with oxymora. The present passage is especially rich in alliteration (17–18, 21, 24, 25, 27).

[2] The lines, also rich in imagery, which the lamenting Constance speaks as she sinks to the ground in *King John* (III, i, 68 ff.) may be compared for their greater poignancy.

[3] For an appreciation of this style cf. A. P. Rossiter, 'The Structure of Richard the Third' *DUJ* (1938), and E. M. W. Tillyard, *Shakespeare's History Plays*, p. 206.

[4] Cf. M. C. Bradbrook, *Themes and Conventions of Elizabethan Tragedy* (1935):

The figures of rhetoric woven into this passage take on new life by being used not merely for stylistic effect but to convey ideas. The connections and correspondences between individual lines and phrases – established by the interweaving figures of rhetoric – are the stylistic counterpart to the links in the chain of guilt.[1] The many repeated phrases help to mirror the recurring cycle within which the evil that is done brings forth fresh evil. The antitheses – which frequently appear in parallel sequences in Margaret's speeches (especially 97 ff.) – are a fitting linguistic medium with which to express the contrast between then and now, appearance and reality, grandeur and abasement. The combination of anaphora and epiphora – for instance in lines 40–46 – emphasizes the regular, inevitable pattern of the crimes. The seven-fold repetition of the final *kill'd him* or *kill him* within seven rhythmically similar lines in which the names always occur in the same places and bear the same accent, hammers home the extent of Richard's sins. In this passage, the concatenation and accumulation of crimes have found a precise counterpart in the patterns of the language.[2]

Use of Names

The accumulation of personal names in lines 38–46, although confusing, was probably deliberate.[3] The use of the same name for

---

'Patterned speech may be defined as verse which, by an elaborate use of alliteration, assonance, balance of epithets and clauses, parallelism and repetition or the use of rhyme, stands out from the rest of the play' (p. 97).

[1] Cf. A. P. Rossiter, *Angel with Horns* (1961), p. 4 ff., and Nicholas Brooke in *The Critical Quarterly* VII (1965), p. 133 ff.

[2] In *The True Tragedy of Richard the Third* the same figure, epiphora, is used, but for merely decorative purposes:

> The Sunne by day shines hotely for reuenge,
> The Moone by night eclipseth for reuenge,
> The stars are turnd to Comets for reuenge,
> The Planets chaunge their coursies for reuenge, . . .
> (1886 ff.)

[3] Cf. A. P. Rossiter, 'The Structure of *Richard the Third*' *DUJ*, 1938: 'The death-lists are so ingeniously varied that one soon gets hopelessly tangled about who-was-who. That, I believe, is the intended effect – one feels there is no end to the blood and treachery.'

different people – now for a victim, now for a murderer – strengthens the impression of an interlinking series of disasters. The relationships are, indeed, so complex and reach so far back into the past that even the audience of Shakespeare's day may have been in some doubt as to who was meant.[1]

Names are frequent throughout the scene (cf. especially 62–69, 145 ff., 273–283). The past events and all who suffered death or incurred guilt are named in this giant summing-up. Marlowe also made frequent use of names (especially in *Tamburlaine*); but he included names solely for their suggestive magic and for their sound, whereas with Shakespeare the names are not simply atmospheric or musical, but are backed by concrete associations.

The mass of new names which Margaret in her first speech finds for Richard carries forward the continuing portrayal of the villain. Besides preparing us for his reappearance (136), these names suggest how we are meant to view his crimes. The animal imagery (*hell-hound, dog, carnal cur, bottled spider, bunch-back'd toad*) continues a catalogue already begun,[2] and stresses the abasement of a murderer who has sunk to the level of the beasts. When Richard is called 'the foul defacer of God's handiwork' (51), his murders are seen as an interference in God's order, an offence against His work of creation. On the other hand, the words: 'excellent grand tyrant of the earth' (52) picture Richard as ruler of the world, as antichrist. Lines 70–73 suggest that Richard's rôle is that of an agent of Hell who is permitted by a higher authority to dispatch others to hell before being claimed in his turn.[3] The culmination of this religious view of Richard as a sinner against Christianity and the climax of the speech comes at line 75:

> Earth gapes, hell burns, fiends roar, saints pray.

Its effectiveness springs from the staccato style, which piles one weighty monosyllable upon another so that the irregularity of the metre makes itself felt.

[1] Cf. J.D.W.'s notes, pp. 230–231.
[2] A. Yoder, *Animal Analogy*, p. 39 f. The chronicle (Holinshed, Hall) had mentioned *toad* in connection with Richard (Boswell-Stone, p. 410). Cf. commentary on I, iii, p. 52 *supra*.
[3] Cf. Sister Mary Bonaventura Mroz, *Divine Vengeance*.

Margaret's Words on Elizabeth (82–115)

But it is less the thought of Richard than the sight of Queen Elizabeth standing before her that quickens Margaret's power of utterance, moving her to speak of the course of destiny, the fall from high to the depths of the present moment. Since classical drama the *topos* 'Then and Now'[1] had been a familiar one in the lament. This, combined with a second *topos*, 'Ubi sunt',[2] is the basis on which Margaret builds her comparisons. The *then* of which she speaks is no climax of happiness but mere appearance and illusion. At the beginning of the play Margaret described her rival as a 'vain flourish'; by using the same words here she reminds us of the accuracy of her prophecy.[3] The wheel has come full circle.[4]

Appearance and Reality in Margaret's Speech

Appearance is set against *reality* in this play in various ways. Richard, of course, is constantly creating situations in which he plays a part and brings others to believe in the deception. But quite apart from any steps Richard may take to dupe his enemies, they themselves are victims of self-deception. Lulled into false security, they fail to see their own danger. Margaret's reproaches to Elizabeth on this score are not altogether justified (for at the beginning of I, iii Elizabeth had already shown doubt as to whether her happiness would last; cf. I, iii, 41); and yet malice or a desire for revenge are not enough to explain Margaret's insistence on the Queen's illusory existence. Only now does the suffering Queen cease to be a 'poor shadow' and a 'painted queen'[5] and

---

[1] Cf. B. Lier, 'Topica carminum sepulcralium latinorum' *Philologus*, 62/63 (1903).

[2] On this *topos* cf. C. H. Becker, 'Ubi sunt qui ante nos in mundo fuere', in: *Aufsätze Ernst Kuhn 7.II.1916 gewidmet*. Cf. also J. Huizinga, *The Waning of the Middle Ages* (1924), and E. M. W. Tillyard, *Shakespeare's History Plays*, p. 207.

[3] Cf. in particular I, iii, 299.

[4] There are other repetitions which reflect the cyclic structure of the play: 'Bottled spider' (81) corresponds to I, iii, 242; 'bunch-back'd toad' (81) to I, iii, 246; 'hell-hound' (48) to I, iii, 289–293; etc.

[5] Margaret repeatedly uses expressions belonging to the world of the stage

come to know her real self. Only misfortune reveals the reality behind the appearance. Thus in a series of contrasts (the symmetry[1] of the style here corresponds to the pattern of thought) Margaret weighs the deception of the past against the reality of the present. Her conclusion expresses one of the fundamental ideas of the play:

> Thus hath the course of justice wheel'd[2] about
> And left thee but a very prey to time.   (105–6)

Conceptions of Fate in Margaret's Speech

Lydgate[3] had already portrayed Fortuna, who casts men down from high estate, as the medium through which divine punishment is administered, though the wheel of fortune, once set in motion, punishes some of the not so guilty along with the guilty. Certain scholars[4] have taken this notion as the central theme of Shakespeare's and his contemporaries' historical plays; it would seem more accurate, however, to regard the concept as only one of those underlying Shakespeare's Histories.[5] In the present scene Margaret does not speak of the 'course of fate' but of the 'course of

---

and the theatre which emphasize her position as a spectator and also underline the illusory and fleeting nature of what she refers to. Cf. *tragic play* (*Qq*, 68), *painted queen* (83), *direful pageant* (85), *to fill the scene* (91).

E. R. Curtius traces the *topos* of *the stage of life, scena vitae, theatrum mundi*, from Plato to Hofmannsthal (*European Literature and the Latin Middle Ages*, 1953, p. 138 ff.).

Cf. also A. Righter, *Shakespeare and the Idea of the Play* (1962), pp. 91, 93.

[1] Cf. also 103–104; this couplet rounds off a long sequence of anaphora, marking a climax before the next lines are uttered with a change of tone and tempo (cf. F. W. Ness, *The Use of Rhyme*, p. 62).

[2] More recent editors (including Al.) follow *F* and read *whirl'd about*, while the Cambridge editors (among others) follow the *Q* readings with *wheel'd about*. Since the 'wheel of fortune' image is common in Shakespeare (cf. Bartlett), and since it is implicit in Margaret's speech, the *wheel'd* reading seems preferable.

[3] Cf. W. F. Schirmer, *John Lydgate*, passim.

[4] R. Chapman, 'The Wheel of Fortune in Shakespeare's Historical Plays' *RES*, N.S.I (1950), p. 1 ff. Cf. P. Reyher, *Essai sur les idées dans l'œuvre de Shakespeare* (1947), p. 245 ff.

[5] Cf. also E. M. W. Tillyard, *Shakespeare's History Plays*, passim.

justice'; for just as the God she invokes is the God of the *Old Testament* (55, 77),[1] so her idea of justice stems from the same source. Margaret, indeed, is the upholder of the point of view expressed in: 'an eye for an eye and a tooth for a tooth'.

Margaret departs from the play, and also abandons the burdens which she has borne, bequeathing them to Elizabeth. Her last rôle in the scene is to teach her successor how to curse (cf. 80), thus completing the circle begun in I, iii, where she herself uttered curses.

Reactions to the Lament from within the Play

As so often in Shakespeare (cf. e.g. I, ii, 115), the characters themselves react critically to the kind of language used in a particular scene. Elizabeth's cry: 'My words are dull; O, quicken them with thine!' (124) draws attention to Margaret's command of language; and the Duchess's question: 'Why should calamity be full of words?' (126)[2] expresses the kind of reservation which is also felt by the modern reader faced with the windy eloquence of the suffering Elizabethan hero. Elizabeth's answer (expressed in artful appositions[3]) pleads that the lament eases the heart,[4] though it 'help nothing else' (131). Such critical consideration of the rhetoric of lament comes as a surprise in the context of this rather traditional rhetorical tragedy. No other Elizabethan dramatist detaches himself from his own work in the same way (cf. I, iii, 287 f.).

[1] Cf. Lily B. Campbell, *Shakespeare's Histories*, p. 316 ff.

[2] The Duchess, who has earlier drawn attention to her own silence in the face of suffering (17–18), is directing this criticism specifically against Margaret's latest and somewhat overblown speeches; it is possible that Shakespeare shared this opinion; cf. *Var.* pp. 323–324 (Mrs Jameson and Furness), and J.D.W., p. 232, who also refers to *3 Henry IV*, V, v, 44.

[3] Here, too, one is conscious of the effort to express one particular thing by a whole series of periphrastic expressions. For discussion of individual terms and of the reading *intestate* cf. J.D.W., H. Spencer, *Var.*, Wright.

[4] The same thought occurs in *Venus and Adonis*, 333–336; *Macbeth*, IV, iii, 209–210; *Tit*, III, i, 233 f. Mark van Doren (*Shakespeare*, 1939, p. 32) sees Elizabeth's lines, especially the end-rhymes at 130–133, as evidence of her 'new-found certainty'.

Pre-Shakespearian Lamentation-Scenes

Pre-Shakespearian dramatic laments draw their material from the common stock of formulae, gestures, and conventions of lament available since classical times. In this scene too we meet with a number of the conventional themes of lament, some of which have already been mentioned.[1] The choric lamentation-scene where various mourners speak in turn is not so common in sixteenth-century drama as is the set speech of lament, which is more appropriate to rhetorical tragedy. Seneca, however, introduces choric scenes of lamentation in which three women take part. In the *Troades*, for instance, we hear (one after the other, and with support from the Chorus) Hecuba's lament for Priam, Andromache's for Hector, and Helen's for Paris.[2] And in pre-Shakespearian drama we find the laments uttered by David, Sadoc, Ahimaas, Jonathan, and Ithay in Peele's *David and Bethsabe* (X 1022 ff.), by Locrine, Guendoline and Camber in *Locrine* (III, ii), and by the three lesser kings Theridamas, Techelles, and Usumcasane for Tamburlaine as he lies dying (*2 Tam.*, 4393 ff.). Medieval liturgical scenes[3] and laments spoken by the Marys in fourteenth- and fifteenth-century mystery plays represent an early stage in the development of the dramatic lamentation-scene; in these earlier dramas the mourning women (in general, three) join in antiphonal lament, each as in the present scene taking up and echoing the turns of phrase used by the preceding speaker.[4]

[1] *Ubi sunt?*; *Then and Now*; Outbidding Formula (34, cf. II, ii, 59); 'How could God permit this to happen?' (24); Address to the Dead (9); 'Hear my Lament!' (14).

[2] The outbidding motif occurs in this scene, just as it does in IV, iv. Cf. *Troas* in Thomas Newton's translation:

> Yet I before most hateful judge
> Dare wel defend my part,
> That I of all your grevous cares
> Sustayne the greatest smart.
> (IV, p. 42)

For further parallels between *Troades* and IV, iv, cf. J. W. Cunliffe, *The Influence of Seneca on Elizabethan Tragedy* (1925), p. 79; E. Koeppel, 'Shakespeares *Richard III* und Senecas *Troades*' *SJ*, 47 (1911), pp. 188–190.

[3] In particular the lament of the three Marys on their way to the Tomb in the Easter *Officium Sepulchri*.

[4] In this connection the lamentation-scenes in the Latin plays of the

In this scene the speeches of the various characters are not interchangeable, as they are in pre-Shakespearian lamentation-scenes.
Moreover, Margaret brings into the lament a note of opposition,
of contradiction, not present in the pre-Shakespearian scenes of
this type. And finally, in Shakespeare the emphasis is less on pure
lament than on presenting a summary of the total situation. While
pre-Shakespearian dramatic laments were sudden lyrical or melodramatic outbursts of feeling or verbal exuberance, here, despite
the melodramatic rhetorical treatment, the subordination of the
part in favour of the total structural design is maintained. Shakespeare is more economical with words, more concrete, less given
to pure expression of feeling divorced from action.

Lamentation-Scenes in Classical Drama and in Shakespeare

Scholars have more than once noted the similarity between this
lamentation-scene and similar scenes in classical drama,[1] basing
their comparison on the lofty pathos of these three mourning
figures. But close examination reveals more differences than
similarities. Shakespeare, it is true, is closer to the Greek dramatists than to the English classicists in setting stricter bounds to the
lament, in including an opposing voice (that of Margaret), and in
combining the lament with other themes. But since the extent of
Shakespeare's knowledge of Greek drama is uncertain – he had
probably read a play of Euripides in translation – the question of
direct influence must remain open. Lamentation-scenes in Greek
tragedy are so varied that it is difficult to generalize about them.
One characteristic feature of classical lamentation-scenes,[2] however, is the close link between lament and action, the lament rising
out of what is actually taking place on the stage.[3] The lament,

---

University Wits should be mentioned. In Gager's *Meleager* (1580), for instance, the 'Matres Calydonides' lament Meleager's death in four lengthy
stanzas (cf. *SJ*, 34, 1898, p. 235).
    [1] e.g. F. E. Schelling, *The English Chronicle Play* (1902), p. 93 (cited in
Var.); F. Gundolf, *Shakespeare, Sein Wesen und Werk* (1928), vol. 1, p. 154.
    [2] This term as used here refers to Greek tragedy only, excluding Seneca.
    [3] Cf. for instance the connection between lament and action in Euripides'
    o

therefore, tends to be very concise, and so interwoven with the events of the play that it is hard to isolate anything that could rightly be called a lamentation-scene. Shakespeare, on the other hand, fashioned his lamentation-scene in the manner of a *tableau*, a clear-cut and static spectacle in marked contrast to the lively, eventful sequence with Richard which follows. The three women meet in order to lament, and their laments are in part caused by events from the distant past. Shakespeare's lamentation-scenes, unlike those of classical drama, seek to systematize, to summarize and survey. Nowhere in classical drama can we find the equal of Margaret's logical and almost schematized presentation of the relationship between guilt and suffering. Nor does Greek drama afford an illustration of such a systematic use of rhetoric – a feature derived from Seneca.

Past and future are brought into the lamentation-scenes in classical tragedy, but the situations alluded to are concrete ones. Shakespeare moves in that direction when, for instance, Margaret asks Elizabeth 'Where be the bending peers that flattered thee?' (95). Only later, in the great tragedies, does Shakespeare make his suffering characters conscious of their everyday surroundings as Greek tragedy had done.[1]

In the lamentation-scenes of Attic tragedy the mourning figures are always balanced either by the chorus or by other characters. In pre-Shakespearian drama, however, no such counter-voice is heard, nor is there any movement on the stage such as we have here when the three women sit on the ground or when Margaret steps forward. Yet the three women take their place on the ground one after the other, so that even this movement takes on a stylized form foreign to Attic tragedy,[2] where movement springs from impulses arising out of the speaker's own rôle.

Heracles, the nurse's lament in Sophocles' *Trachiniae*, and that spoken by the chorus in Euripides' *Troades* as well as in *Medea* and *Electra*.

[1] Cf. e.g. *Troades*, 946 ff., 970 ff., *Hippolytus*, 177 ff., 819 ff.

[2] e.g., when Hecuba, gazing at the ruins of Troy, rises with the words:

> Rise thou, unhappy, from the cold ground raise
> Thy head, thy neck. This is no longer Troy.
> (Euripides, *Troades*)

Cf. the lamentations of the wounded Hercules (Sophocles, *Trachiniae*,

The Scene with Richard (136–197)

The actionless, dialogue-filled wooing-scene is preceded by the
noisy war-like entry of Richard and his train *marching with drums
and trumpets* (Richard's exchange with the three noblewomen is
twice interrupted by martial music). Once again Richard's entry
is announced before he appears (135), while at the same time we
are prepared for the 'bitter words' awaiting Richard (133–134).
These lines mark the transition from lament to arraignment and
execration (cf. I, ii).

The laments and curses of the foregoing sequence now appear
in a new context, made dramatic by the fact that they are addressed
directly to Richard. Margaret, for instance, made use of the lament
topos 'Ubi sunt?'; and now the sufferers put this same question
directly to the murderer (141–147). The portrayal of Richard's
character begun earlier in the scene by Margaret is carried forward, especially in the Duchess's accusation of her son. The clear-
cut pattern of her speech is striking: lines 167–172 trace Richard's
life history from his 'birth' through 'infancy', 'school-days',
'prime of manhood', up to his 'age'.

These lines revive the past; the Duchess's next (and last) speech,
of almost equal length (183–195), in which she turns to the future,
is the complement to the preceding one. The sequence of curses
again draws our attention to the elaborate chain of involvement
underlying *Richard III*. Moreover, the Duchess's curse upon her
own son anticipates the fifth act and especially Scene iii of that act,
where everything uttered here comes to pass. Lines 190–194 prepare us specifically for the ghosts who appear in V, iii. Here, then,
the development which leads to Richard's end is indicated with
great exactitude. The Duchess rounds off her prophecy in the last
couplet (194–195); the aphoristic turns of phrase, the elaborate
use of antithesis and rhyme all combine to heighten the impres-
siveness of this supra-personal pronouncement.

Different types of style and verse mingle here. Richard's character is depicted in lines rich in multiple rhyme, parallel construc-

1023 ff.) and those of Hippolytus in a similar situation (Euripides, *Hippolytus*,
1348 ff.). Their words precipitate a series of movements.

tion, antithesis, anaphora, alliteration, epithet, and end-stopped lines. The curse which ends the passage is characterized by longer sentences (four units of mounting intensity), accentuation of significant words, and a stately and ceremonious tone. At the same time this rhetorical diction is continually interrupted by agitated questions, cries, retorts, and demands. A pattern of interweaving half-lines adds to the speed and variety of the exchange, and occasionally bold irregularities interrupt sharply the flow of the conversation – for instance the four stressed syllables of the Duchess's question 'Art thou my son?' (154) or Richard's sudden monosyllable 'So' (182). Thus the styles conventionally used in rhetorical tragedy are powerfully combined with everyday speech.

In earlier scenes Richard had made use of his superior verbal dexterity and mastery of argument to counter the attacks of the royal ladies. But now, instead of answering, he threatens these 'tell-tale women' (149) and silences them with trumpet-blasts – behaviour which has been thought to indicate a dwindling self-confidence.[1]

The Wooing-Scene between Richard and Elizabeth (198–430)

This so-called 'second wooing-scene', in which Richard pleads with Elizabeth for the hand of her daughter, is unsatisfactory both from a psychological viewpoint and as dramatic art.[2]

The modern spectator or reader will almost certainly be struck by the fault noted by Dr Johnson[3] – the psychological improbability of the whole proceeding; for there are fewer compensating aspects than in I, ii.[4] There Anne was gradually won over by a succession of methods; but here Elizabeth stands firm almost to

[1] H. Spencer: 'The old Richard would have argued it out; this is the baffled villain, not so confident of his intellectual gifts and obliged to fall back on force' (p. 217).

[2] It has recently been argued that this wooing-scene does not fit into its context: cf. L. E. Dollarhide, 'Two Unassimilated Movements of *Richard III*: An Interpretation' *MissQ*, XIV (1961), pp. 40–46.

[3] 'Part of it is ridiculous, and the whole improbable' (*Notes on the Plays – Richard III*).

[4] For a more recent defence of the scene, cf. J. Palmer, *Political Characters of Shakespeare*, p. 104 f.

the end. Anne had been on the defensive, but here Elizabeth attacks throughout with bitterly scornful words, and, unlike Anne, maintains control of the dialogue right up to the end. Moreover, Elizabeth shows herself intellectually superior to her opponent. Since in the course of the play we have seen what Elizabeth has suffered at Richard's hands, we feel justified in assuming that she understands her enemy more clearly than Anne did. There is no reason, therefore, for her sudden, astonishing final acquiescence.

On the other hand, it is possible to find reasons for the insertion of this lengthy scene so late in the play. By comparing it with I, ii certain aspects of the scene will be illuminated. Yet it remains unsatisfactory. The following discussion should not distract our attention from this underlying reservation. Analysis can reinforce but never replace artistic judgment.

It may be argued that Elizabeth only *pretends* to yield in order to gain time; for in the very next scene (IV, v, 7 f.) we hear that she has promised her daughter to Richmond.[1] If we accept this explanation, we must view Richard's contemptuous final verdict on Elizabeth as cruelly ironic, for the deceiver fails to observe how he is being deceived. Plausible as this argument is, it fails to account for the fact that in the plays of his early and middle periods Shakespeare never fails to let us into the secret of any sudden and extraordinary dissimulation of this kind. Yet here we are provided with no explanatory aside, nor has Elizabeth previously been portrayed as a dissembler. It is surely rash to argue that Shakespeare, writing hastily, omitted to add the expected aside, or that the 'slightly corrupt' line 428[2] hints at the existence of such an aside and that in consequence Cibber was right to insert an explanatory one into his new version of the play.

---

[1] This view has been held by such German critics as Gustav Freytag, W. Oechelhäuser, Gervinus, Delius, and Elze. For a fuller discussion of the problem, cf. Oechelhäuser, 'Essay über *Richard III' SJ*, 3 (1868). Cf. also Hudson (*Var.*), E. K. Chambers (*Shakespeare. A Survey*, 1925/1947), and H. C. Goddard (*The Meaning of Shakespeare*, 1951, p. 38). For the opposite interpretation see A. Hamilton Thompson (*Arden*), Sir George Macdonald (*Warwick*), H. Spencer.

[2] Cf. J.D.W., p. 238: 'L. 429 halts and is I suspect slightly corrupt' (line 429 here corresponds to line 428 in Alexander's edition).

Richard's final scornful reference to Elizabeth ('Relenting fool, and shallow, changing woman!' 431) seems, after all, a normal Shakespearian 'objectively accurate statement'[1] which we are meant to accept and which also hints that Elizabeth, 'changing' as she is, may perform yet another *volte-face*. Richard's final comment on Elizabeth is, in addition, self-revelatory, showing how he has lost the ability to judge the success of his manœuvres; he overrates both himself and his enemy and so for the first time deludes himself.

It may also be argued that the very structure of the play demands a piece of bravura towards the end, some villainy out-doing all that has gone before, and that in any case Shakespeare was more interested here in rhetorical effectiveness than in psychological persuasiveness. Yet this latter point is not supported by a similar sacrifice of psychological validity earlier in the play, nor would it explain the extraordinary length of this scene; for although less happens here than in I, ii, and though the tactics of persuasion are less varied, the episode is nevertheless almost a third longer[2] than the altogether superior earlier wooing-scene.

Similarities and Differences between I, ii and IV, iv

The wooing-scenes are related by a number of parallels, which are characteristic of the structure of this play: in each scene a woman is to be won over to something which at first would seem quite impossible; in each instance the suitor has murdered the woman's nearest relatives, and each time we see her plunged in grief at her loss, consumed with hatred of the murderer; in both scenes the action scarcely progresses at all. For it is the *manner* in which the wooing proceeds that is important.

Richard uses parallel tactics in the two scenes: in each he appeals to feminine feelings (to beauty in Anne's case, to mother-love in Elizabeth's: I, ii, 122, 149, etc.; IV, iv, 241, 427); he denies, and then in each case confesses, his guilt (I, ii, 88, 101, 179; IV, iv, 221, 291 ff.); he shifts the responsibility for his deeds on to the woman he is wooing (I, ii, 122, 182; IV, iv, 288); and he sur-

---

[1] L. L. Schücking, *Über einige Nachbesserungen*, p. 28.
[2] IV, iv, 198–430; I, ii, 49–225.

ACT IV, SCENE IV

renders himself to either death or execration at her hands (I, ii
174; IV, iv, 397 ff.).

Yet in spite of these similarities, the two scenes are dissimilar
in some fundamental ways. For one thing, the tone of the second
scene is far more rational, if only because Elizabeth is more
determined in her opposition to Richard, so that Richard can have
little hope of prevailing through appeals to her emotions; in any
case, rational arguments are more fitting where a mother is concerned with her daughter's future, and where, moreover, she is a
mere intermediary and not, like Anne, the immediate object of
Richard's intentions. Apart from that Elizabeth herself reacts
more rationally than had the young widow: Anne's response to
Richard's flattery and self-justification lies in taking up his words
only to hurl them back as curses and accusations; Elizabeth, on
the other hand, carries Richard's train of thought forward in
directions he had not intended, wilfully misunderstanding him;
so while her replies frequently sound like logical answers to what
Richard is saying[1] and sometimes like a deliberate 'confounding
of his meaning' (261), they rob his remarks of all their force and
actually disprove them. In I, ii Richard's adroit use of maxims and
the 'keen encounter of wit' enables him to put Anne at a dis-
advantage and drive her into a useless outburst of anger. But these
tactics are useless here; Richard's hypocritical attempts to clear
himself by citing general adages (cf. 217/218; 291) only elicit
Elizabeth's clever rejoinders. Anne's speech is a succession of
disconnected impassioned laments and accusations; but Elizabeth's speeches are reasoned and logical. Elizabeth is never guilty
of vehement outbursts and exaggerations; the result is a certain
coldness and artificiality in some passages (343-365). Richard, too,
displays a greater rationality in Scene iv. In I, ii his speech is full
of flattery and conventional phrases; but in IV, iv he speaks more
concisely, rationally – indeed, his great conversion-speech opens
quite baldly in a colloquial manner ('Look . . .'), gradually shifting over to a more elevated diction (321 ff.). In the later scene
Richard comes to his main point at once (203 ff.); indeed, he

---

[1] Cf. for instance I, ii, 75/78; 81/83 with, on the other hand, IV, iv, 241:
Richard: 'Th' advancement of your children, gentle lady.' | *Eliz.:* 'Up to
some scaffold, there to lose their heads?' Or 255/258.

speaks sharply to Elizabeth – and not only at the beginning ('Stay, madam, . . .' 198)[1] – in much the same way as he addresses the coffin-bearers in I, ii ('Stay . . .', 33).

It is possible that this conversation between Richard and Elizabeth is designed to underline Richard's isolation[2] (thus preparing us for Act V) and to demonstrate the weakening of Richard's persuasive powers.[3] Anne is completely won over, whereas this success is only partial, for Richard's airy confidence has deserted him. But in spite of our attempts to see the scene in relation to the total play, in spite of the scattered ironies,[4] and in spite of the recapitulation of Richard's guilt, the episode remains over-long, artificial, and unconvincing. Its climax, Elizabeth's final yielding, is quite irrelevant to the ensuing action, so that for the first time we witness an event not followed up at some later stage.

The Seven Messenger Episodes (432–540)

The successive entries of seven messengers occupy the last part of the scene.[5] During the lamentation-scene and the wooing-scene, the action stands still; but now action breaks violently in upon the closed circle of the dialogue – decisions must be made, and new plans forged for the future. The succession of messengers reminds us of the 'serial technique' employed in morality plays and also for messenger-scenes in chronicle plays.[6] In this passage, however, the short episodes are distinguishable from one another; each illustrates Richard's reaction to a particular piece of news,

---

[1] Compare this with the flattery in 'Sweet saint' (I, ii, 49).

[2] Cf. 369 ff.; 399 ff.

[3] Cf. J. Palmer, *Political Characters of Shakespeare*, p. 105.

[4] The following are especially noteworthy:

> 'All unavoided is the doom of destiny.' (217)
> 'What! we have many goodly days to see.' (320)
> 'Bound with triumphant garlands will I come . . .' (333–336)

Richard's curse upon himself (397–403), though not meant seriously, in fact comes to pass, and may therefore be ironic. Cf. Anne's (unwitting) curse against herself (I, ii, 26 ff.), and Buckingham's at II, i, 32 ff.

[5] Cf. Clemen, *Wandlung des Botenberichts*.

[6] e.g. *Troublesome Reign of King John*, Part II, Scene vii.

thus continuing the portrayal of his character. Three of these messengers have already appeared in the play.

Ratcliff's opening lines (433 ff.) recall once more the world of geographical and political reality, providing a precise account (complete with locations and names: *on the western coast, to our shores, Richmond, Buckingham*) of the advancing enemy. Richard's uncertainty and disquiet are apparent in the contradictory commands he issues to his followers in the ensuing 'instruction-scene' (the indirect stage-directions suggest lively acting).

Stanley, the second messenger, does not simply deliver an objective report such as he would have done were this a conventional messenger-scene; the manner in which he skilfully parries Richard's questions and conceals his own opinion behind bald statement makes us feel that he is not impartial. What matters here lies below the surface. Each speaker confronts the other mistrustfully, warily counters his remarks and seeks to sound him, at the same time adjusting his own behaviour to the developing situation. There are similar dialogues in pre-Shakespearian drama – in the *Spanish Tragedy*, for example, though antitheses and parallelisms render this dialogue artificial. But conversations like this one between Richard and Stanley contain elements which were to assume greater importance in Shakespeare's comedies and tragedies: the art of expressing much through the very failure to mention certain things, the art of diplomatic talk, which in the Renaissance had come to be appreciated anew.

Stanley is the only one of those who have close dealings with Richard to conduct his affairs so skilfully[1] that, although the King feels that Stanley will betray him, he cannot pin him down. Thus the bringing of tidings is merely a framework for the submerged

---

[1] Stanley is the only one of Richard's opponents who is his match in wit and cunning. He shows tact and skill in I, iii in his mild and diplomatic reply to Elizabeth's attack on his wife. In III, ii it is he who first sends a messenger and then comes himself to warn Hastings, making it clear that he views the situation with grave misgivings. In III, iv, his attitude to the question of fixing the coronation date is very reserved (44). His reaction to Hastings' rash assurance is one of dubious caution; he acts as a foil to the former's blind trust and confidence. Though he stands at the centre of the growing conspiracy against Richard (in IV, i), he himself – doubtless to stave off suspicion – brings Richard the news of Dorset's flight (in IV, ii), an event which he had helped to make possible.

conflict between Richard and a subject about to desert the cause.[1] Richard adds to his earlier rashness in breaking with Buckingham yet another tactical error – that of releasing Stanley (though Stanley's son remains as hostage). Richard's prudence and mastery are, as we see, on the decline. The rain of questions which Richard here (and nowhere else in the play) lets fall on his opponent reveals his doubt and impatience. It is certainly ironical that Richard should seek support in the fact that he is the anointed king,[2] though this concept still carried great weight in Shakespeare's day.[3]

Richard strikes the fifth messenger before he has time to give his news. But his are the first good tidings to follow a succession of messengers of woe, and mark the sudden change for the worse in Buckingham's fortunes. The next messenger also brings good news. As in his later tragedies, Shakespeare avoids tracing a direct line towards the final catastrophe. We always have the moment when all may still go well.[4] But these interruptions (which mainly concern externals) in fact only emphasize the unalterability of the path along which destiny runs its course.

The final report contains both good *and* bad news, so that the scene ends on an inconclusive note, its ambivalence expressed in Richard's prophetic words: 'A royal battle might be won and lost' (538). In *Macbeth* (I, i, 4) Shakespeare may have consciously echoed this phrase.[5] The many names, places, and concrete details in this final passage sketch in the new tactical situation which prevails in Scene v and during the final struggle in Act V.

The bad news carried by the messengers and in particular the news of Richmond's landing at Milford Haven, shows that resistance to Richard is gaining force. The avenger is at hand

---

[1] Some key-words provide guidance to the real subjects of concern: cf. *guess*, 466, 467, 475, 477; *friends*, 484, 485, 489; *fear, mistrust, trust, friendship, false, faith, true.*

[2] Cf. Clemen, 'Shakespeare und das Königtum' *SJ*, 68 (1932); R. L. Anderson, 'Kingship in Renaissance Drama' *SP*, XLI (1944).

[3] Cf. also 150 and V, iii, 12, where there is further irony in Richard's use of an image from the Bible: Proverbs xviii, 10, 'The Name of the Lorde is a strong towre' (Noble, p. 137).

[4] Cf. III, ii, in which Stanley warns Hastings, and III, vii.

[5] And cf. IV, iv, 460 'neither good nor bad' with *Macbeth*, II, iv, 41 and I, iii, 131.

though he makes his appearance very late in the action. But if this
is a 'tragedy of revenge', we hardly think of this revenge as coming
from Richard's pale and feeble opponents. Shakespeare has in fact
transformed the tragedy of revenge by showing that Richard's
punishment comes not, as we might expect, from his enemies, but
from another, superhuman sphere.

SCENE FIVE

Act IV closes with a dramatically flat scene, the purpose of which
is to impart information; in it we hear, for the first time, *only* the
voice of the opposition (i.e. Richmond's party). The fact that
particular characters are conversing with each other is incidental –
it is only important that the latest news be conveyed to the
audience. The lack of drama in this episode provides a foretaste of
the colourless, unindividual portrayal of Richmond and his followers in Act V.

The mention of the 'most deadly boar' (2) takes us back to
Stanley's dream (III, ii); the same motif will be further (and more
realistically) developed in V, ii. Otherwise, the information im-
parted by this scene is largely disconnected and inconsequent, the
scene disunified. The listing of names recalls the detail-filled lines
of all three parts of *Henry VI*. The most important piece of news is
certainly that Elizabeth has promised her daughter to Richmond
(raising questions about Elizabeth's compliance in the previous
scene; cf. p. 191 f.); the Queen's hitherto ineffectual party has, it is
clear, thrown in its lot with the powerful Richmond.

Act V

━━━⟨⟨⟨⟨⟨⟨⟨❮❮❮ ❯❯❯❯❯❯❯❯❯❯❯━━━

SCENE ONE

This undramatic scene is, in fact, a 'one-man scene', almost a soliloquy, the Sheriff appearing purely as an attentive escort. The situation is now a familiar one; condemned to execution, their eyes at last opened, Richard's victims utter a few final words recalling and reflecting on the past (cf. III, iii; III, iv). The choric quality of this speech is similar to that of the frequent speeches in pre-Shakespearian drama uttered by those about to die. Here, as in those earlier speeches,[1] Buckingham objectively examines himself and his situation, as though wanting to explain to the audience the significance of what has happened to him. The speakers of the *Complaints* in the *Mirror* (and Buckingham is one of them; *Tragedy*, 22, p. 318 ff.) had expressed themselves in much the same manner.[2] Buckingham, however, does not seek, as he had done in the *Mirror*, to enlarge upon the whims of fickle and envious Fortuna; he speaks here of the accurate fulfilment of former portents and curses, the just expiation of his own guilt. 'Since I acted and spoke like that, this is what I must now suffer' is the tenor of his words (cf. 19, 25); they express much the same conception of justice as had been evident in Margaret's speeches.

The opening lines of Buckingham's speech, an invocation to Richard's dead victims who suffered similar or parallel destinies (III, iii; III, iv), make it clear at the outset that the purpose of the

---

[1] Cf. M. C. Bradbrook, *Themes and Conventions of Elizabethan Tragedy* (1935), ch. III.

[2] For an example of such a speech in pre-Shakespearian drama, cf. *Locrine*, IV, ii, 1426 ff. (Estrild's speech as she is led captive across the stage).

speech is to explain, to clarify. This explanatory intent also underlies the passage concerning the four-fold fulfilment of destiny.
Buckingham sees this All Souls' Day as the judgement day he had
wished upon himself when he was found false to Edward's
children (14–15); it is the day on which he wishes to fall by the
false faith of Richard, whom he trusted most (16–17); it constitutes the determin'd respite of his wrongs (19); and finally, it is
the day on which Margaret's curse and prophecy are fulfilled
(25–27). Once again a subsidiary phase of the action is carefully
brought to its conclusion, rounded off with the customary review
and summary.

Buckingham's statement that God has given in earnest what he
begg'd in jest (22) points to something characteristic in the play –
the tendency of Richard's and Buckingham's ironic utterances to
gain their significance retrospectively; thus a special linguistic and
dramatic device is used to express the workings of destiny.

The final proverb-like line[1] expresses once more the balance
between guilt and expiation. The rhyme in the last couplet assures
an emphatic conclusion to this summarizing scene. Buckingham's
end sets in place the final link in the chain of lesser 'Nemesis
Actions' which precede Richard's downfall.

SCENE TWO

The appearance of Richmond in person, after the repeated
references to his approach, heralds the beginning of Richard's
end. It also ushers in the last phase of the play, in which Richmond
plays the dominating rôle.[2]

Richmond's late entry is symbolic of his position in the play, for

---

[1] Wright compares this line with 'right for right', IV, iv, 15.

[2] Johnson thought that Act V ought to begin with this scene, since
Buckingham's end in the previous scene concludes an earlier strand of
action.

he is not an antagonist in the ordinary sense of the term but merely
the agent of a destiny unconnected with his own person. Indeed,
the play has no antagonist; Richmond is there simply to carry out a
specific function, to lead the open opposition which is at last able
to gain ground now that Richard's downfall is upon him. Margaret's words: 'till thy sins be ripe' (I, iii, 219), along with a
number of other lines (e.g. IV, iv, 71 ff.), now take on fuller
meaning.

The flatness of Richmond's portrayal can be attributed to the
fact that he is only an instrument of fate. Indeed, he has little more
to do than speak three very conventional addresses – V, ii and V,
iii (common patriotic concluding speeches), and V, v. We never
see him making a personal decision or facing the difficulties of
the earlier part of the campaign, for, when he first appears, his
position is already assured. Nor do we see him face to face with
Richard. Thus a comparison of these two as 'characters' must
prove misleading.

This scene, like V, i, is undramatic, again almost a one-man
scene, for the three lords are there to act as listeners, to express
agreement at the end of Richmond's rousing cry to action, and to
reinforce his confidence. They comment on the overwhelming
support Richmond can expect to reap, but their observations can
hardly be called conversation.

The Incitement-Speech

In pre-Shakespearian drama, the 'incitement-speech', an *adhortatio*
belonging to the *genus deliberativum*,[1] often occurred in conjunction
with some appropriate spectacle, in this case Richmond's ceremonial entry. The speech itself is constructed along the usual
lines with three main sections, each treating a different subject.
The introductory lines (1–4) simply make clear the situation in
which Richmond and his followers find themselves;[2] lines 5–11

---

[1] Cf. the division – following that laid down by Quintilian and Cicero –
in Wilson's *Arte of Rhetorique* (ed. G. H. Mair, 1909). Cf. also Clemen,
English Tragedy before Shakespeare, ch. 3.

[2] The summary account of Richmond's advance is all that is needed, for
the various stages in the campaign have been fully reported (IV, iv, 463,

recount the latest news, and finally, in lines 14–17, comes the incitement to further exertions. This sort of report was often used in pre-Shakespearian plays to inform the audience of how things stood; here, in the exhortation, the audience's attention is also directed towards the future.

The language, as well as the structure, is conventional and impersonal, its rhetorical ornament suited to a public address. The rather stilted two-fold apostrophe, expanded by a participial clause, as well as the inversion (4) and the periphrases (*bowels of the land, yoke of tyranny*) lend even the first sentence a weighty air. In the second, the main stylistic devices are the doubled phrases (*fair comfort and encouragement*, 6; *summer fields and fruitful vines*,8), triple epithets (*wretched, bloody, and usurping*, 7) alliteration (7, 8, 9, 15), the repetition of the subject (10), and the antitheses (e.g. 15–16).

Though undramatic, this scene is nevertheless an organic part of the play, carrying forward certain themes and key-words, sometimes putting them to new use. The metaphor of the savage boar, for instance, familiar from previous scenes (III, ii; III, iv), appears here in an expanded form (7–11). The words *bloody* and *blood* are scattered over Richmond's speech (7, 9, 16), as is the word *friends*, referring on the one hand to Richmond's 'most loving' and 'courageous' friends (1, 14), and on the other to Richard's 'friends for fear' (19–20). The antithesis *peace – war* with which the play had opened gains a new significance in the closing lines of Richmond's speech. For in this play both Richard and his opponents tend to lay claim to the same virtues, so that Richard, the 'troubler of the poor world's peace' (I, iii, 221), though he ridicules 'this weak piping time of peace' (I, i, 24), can even so refer to 'the peace of England' (III, v, 45) to justify his deeds of violence before the people. With unparalleled cynicism he speaks of 'fair England's peace' in the second wooing-scene (IV, iv, 343), and poses in the pseudo-reconciliation scene as a peacemaker (II, i). In the ensuing scenes Richmond, the true harbinger of peace,

---

469, 524–529, 534 f.; IV, v, 9). Unlike Marlowe, Shakespeare is careful to prepare for his changes of locality and usually keeps track of his characters' movements both off-stage and between the acts and scenes.

often refers to it, as do the ghosts in V, iii who prophesy and invoke *peace* on Richmond's behalf (cf. commentary on V, v, p.235).

The word *conscience* also occurs in an almost aphoristic statement: 'Every man's conscience is a thousand men, | To fight against this guilty homicide' (17–18). Richard later provides the reversal of this sentiment when he seeks to encourage his men with the admonition: 'Conscience is but a word that cowards use' (V, iii, 309).

Finally, it is worth noting that just as Richard's spirits had been raised by the thought of swift action (cf. the conclusion of IV, iii), so now Richmond looks to the speedy fulfilment of his hopes; and in each case the same words are used to form the same rhyme:

Richard: Then fiery expedition be my wing,
　　　　　Jove's Mercury, and herald for a king!
　　　　　　　　　　　　　　　(IV, iii, 54 f.)

Richmond: True hope is swift and flies with swallow's wings;
　　　　　　Kings it makes gods, and meaner creatures kings.
　　　　　　　　　　　　　　　(V, ii, 23 f.)

The image of hope flying with swallow's wings could even contribute to the impression that the end is approaching.

SCENE THREE

With this scene the play reaches its final climax. The two concluding scenes (iv and v) merely tie up loose ends.

The scene is dramatically impressive, yet it lacks the element of conflict between persons or factions which, theoretically, is necessary for dramatic effect. But Shakespeare not infrequently contradicts dramatic theory, and in this case a direct conflict between Richard and Richmond is replaced by a series of contrasts. Contrast and symmetry, favourite techniques in the play, are partic-

ularly evident in this scene. Although there is no contact at all between Richard and Richmond during the whole of this scene,
they are, in the centre section, seen together in relation to the
supernatural which holds them both in its sway. Thus a connection is established between these two separated figures, and
this connection is strengthened by the many other links established in the course of the scene.

The action takes place on the evening and night before the
battle of Bosworth Field, the preparations for which keep the
coming battle constantly before our eyes. Beyond this, we are
shown the presentiments and state of mind of both Richard and
Richmond before the event which will decide their destinies, while
the curses and blessings spoken by the ghosts anticipate the outcome. This scene, then, prepares us for the future in a variety of
dramatically effective ways. The shift of emphasis on the situation
before the decisive event is a characteristic feature of Shakespeare's
work, especially of his great tragedies.

The confrontation of human and superhuman at the end of the
play gives the fate of Richard a new significance previously only
hinted at, and now conveyed in highly original fashion: for, taken
as a whole, the scene is unrealistic, the spectacle on the stage is
improbable in the extreme (nowhere else in Shakespeare's early
plays does the supernatural play so large a part); yet the individual
episodes that make up the action are presented in a markedly
realistic manner – a realistic dramatic technique is used within the
context of the unrealistic, simultaneous staging (a feature of the
earlier morality plays). The result is a scene which transcends the
normal natural bounds, a symbolic panorama which includes both
earthly and supernatural elements. At the same time, however, the
spectator remains convinced of the reality of what he is seeing.
For the first time Shakespeare produces his unique combination of
real and unreal, earthbound and transcendental. He makes use of
the possibilities offered by the stage tradition of his own day, both
primitive and sophisticated,[1] and of the earlier morality and
mystery plays with their multiple staging.[2] *Hamlet, Macbeth,* and

[1] Cf. S. L. Bethell, *Shakespeare and the Popular Dramatic Tradition* (1944).
[2] Cf. R. Stamm, *Geschichte des englischen Theaters*, 1951, p. 29 f. E. K.
Chambers gives numerous examples of multiple staging in the Elizabethan

P

The Tempest provide us with later and vastly subtler examples of this same complex art.

Symmetry and Simultaneous Presentation

The symmetrical construction of the scene corresponds to the symmetry of the stage setting; one after the other, Richard and Richmond are twice each allotted a short episode, after which the ghost-scene continues in the same symmetrical manner. The scene closes with two more episodes, one for Richmond and one for Richard. Richard's monologue (177–206), however, is not balanced by a corresponding monologue from Richmond; and the passage which precedes Richmond's oration describing his good sleep and fair dreams, does not, as we might expect, correspond to the dialogue preceding Richard's oration (271–313), but to Richard's earlier description of his dreams and fears following upon his soliloquy (207–222). In *Henry V* and *1 Henry IV*, and later in *Julius Caesar* and *Antony and Cleopatra* we have examples of two enemy camps being presented within one act; yet these are presented *in turn*. Here, however, Shakespeare shows us both camps simultaneously.[1] For throughout the scene we see, side by side, the tents of the two commanders,[2] the focal point of each camp. The frequent alternation between the use of one side of the stage and the other creates the illusion of events happening simultaneously. Moreover, the middle section where the ghosts appear makes necessary the simultaneous presence on the stage of both protagonists. The central position on the stage occupied by these ghosts corresponds to their rightful superior position in

---

theatre in his *Elizabethan Stage*, III, ch. XIX, XX. For observations on the dramaturgy of this scene the author is indebted to Werner Habicht.

[1] There is a similar instance of this side-by-side technique in Act V of *Histriomastix*, where we see Fouchier in his study and Velure in his shop, both in conversation with others (A. I. P. Wood, *The Stage History of Richard III*, p. 45. Cf. also G. F. Reynolds, 'Some Principles of Elizabethan Staging' *MP*, III (1905), pp. 69–97.

[2] But cf. A. B. Weiner, 'Two Tents in *Richard III*?' *SQ*, XIII (1962) pp. 258–260: 'The tent scene could have been adequately and theatrically staged with one tent against the tiring house wall for Richmond, and a table and chair on the platform for Richard.'

relation to the two men, on whom they are to pass a supernatural
judgement. They embody the transcendental powers invoked by
Richmond in his prayer; and their apportionment of curses and
blessings determines the destiny of both Richard and Richmond.
These blessings and curses are, of course, facets of the same judgement, so that a simultaneous presentation is called for by the logic
of the situation.

Any attempt to purge the scene of its unrealistic features
through the use of a revolving stage is therefore ill-advised, for
the symbolic triangular pattern should be kept before the audience
at this critical moment in the play. Moreover, the contrast between the camps would lose in effectiveness if they were shown in
turn instead of together.

Section One (1–117): Indications of Locality and Time

The four short episodes which make up this first section are full of
realistic detail and form a concrete background for the subsequent
ghost-scene. They all begin with a mention of the locality and
contain definite indications of time. The arrival of Richard and his
army on Bosworth Field provides the sequel to his words at the
end of IV, iv, while Richmond's arrival follows upon his summons to his men at the end of V, ii. Both commanders reach their
goal (which has previously been indicated in a general way) towards evening. Richard orders his tent to be set up 'even here in
Bosworth field' (1), while Richmond's words make clear that he is
standing outside his tent, and that he retires into it with his
followers at the end of the episode (46). The actual situation outside the tents is also described. In the Richard episodes we are told
the strength of the opposing armies (10–11), that sentinels are to
be posted (54), that Richard intends to survey the terrain with his
officers (14 ff.), and that Surrey has been 'cheering up' the soldiers
(71). Stanley's troops are half a mile away from Richard's (37), but
his visit to Richmond (79) and the sending to him of both
Richard's and Richmond's messengers bring his camp too within
the scope of the action.

The time as well as the locality is fixed with some precision. We
are, moreover, made conscious of the rapid passage of time, and

our curiosity about the events of the next day is not allowed to wane. Once again, although the overall time-structure of the scene is unrealistic, the individual episodes preserve the passage of 'real' time. The scene begins in daylight (otherwise Richard could not survey the ground); but the ghosts appear in the deep of night, for when Richard wakes from his dreadful dream it is 'dead midnight' (180). When Ratcliff arrives some time after, the early cock has just crowed (209), but – as Richard notes – the dawn has not yet come (' 'Tis not yet near day', 222). Richmond delivers his speech to the soldiers just after the clock strikes four (235), and somewhat later, when Richard speaks with Ratcliff, it is an hour after sunrise (276–279). Obviously a considerable period of time is compressed into these four short episodes, and mainly into time lying *between* the episodes.[1] For instance, the interval between Richard's two entrances is occupied with putting up the tents, surveying the ground, and in Surrey's going the rounds 'about cock-shut time, from troop to troop' (70). All that could scarcely have taken place during the 26 lines of the Richmond episode. Between Richmond's first and second entries the messenger leaves to find Stanley who then waits till it is quite dark before making his way to Richmond's tent – equally impossible. Yet *within* each episode, the passage of time is as it could in reality have been; these episodes form seemingly realistic segments of time inserted into the unreal timing of the scene, so that the audience is unconscious of the telescoping that has taken place. Their attention is directed rather towards coming events, usually precisely fixed in time. Directions and orders, too, are generally linked with some indication of time (31, 56, 61, 77, 88). When the two commanders think forward to the morrow, Richard's words 'Here will I lie to-night; | But where to-morrow? Well, all's one for that' (7–8)[2] and 'For, lords, to-morrow is a busy day' (18) are in clear contrast to Richmond's confident assertion: 'The weary sun . . . gives token of a goodly day to-morrow' (19–21). The ghosts speak only to Richard of *to-morrow*, and always linked with

---

[1] M. Buland sees in this scene 'the genesis of the double-time movement' for Shakespeare's entire subsequent development as a dramatist ('The Presentation of Time in the Elizabethan Drama' *YSE*, XLIV, 1912, p. 101).

[2] Cf. *Macbeth*, V, v, 19.

heavy and *despair and die*. Richard himself mentions *to-morrow* for the last time when he speaks of 'to-morrow's vengeance' (206). The idea of the future is, moreover, inherent in the many and varied preparations for battle which we hear discussed and which enliven the scene with concrete detail (16, 22, 23, 51, 64–65), as well as in such statements as Richard's 'Norfolk, we must have knocks; ha! must we not?' (5) or Richmond's prayer for victory (108 ff.).

The way in which these two antagonists use the time before the battle is another area of contrast between them. Richard urges his followers to bestir themselves (17, 53), does not give himself time for supper (48), asks impatiently what o'clock it is (47) – ironically enough he put Buckingham off with this same question in the previous act (IV, ii, 113) – and orders a 'watch' (a nightlight notched to mark the passing hours) to be set in his tent. Whereas Richard, who sits down to write, tells Ratcliff to return 'about the mid of night' (77) to help him on with his armour, Richmond plans to sleep until 'the second hour in the morning' (31). Thus the difference in behaviour (and in mode of expression) of the two commanders emphasizes the contrast between the anxiety of the one and the calm of the other (see below). Even where Richmond admits to 'troubled thoughts' (in the disputed lines 104–105[1]), his measured mode of expression and his diction remain unaltered. Indeed, his 'I'll strive with troubled thoughts to take a nap' (104) could be taken to indicate the degree of firmness with which he handles his natural anxiety on the eve of a battle.[2]

The atmosphere of particular phases of day and night permeates this opening section. At the beginning of the first Richmond episode, Richmond refers to the brilliant sunset; at its close, the coolness of the evening ('the dew is raw and cold', 46) causes him and his officers to enter his tent. Richmond greets his father-in-law with 'all comfort that the dark night can afford' (80) and Stanley's poetic lines 'The silent hours steal on, | And flaky darkness breaks within the east' (85 f.)[3] combine a description of the

---

[1] F: 'troubled noise'; for a discussion of the two readings see *Var.*, p. 389 f.; J.D.W., p. 245, H. Spencer.
[2] It is possible, as Vaughan does, to interpret *strive with* as 'strive against'.
[3] The explanation offered by F. A. Marshall (1888) that this line indicates

night sky with a reminder that the hours are swiftly passing. Richard's one reference to night does not describe the night through which he is living but the night of death that threatens George Stanley ('lest his son George fall | Into the blind cave of eternal night', 61 f.). Yet even these words contribute to the atmosphere of night, while at the same time they ironically point forward to Richard's own death. Richmond's rather formal and confident reference to the setting sun (19) at the beginning of the scene is matched by Richard's impatient question the following morning: 'Who saw the sun to-day?' (277), and his anxious statement:

> The sun will not be seen to-day;
> The sky doth frown and lour upon our army.
>
> (282–3)

Further Points of Contrast between Richard and Richmond

The contrast between ease and uneasiness, calm and frenzy, is heightened by the brisker handling of the characters and dialogue in the Richard-episodes. In the Richmond-episodes speeches tend to be much longer and movement on the stage rarer.[1] Since more time is given to each statement, the diction is richer in epithets and the syntax more involved than when Richard or one of his

---

the break of dawn ('The mass of darkness begins to break into irregular pieces . . .', *Var.*, p. 388) is not altogether acceptable, for it is still *before* midnight and the ghosts have not yet appeared. Stanley's words may, however, mean that he is so impressed by the swift passage of time ('steal on') that he is speaking of dawn as though it had in fact already broken. He sees the signs of daybreak while it is still some hours off. In comparison to other passages in Shakespeare which use similar images to describe the dawn (*Romeo and Juliet*, II, iii, 1 ff.; *Much Ado*, V, iii, 25 ff.), Stanley's lines show a marked degree of concentration; he has no time for more detailed description such as we find in *Romeo and Juliet*.

[1] In the first 18 lines of the first Richard-episode there are 9 changes of speaker, but in the 28-line Richmond-episode there are only 5. In the second Richard-episode (47–78) there are 17 changes within 32 lines, whereas for Richmond's 39 lines (79–117) the total is only 4. The Richard-entries contain 17 single-line speeches as against only 1 in the Richmond passages.

party speaks. For example, Blunt takes his leave in two sentences (42–43); but Norfolk, in a similar situation, simply says 'I go, my lord' (55). His answer to Richard's inquiry about the strength of the enemy (10) is equally laconic, whereas Blunt replies to a query from Richmond in four rather wordy lines (35–38). Richard dismisses his followers with a curt: 'Leave me, I say' (78), which is quite unlike Richmond's: 'Good night, good Captain Blunt' (44) and his final word to Derby (102 ff.) and to his suite (107). Again, Richard's abrupt order: 'Give me some ink and paper' (49) is matched by Richmond's complete pentameter: 'Give me some ink and paper in my tent' (23), to which he adds three lines of precise, almost punctilious, explanation.

Richmond's very first lines illustrate the difference between the two men. Whereas Richard's first words are a short, single-line command, followed by his abrupt question to Surrey, 'why look you so sad?', Richmond begins his neatly constructed speech with an extended three-line nature-image reminiscent of the more lyrical passages in *Venus and Adonis* or *Romeo and Juliet*. Instead of Richard's anxious haste, Richmond displays a calm confidence that allows time for the contemplation of nature before passing on to practical preparations for battle. Richmond's mode of expression is altogether smoother and more formal than Richard's very individual way of speaking. Richmond's well-balanced lines with their conventional epithets (e.g. *weary sun; golden set; bright track; fiery car, dark night, leaden slumber*) might come from any Elizabethan epic or lyric poem, but Richard's speech bears the unmistakable stamp of his personality. The images which Richmond uses (*wings of victory; windows of mine eyes*) are fairly conventional; far more poignant is the impact made by Richard's one poetic image, 'the blind cave of eternal night' (62). The one original and striking image to be found in the Richmond-episodes ('And flaky darkness breaks within the east', 86) is spoken by Derby.

In contrast to Richmond's logical and clearly structured speeches, Richard's thoughts leap to and fro; we find him losing the thread, forgetting what he intended to say. At the very beginning Richard addresses first Surrey and then Norfolk, suddenly thinks about where his tent should be placed and breaks the thread of his next speech by impatiently repeating his order: 'Up with my tent!' (14). Richard calls on Norfolk only, it seems, to have his own statement confirmed: 'we must have knocks; ha! must we not?' No information is conveyed here, no command is spoken, no question posed. Richard's almost monologic utterance gives expression to some idea which has risen to the surface of his mind, and which he wants Norfolk to confirm. His words: 'But where to-morrow? Well, all's one for that' (8) are spoken as though to himself. He gives vent to whatever is passing through his mind, even though in doing so he repeats himself (cf. 63, 72; 76, 78; 7, 14). Thus even before the ghosts appear Richard's utterances prepare us for the altered manner we encounter in his great soliloquy.

Metrical Contrasts

The abrupt, staccato quality of Richard's speech is emphasized by the metre. In both Richard-episodes the blank verse is irregular, the caesura often seeming to interrupt the flow and the logic of the thought. There are eight shortened lines which cannot be combined with others to form a complete pentameter, whereas we find no such lines in the Richmond-episodes. Richard's lines which hardly sound like blank verse at all, become even less regular towards the end of the second Richard-episode, where the metre begins to disintegrate. Earlier scholars ascribed such lines as 72 or 76 to inattention on Shakespeare's part,[1] or saw them as signs of a corrupt text; but the conscious artistic design behind them is now recognised,[2] so that emendations to such passages made by former editors[3] are to be rejected.

[1] On line 72 Malone writes: 'In speeches of this description, where minute orders are given about trifles, the poet appears to have paid little attention to metre, and to have interposed sentences of mere prose' (*Var.*, p. 386).

[2] Cf. R. Flatter, *Shakespeare's Producing Hand* (1948); Th. Finkenstaedt, 'Zur Methodik der Versuntersuchung bei Shakespeare' *SJ*, 90 (1954).

[3] For instance, Pope's smoother version of line 76 was 'Bid my guard watch *and* leave', while Keightley read 'So leave me'. At line 75 Pope placed a *There* before 'Set . . .', while Capell, Malone, Steevens and others inserted *So*. At line 78 Pope sought to restore the iambic metre by adding *now*: 'Leave me now'. Cf. *Var.*, p. 387.

In any case Richard's lines, perhaps precisely because of their unconventional restlessness, are an ideal medium for the actor. They invariably postulate some accompanying gesture – looking round, pointing, turning away, impatiently turning to the servants (e.g. the sudden 'set it down' in line 74), trying on a helmet (50), seizing and emptying a bowl of wine, anxiously striding up and down. Richmond, however, seems less given to movement and his words suggest no more than a few conventional gestures. What Richard says and does shows a greater concern with himself (7–8, 48, 50–51, 63–65, 73 f.), whereas Richmond's preparations for battle are of a general nature. Richard's state of mind is thus vividly put before us (cf. especially 73–74), while Richmond remains a vaguer figure – though it is he and not Richard whom we see alone and absorbed in prayer at the close of the four episodes. Richmond, however, utters this prayer as the spokesman of his entire army; he speaks and thinks of himself as God's 'captain' (108), using not only *I* and *my*, but also *our*, *us*, and *we*. Of all the addresses to God so far, this is the fullest; it is, moreover, a complete prayer, not simply an invocation.

The Ghost-Scene (118–176)

This scene, far from interrupting the parallel portrayal of Richmond and Richard, continues it in a different manner. The extreme regularity of this parade of Richard's eleven victims, each cursing and blessing the two commanders with the same phrases and formulas,[1] causes the passage to stand out of its context. The echo effect, familiar from the scenes of lament, sounds more loudly here. It would be mistaken to dismiss the strict pattern and stereotyped expression of the ghost-scene (reminiscent of the serial technique of morality plays) as a primitive artistic device, or to assume that this scene is not Shakespeare's at all.[2] In this scene,

---

[1] The lines addressed to Richard always end with *despair and die*, and almost as often include *think*, or *think upon*; cf. also 'fall thy edgeless sword' or 'fall thy lance', 135, 143, 163. The lines addressed to Richmond usually contain such words as 'good angels' or 'God and good angels', 138, 156, 175; 'live and flourish', 130, 138; the repeated *awake* is then addressed to both of them (144, 145, 146, 149).

[2] E. K. Chambers holds this view (*Shakespeare*, I, p. 303) and calls the scene

as in IV, iv, the recurring pattern of incident and phrase emphasizes the ritual and ceremonial, the supra-personal quality of the sequence and thereby heightens its effectiveness.[1]

The ghosts appear in the order in which they were murdered,[2] so that Richard's deeds of violence are once more reviewed. As so often before, past and future are linked together. We are reminded of Margaret's imprecations, for the ghosts speak of Richard's past crimes, and their curses like their blessings, look forward to the future. The blessings invoked for Richmond extend into a future beyond the compass of the play: he is to triumph on the morrow, and, beyond that, he is to 'beget a happy race of kings' (157).[3]

Shakespeare made it quite clear what precise effect the ghosts were meant to exercise on Richard's future. Unlike the pre-Shakespearian spirits of revenge (see below) with their curses and demands for vengeance, these ghosts only wish to be present in Richard's *mind* on the morrow,[4] weighing him down with their accusing presence, sapping his courage, causing him to despair. What they intend is couched in precise pictorial terms: 'Let me sit heavy on thy soul to-morrow' is three times repeated (118, 131, 139), while the two princes picture themselves as lead within his breast to weigh him down.[5] Richard's arm is to be weak and his sword 'edgeless' (135, 163), and he is, at last, to feel guilt (142, 146). Richard first speaks of his troubled conscience in the

---

'a spectacular theatrical addition'. On this point cf. J.D.W., *Introduction*, p. xxxiv, and the explanation by Maxwell cited there. The fact that from line 48 to the end of the play F follows the text of Q_3 without collation with any other MS might provide support for doubts about the authenticity of certain passages.

[1] Cf. M. van Doren, *Shakespeare* (1939), pp. 23–24.

[2] The order is altered in the *Quartos*, possibly for the sake of emphasizing the symmetry; for first come three entries of a single ghost, then two groups of ghosts, and finally three more single entries.

[3] The ghost of Henry VI, indeed, recalls his own former prophecy that Richmond shall be king (cf. IV, ii, 98 f.).

[4] *think on me* occurs eight times with only slight variations.

[5] It is possible to see in Richard's order that his staves be not too heavy (65), and in his cry 'What, is my beaver easier than it was?' (50), an unconscious desire to throw off a burden, in ironic contrast to the burden which is to fall upon him.

soliloquy that follows, but the ghost-scene has already prepared us for this awakening of Richard's sense of guilt. In addition to conscience, the subject of sleeplessness or broken sleep[1] is mentioned by the ghosts and stressed through the implicit contrast with Richmond's peaceful, undisturbed slumber (160–161; 130, 155, 164).

Whereas Richard will be burdened by conscience, Richmond can expect comfort, fresh energy, and help (121 f., 130, 137, 144 f.). Similarly such words as *destruction, dread,* and *guilt* addressed to Richard are matched by contrasting words (*victory, joy, peace,* and *comfort*) spoken to Richmond. The opposing values are impressed upon the audience by repetition (often within a line or couplet[2]), by rhetorical emphasis laid on certain lines,[3] by rhyme and alliteration, and by the use of key-words familiar from repeated occurrences throughout the play.[4] Buckingham, who had remained longest at Richard's side, is given the longest speech, a speech in which rhyme (171–176) and an accumulation of rhetorical devices (171–172) help bring about a moment of heightened intensity at the close of this ghost-scene. His last two lines (175–176) round off the episode with an objective and explicit, indeed a choric, commentary on the fate of the two commanders.

That the two sleepers have heard the ghosts' voices in a dream is apparent from their reactions on waking; yet unlike Clarence's dream, this one is objective and lacks the dream atmosphere. Indeed, the rigid sequence, the symmetry, the markedly rational and similar speeches of the ghosts make us forget that this is supposed to be a dream. Had the ghost-scene been played out before wide-awake witnesses it would not have needed altering. It is doubtful, therefore, whether this scene can usefully be considered as an example of a dream.[5] However, Clarence's dream and this one are not altogether without similarities: the dead accusers of the earlier passage seem here to have taken on visible shape, come to rouse the conscience of a man more guilty than poor Clarence.

[1] Cf. Margaret's curse at I, iii, 225; and IV, i, 83–85.
[2] e.g. 144–145, 146–147, 149, 164, 171.
[3] e.g. 146–147, 172.
[4] For example, *deadly – death, fear, bloody, quiet, peace, joy.*
[5] A. Arnold ('The Recapitulation Dream in *Richard III* and *Macbeth*' *SQ,* VI, 1955, pp. 51–62) has made a comparison between Clarence's dream, this

Objective Reality of the Ghosts

The nineteenth century took an exclusively subjective view of the ghosts, regarding them as manifestations of Richard's awakened conscience; the present century, however, has maintained that they exist outside Richard's mind.[1] No attempt will be made here to discuss these two standpoints more fully, though a number of arguments can be used to support either view. The present writer is convinced that Elizabethan theories about ghosts put forward in discussing this scene throw less light on Shakespeare's ghosts than do considerations of dramatic and artistic effect. The 'Elizabethan background' – approach to Shakespeare's work tends to assume that simply by applying a knowledge of contemporary ideas we arrive at a correct understanding of much that is difficult in Shakespeare; this is to overlook the fact that a dramatist of genius often makes use of conventions and contemporary views as a mere

---

scene, and Lady Macbeth's sleep-walking scene (*Macbeth*, V, i); he notes that in contrast to pre-Shakespearian dreams, which are always prophetic, these three also look to the past and involve recapitulation. Compared to the rational and strictly ordered presentation in *Richard III* (in both I, iv and V, iii) Lady Macbeth's dream gets much closer to the real world of dreams; it 'is characterized by a distortion of time sequence and a confusion of events', and thus gives us 'the illusion of the dream world as we know it, in which time and events are often distorted and telescoped'.

[1] E. E. Stoll adopts this standpoint (see his full treatment in *Shakespeare Studies*, 1942, ch. V, and also 'The Objectivity of the Ghosts in Shakspere' *PLMA*, XXII, 1907, p. 201 ff.). In Stoll's view these ghosts (like those in every Elizabethan play) are vengeful spirits who appear for the sole purpose of wreaking personal vengeance. He opposes any expansion of the idea of Nemesis in Shakespeare's work. It must be pointed out, however, that though Richmond in particular has *no* personal grounds for revenge, the spirits support his actions; thus they, like Richmond, participate in fulfilling that higher plan. But the objective reality of the ghosts – Stoll draws attention to the detailed description of certain physical circumstances accompanying the appearance of the ghosts (180–181) – does not necessarily mean that they have no subjective significance. Stoll disputes that they have anything to do with Richard's conscience and interprets his 'obscure and awkward speech' as no more than an attempt to shake off the apprehension with which his dream has filled him. The idea that Richard is brought face to face with his own conscience is categorically denied ('What has he, a thorough Machiavel . . . to do, before this or after, with conscience and remorse?' p. 225). Bradley, Herford, and Moorman (*MLR*, I, 1906) regard these ghosts as subjective apparitions.

springboard for his own artistic ends. When ghosts appeared on
the stage the contemporary theories about ghosts[1] were no doubt
present in the mind of the audience. Indeed, every dramatist
must reckon with the expectation aroused in his audience by his
use of dramatic conventions. Yet more than once in *Richard III* the
audience is led from the familiar to the unfamiliar:[2] so, in this case,
the ghost-scene is unconventional in that it performs an unusual
function within a larger dramatic pattern. The audience, for its
part, would probably have responded to what was new as well as
to what was familiar in the episode; for wherever Shakespeare
puts certain conventions to use for a new purpose, he does so on
the understanding that his audience already has preconceived
notions about these conventions, with the result that the new
aspects he introduces produce a complex effect and act on many
levels at the same time.

To pose the question, whether the ghosts here or the witches in
Macbeth are real and objective *or* subjective and symbolic is to
oversimplify the issue. For both possibilities are present in these
ghosts. Shakespeare realizes that an apparition existing outside of
a conscience-stricken mind may, without losing its reality, at the
same time be a symbol for conflicts within the mind of the pro-
tagonist.

Considered from the point of view of the first part of the scene,
the ghosts are not intruders breaking in upon the stream of the
action; rather they help to carry forward the contrasts in the state
of mind of the two men set up in the foregoing parallel episodes.
Richard must, in any case, once more mentally review the long
list of his victims so that sentence may be pronounced upon him
when he is fully conscious of his crimes. Furthermore, the
cyclical pattern of the entire drama justifies this retrospective
summary of the past at the close of the main chain of action. We
may also recognize the familiar tendency to draw up the balance,
to assess what has taken place. What we do not find here are the

[1] Cumberland Clark, *Shakespeare and the Supernatural* (1931); P. S. R.
Gibson, *Shakespeare's Use of the Supernatural* (1908); A. de Berzeviczy, *Le
Surnaturel dans le théâtre de Shakespeare*, Paris (n.d.); R. H. West, 'Elizabethan
Belief in Spirits and Witchcraft' *Studies in Shakespeare, UMPEAL*, 1 (1953).
[2] Cf. Clemen, 'Tradition and Originality in Shakespeare's *Richard III*'
SQ, V (1954), p. 247 ff.

conventional cries of the murdered for vengeance; indeed, the word *vengeance* does not occur at all.

Up till now Richmond has been an isolated figure; now, at last, the forces standing behind him are made explicit. And just as the ghosts do not speak to Richard of vengeance, so their words to Richmond show that they are not spirits of revenge but prophets of good fortune and peace. Conventional vengeful ghosts are not entrusted with such messages. Richmond is in no sense an avenger of any wrong done personally to him; he is God's 'captain', fulfilling a behest from above to restore the order that Richard has defied and disrupted. The fact that the ghosts appear immediately after Richmond's prayer and to *both* men suggests that they are indeed agents of a transcendental power – a power, invoked by Richmond, which is now to pronounce the fate of both men. From this point of view, then, the ghosts do possess some objective reality; but in saying this we have not exhausted the subject.

For only as Richard relives the dreadful experience in his ensuing soliloquy do we grasp the full effect on his mind of what he has seen and heard: Richard's conscience now responds to the burdens heaped upon it in the ghost-scene. Indeed, the sequence must be regarded as one whole: the soliloquy provides an appropriate medium for expressing the processes of Richard's mind. The revelation of subjective experience would have been totally out of place in the ordered symmetrical rhythm of the ghost-scene, with its rhetoric and rational bent. Thus both elements, the objective and the subjective, are present in this extraordinary scene where conventions are used for unconventional ends.[1]

---

[1] E. E. Stoll complains that ghosts in Elizabethan drama are portrayed in a manner that demonstrates an 'inability or unwillingness to discriminate things subjective and things objective' (*Shakespeare Studies*, 1942, p. 223). But, from another point of view, it is the modern critic who errs by setting up unnecessary alternatives; the Elizabethan consciousness was able to encompass both possibilities. For further discussion of the ghosts cf. also Hardin Craig, *An Interpretation of Shakespeare* (1948), p. 74.

Pre-Shakespearian Ghost-Scenes

In Senecan drama the ghost-scene is not integrated into the dramatic action, and only gradually do such links appear;[1] in Shakespeare the connections are for the first time firmly established. Before Shakespeare ghost-scenes either form a prologue (as in Seneca's *Thyestes* and *Agamemnon*, and in *Herodes* and *Solymannus*), or, functioning as both prologue and epilogue, they frame the drama. In addition we find ghost-scenes inserted between the acts, where the ghost is a choric figure, a spectator, a commentator, or a witness. The *Spanish Tragedy* is the best example of this technique. But the ghost-scene in this play, though it sheds light on the action through its inclusion of the supernatural, remains none the less an interlude. The first signs of a relationship appear in the English translations of Seneca's works, where the theme of revenge, so important in the main action, is given a new prominence in the ghost-scenes. But here, too, apart from stating their claim to vengeance the ghosts have little connection with the real action,[2] and do not provide the impulse for what then happens.

Even when, later, the ghosts are brought into the body of the play, there is still no interplay between the two levels. The figures on both levels deliver their soliloquies, and the ghost-scene is addressed primarily to the audience. In *Woodstock*, for instance, the function of the ghost-scene (V, i) is not so much to urge Woodstock to flight as to fix the audience's attention on the central theme of 'Fair England', symbolized in the ghosts of Edward III and the Black Prince. *Locrine* does in some measure act as a forerunner to the ghost-scene in *Richard III* in that ghost and living man appear together on the stage. But the prophetic words of warning spoken by the ghost to his murderer elicit from the guilty man only an arrogant protest, and the rhetorically inflated diction used by the ghost is very different from the concise and pregnant utterances of the ghosts in *Richard III*. In both

---

[1] I am indebted for the following paragraph to G. Dahinten's study, *Die Geisterszene in der Tragödie vor Shakespeare* (Palaestra Bd. 225, 1958) which has superseded the earlier study by W. F. Moorman, 'The Pre-Shakespearean Ghost' *MLR*, I (1906), p. 85 ff.

[2] e.g. *Herodes*, *Misfortunes of Arthur*, *Roxana*.

scenes, foreseeing the future plays an important part – but the same could be said of almost all ghost-scenes since Seneca.

Richard's Soliloquy (177–206): Structure and Development

Richard's soliloquy following the ghosts' appearance tips what has been an almost even balance of importance between the two commanders in favour of Richard. This monologue is an astonishing piece of self-revelation, second in importance only to the opening soliloquy in Act I. Touching on a series of topics thrown up from various levels of his consciousness, Richard appears to speak at the very moment of experience.

As Richard opens the monologue, he is still in a dream-world, living out in advance the actual circumstances of his death. His anguished cry to Jesus is the first sign of deep emotion we have had from him. Now fully awake, his consciousness at once asserts itself – it was *only* a dream. Yet in the next line he proceeds to accuse his 'coward conscience', admitting that what he has to contend with is not just an illusion but something within himself.

In the next two lines his attention shifts away from himself to his surroundings. Although the lines convey information only about the time of night and the degree of light present on the stage, they seem entirely in place because Richard's consciousness of his surroundings naturally increases as he puts sleep behind him. Having taken note of his own abnormal state Richard goes on to inquire into its cause ('What do I fear? Myself?'). His words: 'There's none else by' make it clear that he is seeking an obvious, unmysterious cause for his own emotion, yet he cannot believe that he fears himself ('Richard loves Richard; that is, I am I'). The very possibility of such a split within a person is a new and important phenomenon in sixteenth-century portrayal of character. Richard's shrewd logical arguments with himself (both here and later) are a reflection of that delight and skill in argumentation so obvious from the outset, as well as a manifestation of his characteristic attitude towards himself: he has more than once talked to himself as if to someone else, cynically described and encouraged himself. But hitherto Richard's logical skills were a means of refuting and criticizing others; now he is the victim of his own

arguments and faced with his own questions and demands, he falls
into self-contradiction and evasiveness. His initial seemingly valid
answer is repeatedly followed by a second reply which negates the
first, and which is a reluctant admission of some unhappy truth
about himself (cf. 184, 186, 188). Thus the compulsion to admit
the truth to himself breaks through his dialectical defences. This
vicious circle of evasions and admissions ends with line 192; his
exclamation: 'Fool, do not flatter' (192) banishes both self-
esteem and vanity. The two opposing admonitions to the 'fool' in
this one line balance one another and reveal a self-critical attitude
which would have been unthinkable even in IV, iv, where Richard
had scornfully called the Queen a fool (431).

Thus the way is paved for the self-accusation which now
follows (193–199). Conscience, described as 'coward' at the beginning of the soliloquy, has now become a mighty accuser with
'a thousand several tongues'.[1] The catalogue of Richard's sins
mounts to a climax in a dramatic image reminiscent of the allegorical style of the late Middle Ages – these sins, all crying
'guilty, guilty', throng to the bar of justice to accuse him. The
three laconic words 'I shall despair' (echoing the ghosts' ten-
times repeated 'despair and die') show that all attempts to justify
himself have failed. His despair is then deepened by the admission
of his complete isolation; lines 199 to 202 ('There is no creature
loves me; . . . ') refer to the earlier admission, 'Alas, I rather hate
myself' (189). Here we have the tragic answer to this same Richard's triumphant 'I, that have neither pity, love, nor fear' at the
close of *3 Henry VI* (V, vi, 68) and to his

> And this word 'love', which greybeards call divine,
> Be resident in men like one another,
> And not in me! I am myself alone.
> >   (V, vi, 81) ibid.

Now, at the end of his existence, this isolation ('I am myself
alone') has become a curse. The soliloquy thus rounds off the
sequence of variations centring on the key-words *love*, *pity*, and
hate, that has run through the play.

[1] Sir George Macdonald (*Warwick*) compares this with 'Conscientia mille
testes'.

Q

Up to this point the soliloquy mirrors the course of the speaker's own experience, as he talks and disputes with himself. But in the last three lines, which briefly summarize the events of the dream, Richard seems to distance himself from this experience, objectively reviewing what has happened in a manner characteristic of the pre-Shakespearian dramatic monologue. Johnson doubted whether these lines, so out of character with the rest of the soliloquy, were in their right place here.[1] But as elsewhere in the play we find instances of the juxtaposition of different styles, too (cf. e.g. I, iv, 76), it seems somewhat rash to insert these three lines after 212,[2] though they would fit better there and add point to Ratcliff's rejoinder 'be not afraid of shadows'.[3]

Use of Language in the Soliloquy

Richard's various states of mind are reflected in the language of this soliloquy. It opens with three short exclamatory sentences, still pertaining to the dream; then, after a distinct break, the monosyllable *soft* marks a new phase, where the speaker's calmer emotions are reflected in a particularly regular line (179). The next two lines (180–181) with their indications of time, place, and the speaker's own state, are packed with concise and highly evocative phrases. 'Burn blue' has onomatopoetic force, and alliteration lends it special emphasis. The *dead* of 'dead midnight' reminds us of the death predicted for Richard (cf. e.g. 171 and 'despair and die'), and leads on, by association, to the words *cold, fearful*, and *trembling* in the next line.

The dialectical argument with himself on which Richard now embarks (182–192) is stylistically quite different from the con-

---

[1] Cf. *Var.*, p. 405 for other views on this question.

[2] As suggested by R. G. White, and H. H. Vaughan. For discussion of this and other proposals, cf. *Var.* and J.D.W., p. 249. More recently C. J. Sisson has again spoken in favour of this transposition: 'Lines 204–206 . . . seem quite out of place there. He hardly needs to tell himself what he has seen. And this epilogue ruins the unity of his magnificent soliloquy' (*New Readings in Shakespeare*, 1956, II, p. 95 f.).

[3] For a new interpretation of lines 204 to 206, cf. R. Gerber, 'Elizabethan Convention and Psychological Realism in the Dream and Last Soliloquy of *Richard III' ES*, XL (1959), pp. 294–300.

fession of guilt which follows it. The reiteration of the word
myself (epanalepsis), often at the end of a line (epiphora),[1] hints at
Richard's self-explanatory posture. The staccato rhythm of the
short sentences, the short or monosyllabic questions, the interjections breaking up the line have all characterized Richard's
speech earlier in the scene. But as soon as the process of self-
delusion has come to an end (192), the language changes. A more
ordered and deliberate sentence construction follows, in which the
rhetorical figures,[2] the end-stopped lines, and the formal tone
recall the heightened speech of the scenes of imprecation and
lament.

The three curt words 'I shall despair', following immediately
upon the broad, sweeping lines of accusation, represent the total
result of all these reflections. Lines 202 to 203, containing a three-
fold repetition of *myself* in the clause 'Since that I myself . . . ',
conclude Richard's introspective comments on a hopeless,
negative note. The simplicity of the final, smooth three-line
sentence (cf. p. 219) accords with the unemotional reporting
which it contains.

Comparison with Later Soliloquies

The soliloquy ends with the speaker's own name; up to the last
few lines it is far more turned in upon Richard himself than are the
other soliloquies in the play. Even in *Richard II* and *Romeo and
Juliet*, in spite of a richer use of language, the speaker does not
converse with himself to the same extent.

The soliloquies in *Macbeth* and *Hamlet* also reflect what is going
on inside a character. But these later works pierce to deeper levels
of human consciousness, for there the spoken words reflect not so
much what a man is consciously thinking, but the feelings within
him, the images that arise in his mind. Richard's soliloquy presents his thoughts rather than his feelings or visions, even though
behind these thoughts we recognize despair, and even though the

---

[1] *Myself* occurs nine times, *I* eleven times.
[2] The parallelism and echo effect brought about by these figures emphasize
the long catalogue of Richard's sins, all of which are simply variants of the
same crime.

rhythm of his speech reveals his anguish. Logic and dialectical argumentation are in any case in keeping both with his character and with the conventions governing the monologue, which, since Seneca, had always included abstract reflection and the 'debate with oneself'.

The Soliloquy: Development of Richard's Character

Richard's introspective monologue comes as a surprise. Up till now he has assessed every situation purely in terms of the *ex-ternal* gain or loss it might involve, without ever inquiring into his own state of mind. He has made his way through the play as though the inner conflicts which plague other men simply did not concern him; his sole care has been the carrying out of his designs. With each of his victims he assumes a different disguise,[1] never is he himself, never does he examine the workings of his own mind. The tone of his opening soliloquy derives not from any attempt on Richard's part to reveal what is actually going on inside him, but simply from the fact that in this speech he is introducing himself.

The despair which Richard reveals here is not caused by the external situation (which is still favourable, thanks to the greater military strength of Richard's side), but by the hopeless conflict being waged within him. Having known only outward hind-rances, having depended on external might, he now capitulates before an inward obstacle – one which he at first tries to dismiss as a dream.

The play has given us reason to suppose that Richard would finally be defeated by some overwhelming external force, some punishment meted out by Nemesis. Here, however, we see him vanquished and punished by something within himself, and *before* the defeat on the battlefield. More clear-sighted than any of his victims, Richard recognizes the underlying reason for his own despair and ruin.

His situation is not without irony: for the cynical realist is over-whelmed by precisely that factor which he has always considered

---

[1] Cf. T. Bogard, 'Shakespeare's Second Richard' *PMLA*, LXX (1955), pp. 192–209.

an illusion. The apparitions of his dream have now become more real for him than reality itself. The 'shadows' have shaken him more profoundly than could the 'substance of ten thousand soldiers' (216-219). Appearance is once more contrasted to reality; appearance seems more menacing to Richard than even the reality – a last variation on the familiar theme.

Towards Character-Tragedy

Until this point Richard, like all the other characters, is depicted largely in terms of his actions; the development of his character is hardly touched upon. Shakespeare seems to have been more concerned with establishing logical connections, depicting the course of events, revealing the interconnection between guilt and expiation in the lives of individual characters. Revenge and expiation have until now been portrayed as outside forces descending upon the offender rather than as forces within the character. Margaret's curse has accurately foretold each victim's fate, and the offenders (Hastings, Buckingham) regard their allotted end as an expiation exacted by fate for their wrongdoings.

But in this monologue of Richard's the situation has changed. Significantly, he makes no reference to Margaret's curse; his real collapse and fall take place independently of his physical defeat and death – which is what fate has prepared for him. The cause of his destruction is the fact that here he gains a true insight into his own nature. This is something very different from the scruples and remorse occasionally expressed by the typical 'villain'[1] of pre-Shakespearian tragedy, or by Richard as portrayed in the *True Tragedy* (1398 ff.). Even so Shakespeare's move in *Richard III* in the direction of 'character-tragedy', his study of evil entangled in its own coils, is practically unprepared for in the play and comes too late to alter appreciably the dramatic fabric of the play.[2]

The question then arises, whether *Richard III* is not more of a tragedy than a history. Shakespeare and his audience probably saw no clear line of demarcation between the two genres. The

---

[1] e.g. Ateukin in Greene's *James IV* (V, ii).

[2] Cf. T. Bogard, 'Shakespeare's Second Richard' *PLMA*, LXX (1955), p. 198, for a discussion of the technique in Richard's soliloquy.

First Quarto (1597) calls the play *The Tragedy of King Richard the Third*, and though the editors of the *First Folio* placed it among the Histories, they retained the word *Tragedy* on the title-page. If one applies the criteria established by certain modern scholars[1] for distinguishing tragedy from history, *Richard III* might equally be put in either category. Even if we admit that this depiction of Richard's downfall in his soliloquy suggest some of the characteristics of Shakespearian tragedy,[2] this development is not followed up.

The Richard–Ratcliff Episode (202–227)

The episode following the soliloquy once more mirrors the ghost-scene. Though short (a bare 15 lines), it contains more undertones and suggestive phrases than do the longer Richmond-episodes.

Richard, still sunk in his own reflections, is startled by Ratcliff's entry, though he himself has told Ratcliff to come back at this time (77).[3] The latter's greeting tells him that the morning about which he has expressed such misgiving has finally come. Ratcliff's announcement: 'your friends are up . . .' fixes Richard's indeterminate fears on a definite object, so that after mentioning his 'fearful dream', he asks: 'will our friends prove all true?' (the irregular metre brings out the anxiety and uncertainty behind this question). His words recall Margaret's curse[4] and also take up the theme of false friends again.[5] Richard's hesitant 'I fear, I fear' (214) gains suggestiveness through the elliptical nature of the utterance, a technique first introduced into English drama by Shakespeare. Ratcliff interprets the words as still relating to the dream, and

---

[1] Cf. Lily B. Campbell, *Shakespeare's 'Histories'. Mirrors of Elizabethan Policy* (1947), p. 306 ff.; M. Doran, *Endeavors of Art*, 1954, p. 112 ff.; P. Alexander, *Introduction to Shakespeare's Histories*, in: *Complete Histories*, ed. P. Alexander (Collins, n.d.), p. 7.

[2] On the lack of genuine tragedy in *Richard III*, cf. H. B. Charlton, *Shakespearean Tragedy* (1949), pp. 24–39.

[3] Ratcliff's statement that the cock has crowed twice (another indication of time; cf. p. 205) may have a symbolic undertone. St Peter's conscience smote him at the cock's third crow.

[4] Cf. I, iii, 223–224.

[5] Cf. II, i, 36; III, i, 15–16; IV, iv, 216, 435, 485; V, ii, 19.

tries to disperse its impact by his reference to 'shadows'.[1] But *shadows* is ambiguous too, and conjures up for Richard the ghosts who have filled him with such terror (cf. p. 222 f.). And now he quite openly confides his fears and weaknesses to a subordinate; for the first time his words are not chosen for their calculated effect on the hearer. Anxiety and uncertainty, too, lie behind his unkingly intention of eavesdropping on his men. At the same time Richard's project reminds us of the external situation and bridges the gap in time before the next appearance of these two characters.

Richmond, in his short exchange with the anonymous 'Lords', tells how he has dreamed not the 'fearful dream' of Richard, but the 'fairest-boding dreams' (227; cf. also 'so fair a dream', 233); the brief description of the dream (230–231) opens with the same words as the corresponding passage at the end of Richard's soliloquy ('Methought . . . ', 204). This short dialogue serves to introduce Richmond's speech to his men. To appreciate it we must compare it with the corresponding speech of Richard; for the extended contrast which forms the basis of this scene reaches its climax in these two speeches.

The Two Orations Compared (237–270; 314–351)

The orations are roughly equal in length and similarly constructed, both framed by an introductory and concluding passage, both evidencing the traditional division of the central section into *narratio* and *confirmatio*.[2] Both speeches deal with the same themes – they denigrate the enemy, give reasons for fighting, and spur the

---

[1] The insertion of lines 204–206 here (i.e. after 212) would clarify the passage (cf. also p. 220). Lines 212–214 are absent in the *Folio*, which, as was pointed out by Wright, makes Radcliff's following words unintelligible. For a compositorial explanation of the omission of these lines, cf. J.D.W., p. 249. J.D.W.'s suggested emendation of line 213 ('What thinkst thou, will all our friends prove true?') seems unnecessary in view of how frequently metrical irregularity occurs elsewhere – as here – in the interests of emphasis. On the whole passage cf. also C. J. Sisson, *New Readings*, II, pp. 95–96.

[2] On the construction of such speeches cf. M. B. Kennedy, *The Oration in Shakespeare* (1942); for Richmond's speech see p. 114. The most informative contemporary treatises in this field are those of Thomas Wilson, *Arte of Rhetorique* (ed. G. Mair, 1909) and John Hoskins, *Directions for Speech and Style* (ed. H. H. Hudson, 1935).

hearers on to battle. Both make use of rhetorical figures, especially parallelism and antithesis, and of alliteration.

Yet in spite of superficial resemblances, the speeches reflect the essential differences between the two men. Richmond's oration is impersonal, clearly structured, his manner calm and undynamic; Richard's is altogether personal, the language concrete and alive; as his speech progresses, its intensity rises.

The very beginning shows a difference of approach. Both speakers, it is true, refer to what they have already said (237–239; 314). But after a short question Richard leaps forward to his main theme, whereas Richmond devotes two and a half lines (containing a courteous address, which Richard omits) to a drawn-out explanation of why he cannot add more to what he has already said. The doubled nouns ('the leisure and enforcement of the time', 238) are quite in keeping with his slow, unhurried style of speech (cf. 'the form and model of our battle', 24). The lines that follow carry these differences forward. Right at the beginning of his next sentence Richard refers specifically to the enemy ('remember whom you are to cope withal'); he paints a horrifying picture of the foe (in many variations and in nearly every line). Richmond, on the other hand, begins with an abstract idea which stresses the justice of his cause, and then enumerates the unseen array of his heavenly supporters. Richard from the very beginning makes exclusive use of the negative method of vilifying his enemies. Richmond resorts to this technique later in his speech, but only sparingly and with a generous intermingling of positive statement. Richmond's rôle as God's 'captain' makes appropriate his own dependence on a higher order (cf. 254 ff.)[1] and his constant references to a supra-personal force. Richard calls on no principle to prop his arguments. Although up till now he has shown himself a master of argument and twisting logic, here his appeal is based not on reason and principle but on feeling and imagination. He knows that hatred of a dangerous adversary will be more effective in spurring on his men than any recourse to moral argument, which, in any case, his men would no longer accept. For this reason his references to the grim consequences of defeat are more vivid than anything in Richmond's speech.

[1] Cf. E. M. W. Tillyard, *Shakespeare's Histories*, p. 204.

Richmond refers to country, wives, children (257, 259, 261) who must be protected, but in each case he stresses the reward ensuing upon success; Richard's three successive questions are far more dramatic: 'Shall these enjoy our lands? lie with our wives, | Ravish our daughters?' (336–337).

His speech is made additionally dramatic by the sound of the drum heralding the enemy's approach, by his stirring five-fold call to his men, and by the interruption caused by the arrival of a messenger.[1] The war-cry with which Richard's speech ends is far more urgent and impassioned than the one that rounds off Richmond's speech, and at its conclusion the soldiers sweep off to battle before our eyes.

Richard's speech, unlike Richmond's, rises to a climax at the end; and indeed the man we now see before us is not the tortured Richard of the soliloquy. Once more the dauntless, commanding spirit, the fiery will and resourcefulness of the old Richard take over. Our disgust at his crimes gives way to reluctant admiration.

Both language and syntax emphasize the differences between these two speeches. Richmond's is clearly structured, certain sections standing out by virtue of a recognizable internal pattern (lines 253–268 in particular: five sentences of similar construction – a conditional clause followed by the main one). Parallel sentence construction is accentuated by alliteration, anaphora, and other rhetorical figures, and, within the line, chiasmus (247). The preponderance of statements, two lines long for the most part, lends a static, well-regulated air to the speech, which ought, surely, to receive an almost formal delivery.

Though Richard's speech makes use of the same or similar rhetorical figures, it is infused with a completely different spirit. When Richard uses antithetical contrast and parallelism (as in 320–322), he does so not to repeat, but to heighten the intensity. The sentences are of varying length, often rising to a climax and sometimes spanning a number of lines (315–319, 327–331, 332–335); they impose their pattern on the metre much more clearly than do Richmond's. Above all, the frequent questions

[1] Stanley's shift of allegiance, reported by this messenger, is the decisive factor that makes Richmond's victory possible. Though Shakespeare does not stress this fact, it must have been known to at least part of his audience.

and imperatives bring dramatic intensity to the speech, which has more energy and speed than Richmond's oration.

Finally, there is contrast in the choice of words. On the whole, Richmond's language is colourless and abstract; he uses conventional epithets (*holy saints, wronged souls, willing swords, bold attempt*), and only rarely rises to more graphic imagery.[1] Richard's vigorous, direct expression recalls the blunt colloquial tones we heard from him in earlier scenes. Phrases such as *scum of Britaines, base lackey peasants, milk-sop, over-weening rags, famish'd beggars, poor rats*, which he uses to describe the enemy, and verbs such as *bobb'd, thump'd*, and *vomits forth* illustrate this and suggest army slang.

Richmond's exhortation to his followers in V, ii (cf. p. 200) is a conventional one; but these two speeches – which *Q* expressly terms '*Oration to his Soldiers*' and '*Oration to his Army*',[2] use the conventional and impersonal framework of the typical oration for a character-revealing contrast (cf. p. 225, note 2). Moreover, the formal oration, which frequently becomes an isolated rhetorical gem,[3] is here incorporated into the structure and design of the scene. Since the whole scene is a kind of *tableau*, the oration is for once placed in a fitting frame. It must be admitted, however, that the immediate transitions leading to these two speeches are somewhat abrupt.[4]

Richard's great oration (not Richmond's) crowns the scene, rounding off its symmetrical design. For although Richmond is the hero of Act V, Richard is still the hero of the whole play. In his last hours, we do feel some concern for him. This can be attributed both to his oration and to his final appearance in this scene.

[1] Cf. 250 and 258; 'country's fat' derives from Genesis xlv, 18.

[2] J.D.W. notes that though there are contemporary parallels, this is the only instance where Shakespeare marks an oration with a heading in this way (p. 250). Cf. e.g. *Edward I*, 763 ff.: '*Queene Elinors Speeche*'.

[3] Especially in pre-Shakespearian drama: e.g. *Edward I*, 763 ff.; *2 Tamburlaine*, 3243 ff.; but cf. also *3 Henry VI*, V, iv, 1–38. For further examples see Clemen, *English Tragedy before Shakespeare*, passim.

[4] And cf. J.D.W., pp. 250 and 253.

Richard's Last Entry (271–351)

This section, following directly after Richmond's oration, consists of four short loosely knit episodes, Richard's oration, and a final short episode. The four episodes all prepare us in their different ways for what is to follow. Richard's isolation is portrayed from a new angle in the brief, five-line exchange between him and Ratcliff. Ratcliff, who has been eavesdropping on Richard's officers, reports their rather colourless comments on Richmond, in which Richard, if not the audience, finds reassurance. In the next episode Richard regards the sun's absence[1] as an evil omen directed at his army. But recognizing the logical weakness of this first instinctive reaction, Richard ends by comforting himself with the fact that the cloudy sky hangs over Richmond's army too.

The passage is significant not only as another example of how Richard reassures himself, but also because it illustrates the beginning of a process of rationalization of natural omens, a process which becomes more marked in the seventeenth century. In earlier times omens and portents are regarded as unambiguous facts of life. In his earlier Histories Shakespeare too generally uses omens in this manner.[2]

Having overcome his own uncertainty, Richard is able to give a detailed, clear, and concise order to attack, quite unlike the impatient, contradictory commands he gives at the beginning of the scene or in Act IV. Richard has himself in hand again. Viewed against the background of Richard's soliloquy, such decisiveness must fascinate the spectator. Richard is, after all, not only a villain but also the hero of a 'tragical history'.[3] The ordinary Elizabethan villain would hardly have been granted a final appearance of this sort.

[1] Since the sun was the emblem of all the Yorkist kings (and thus also of Richard), the mention of the darkened sun contains a veiled allusion to the ruin of the House of York. Cf. C. W. Scott-Giles, *Shakespeare's Heraldry* (1950), p. 172 f.; and cf. Richard's first words in the play.
[2] Cf. Clemen, 'Shakespeare und das Königtum' *SJ*, 68 (1932), p. 56 ff.
[3] The latter scenes of *Macbeth* contain a far completer transformation of villain to tragic hero. On the question of how much sympathy it is possible to accord a villain, and to what extent such a villain can be the hero of a play, cf. Hardin Craig, *An Interpretation of Shakespeare* (1948), p. 76.

The last episode before the oration serves to emphasize the change in Richard;[1] his views on conscience and dreams, expressed a short time before, now undergo a reversal which, in a scene where conscience has confronted him in visible form, seems almost paradoxical. The audience will therefore feel inclined to take Richard's scornful 'Let not our babbling dreams affright our souls' and his aphoristic remarks on conscience (recalling 179 and 193 as well as 216 to 219) in an ironic sense. The use of *our* twice in line 308 draws attention to the fact that Richard is putting what concerns only himself on a general level, as though it were the concern of many. Moreover, here, as elsewhere (e.g. III, i, 79, 94), Shakespeare takes a phrase with a proverbial ring and uses it as a warning. This is the last of a series of prophetic statements, couched in various forms, scattered throughout the scene.[2]

Richard's last lines before the oration,

> March on, join bravely, let us to it pell-mell;
> If not to heaven, then hand in hand to hell.
>
> (312–313)

reveal inflexible determination, but also extreme cynicism.[3] The language is similar to that which he had used in contemplating Clarence's murder ('pack'd with post horse up to heaven', I, i, 146; cf. also I, i, 119); but his last remarks at the end of the scene are devoid of cynicism, showing him to be further removed from despair and irresolution than at any other point in the scene. In these final lines Richard, like Richmond in his oration, invokes St George; but whereas Richmond had called out 'God and Saint George' (270), Richard begs the saint to inspire his side with 'the spleen of fiery dragons' (350). It was the fiery dragon, however, a symbol of the powers of Hell, which St George succeeded in vanquishing.

[1] For discussion of the stage-direction *He showeth him a paper* (found only in *Q*) cf. J.D.W., p. 252, and C. J. Sisson, *New Readings*, II, p. 96.

[2] Cf. 5, 18, 21, 73, 120 ff., 177, 201, 206, 214, 231, 280, 282.

[3] In 1903 G. B. Shaw wrote to the actor Forbes-Robertson: 'All Nietzsche is in the lines "Conscience is but a word that cowards use . . ." [ll. 309–311]. And after all the pious twaddle of Richmond his charging order is delicious: "let us to't pell-mell; | If not to heaven, then hand in hand to hell" ' (cited by J. Palmer, *Political Characters*, p. 115 f.).

SCENE FOUR

In thirteen lines and a stage-direction preceding V, v, the action of
the play is rounded off. As in some of the great tragedies, the external events – Richard's defeat and death – are swiftly and
summarily carried to their conclusion once essential issues have
been settled.

This play (unlike all three parts of *Henry VI*) has so far contained no battle-scenes with one or more groups fighting or fleeing
across the stage and exchanging news to the blare of trumpets
(*Alarum*). Such scenes are frequently to be found in pre-Shakespearian popular drama and in the early chronicle plays,[1] and continue to occur in Shakespeare's work, though in his later battle-
scenes – for instance *King John* (III, ii; V, iii); *Julius Caesar* (V,
i–v); and *Antony and Cleopatra* (III, viii–x, IV, vii, x–xii) – new
techniques and new purposes have been introduced into such
episodes. The present scene falls into two almost parallel and
equal halves; in the first, Catesby's words conjure up the battling
king, preparing us for the second half in which he appears before
us. Shakespeare often leads up to the entrance of his hero or other
important character with a passage describing the situation he is
in[2] – a variation, in fact, of the messenger's report which is then
given dramatic form in what follows. The preparatory report
often serves, as in the present scene, to portray what would be
difficult to act out on the stage but is nevertheless a necessary part
of the picture to be conveyed.

Catesby's words follow immediately upon Richard's oration
and call to battle at the end of V, iii, so that the audience receives
the impression of a breathlessly intense, uninterrupted final sweep

---

[1] Realistic brawling, tumult, and war-like demeanour play an important
part in these scenes; e.g. *Horestes* (1567); *Locrine, The Wounds of Civil War,
The Battle of Alcazar, Tamburlaine*; cf. A. I. P. Wood, *Stage History of Richard
III*, p. 49.

[2] The most notable instance of the many in the tragedies is in *Lear* (III, i,
4 ff.). But see also *Romeo and Juliet* (I, i, 116 ff.) for this aspect of the art of
anticipation.

of action. *All* our attention is concentrated on Richard. The admiration which we feel for him at the last is evidence of Shakespeare's expert manipulation of our sympathies. The scene in which Macbeth dies in battle (V, viii) is in many ways similar, though Macbeth's heroic end is more skilfully and convincingly brought about.[1]

Catesby's second line at once begins to build up this heroic image of Richard in our minds: 'The King enacts more wonders than a man' (2). Nor is it Richmond who is represented as the intrepid attacker; on the contrary, Richard, seeking Richmond, has already slain five men whom he has mistaken for his antagonist. The very fact that Richmond has disguised so many others in armour resembling his own (no doubt a usual and acceptable stratagem in war at that period) hardly helps sustain an image of the fearless avenger.[2]

With his famous cry – perhaps the best-known line from Shakespeare's early Histories – Richard offers everything he has achieved with so much effort and spilt blood in exchange for a horse. At the end, fighting desperately for his bare life, the great gambler stakes all he has upon this final cast. Richard's metaphorical use of the gambler's terminology (*cast* and *die*) to describe his own situation makes explicit what had not yet been expressly formulated – Richard's reckless gambling nature.

That these should be the last words uttered by Richard before he dies is unconventional. For the Elizabethan tragic hero in his last moments almost always speaks of his own end. In most cases, indeed, he delivers a 'dying-speech'.[3]

[1] D. A. Stauffer discusses a certain lack of credibility in Richard's character in *Shakespeare's World of Images. The Development of his Moral Ideas* (1949), p. 30.

[2] Cf. H. Spencer, p. 235.

[3] Cf. Th. Spencer, *Death and Elizabethan Tragedy* (1936).

SCENE FIVE

Conventional Motifs in the Final Scene

Certain motifs often found in the closing section of Elizabethan tragedies are used here to support the particular purposes which Shakespeare was pursuing in this play; still others are ignored. Thus the usual obituary on the hero is dispensed with, and there is no farewell or dying-speech, no funeral march with the customary ceremonial for the burial of the fallen. (Richmond takes care of this matter with a word or two, 15). In contrast to some of the other Histories, there is no crowd-scene at the end and the army is no longer on stage. The 'state-scene', in which the crown is passed from the slain 'bloody dog' to Richmond, is kept within modest limits and involves comparatively few persons, for the new era which Richmond represents is obviously not to disturb the play's focus on Richard's dreadful career.

On the other hand, almost all the motifs that *do* occur in this scene are those which normally characterize the ending of a pre-Shakespearian or Elizabethan tragedy. The concluding episode frequently includes a decisive battle between two armies or a duel in which the guilty party falls, his death satisfying at least outwardly the requirement of retribution (the avenger and legitimate heir being victorious); even in his later tragedies[1] (*Julius Caesar, Hamlet, Macbeth*) Shakespeare does not neglect these particular events. The restoration of order and the resulting onset of a new and better era for the state as well as for the individual is a prevailing theme in Elizabethan tragedy; as in *Richard III*, we are led into a world of disorder and catastrophe, but at the end the

[1] In *King Lear*, the duel between Edmund and Edgar towards the end is a case in point; in *Antony and Cleopatra*, the great battle takes place as early as Act IV. *Misfortunes of Arthur* keeps to the convention of English classical drama in bringing this duel and the battle only indirectly before us in a retrospective account; in *Orlando Furioso* the duel between Orlando and Sacrepant in which the latter, the 'villain', falls, forms an introduction to the final scene (1370).

prospect seems bright for a healing of wounds, a reconciliation of the contending parties, and a restoration of normal conditions.[1] This restoration of order is often linked to the accession and coronation of a new and legitimate ruler.[2] There is at the play's ending a patriotic emphasis on the affairs of the nation as opposed to those of individuals; the fate of the whole country is seen to be connected with the destiny of the man whose end we witness.[3]

The unobtrusive prayer woven into Richmond's final speech is a convention which goes back to the morality plays; it is often used there to round off a serious play.[4]

The Initial Stage-Direction

A short pantomime indicated in the stage-direction which precedes Scene v[5] allows us to witness Richard's death at Richmond's

[1] As in *James IV*, *David and Bethsabe*, *The Troublesome Reign*, *Jew of Malta*, *Massacre at Paris*; cf. Shakespeare's variants of this theme in *Romeo and Juliet*, *Julius Caesar*, *Hamlet*, *Macbeth*.

Th. Spencer sees the disruption and final restoration of order as the recurrent basic pattern of *all* Shakespeare's Histories: 'An existing order is violated, the consequent conflict and turmoil are portrayed, and order is restored by the destruction of the force or forces that originally violated it' (*Shakespeare and the Nature of Man*, p. 73).

[2] As in *Edward II*, where the new king is also (like Richmond) the guarantor of future peace and order; in *David and Bethsabe* Solomon is chosen as the new king and successor, in the *Battle of Alcazar* it is Muly Mahomet Seth; in *2 Tamburlaine*, Tamburlaine makes the crown over to his son; *The Troublesome Reign* and *King John* both conclude with Henry's coronation. And cf. the endings of *Hamlet* (Fortinbras), *Macbeth* (Malcolm), and *Henry IV*.

[3] Cf. in particular the ending of *The Troublesome Reign*, the final speech of the spirits of revenge in *Misfortunes*, Eubulus's speech at the end of *Gorboduc*, and the endings of Shakespeare's *King John* and *Henry V*. The *True Tragedy* devotes much more space than does *Richard III* to this patriotic theme and to the promise of peace at the end.

[4] The final prayer was not usually part of the action, but more like an epilogue; later it was often combined with homage and praise offered to Queen Elizabeth or to the current head of state. Cf. *Mankind*, 894 ff.; *Mundus et Infans*, 978; *Nice Wanton*; *Hyckescorner*; *Foure PP*, 1223 ff.; *Everyman*; *Locrine* (Ate's epilogue); Bale's *Kynge Johan*; *Appius and Virginia*; *Cambises*.

[5] For critical consideration of this stage-direction, cf. *Var.*, p. 423 f. and J.D.W. Marshall's suggestion (*Var.*) that the stage-direction be divided, so that Richard and Richmond's final encounter is added to the end of Scene iv, and Scene v begins with *Enter Richmond, Derby bearing the crown* deserves notice, but is of no practical importance if the play proceeds, as at least in

hand. The pantomimic presentation of important parts of the
action is rare in pre-Shakespearian drama, though some parallels
do exist.[1]

Richmond as the Mouthpiece of the Higher Powers

The final scene is an undramatic epilogue in which Richmond,
even less individual than in the earlier scenes, once more becomes
the mouthpiece of a higher power.

The order which Richard has disrupted is now restored. For the
play is not simply the 'tragical history' of its chief hero; the fate of
England, the larger pattern of history, and indeed the whole
divine order of things in the world fall within its scope and
receive particular attention in this final scene.

The scene begins with an invocation to God and ends with the
words *God say amen*; during its course Richmond calls upon God
more than once – indeed, some of his lines seem almost like a
prayer (39 ff.). It is not accidental that Richard's ironic pro-
clamation of peace in his opening soliloquy is now matched by
Richmond's genuine promise of peace made in God's name at the
end.[2]

The Concluding Speech

Richmond devotes little time to asking questions (George
Stanley's fate, 9; the names of those slain, 12) or making arrangements (the burial of the dead, 15; an amnesty for the soldiers who
fled, 16), but moves quickly on to survey the approaching union of
the White Rose and the Red, the union of York and Lancaster,
that promises to restore England to health. Not a word of the
final speech is devoted to Richard; 'The bloody dog is dead' (2)

---

these scenes it ought to, without a break. On the question of stage-directions
in Shakespeare, cf. Chambers, *Shakespeare I*, pp. 118–122, 201–203, 300 etc.

[1] Cf. D. Mehl, *The Elizabethan Dumb Show* (1965).

[2] Specific turns of phrase, too, balance one another; e.g. 'Grim-visag'd
war hath smooth'd his wrinkled front' (I, i, 9) and 'smooth-fac'd peace' (33).
On this last expression, cf. A. S. Venezky, *Pageantry on the Shakespearian Stage*,
p. 179.

R

replaces the customary obituary on the tragic hero; 'from the dead temples of this bloody wretch' Derby has plucked the now superfluous crown.

Richmond is Richard's punisher and the restorer of the order Richard has disturbed; but beyond this he is the initiator of an order reaching down to Shakespeare's own day. With this final scene the age-long strife between York and Lancaster is brought to an end; yet neither of the two parties has prevailed, for Richmond (the first Tudor king) in marrying Elizabeth of York lays the foundations of a dynasty whose legitimacy is particularly stressed – 'The true succeeders of each royal house' (30). These final lines, infused with the point of view known as the 'Tudor myth', point to the new and auspicious age ushered in by Richmond's accession to the throne.

It seems reasonable to assume that the Elizabethan audience was fully alive to the veiled references to their own age contained in Richmond's epilogue, to the hints of present dangers, contained in the final prayer. The play itself hardly justifies the extreme urgency with which God's aid is sought against 'traitors', nor does it seem likely that the play would have ended on this particular note if contemporary issues had not been involved.[1]

The last two lines stress once again that peace – a concept that has appeared in such varied and often paradoxical contexts in the course of the play[2] – is restored: 'peace lives again'. Thus is the circle closed which had opened with Richard's ironically malicious talk of the coming of peace at the outset of the play. Peace can in truth return now that Richard, 'the troubler of the poor world's peace' (I, iii, 221), has been destroyed.

---

[1] Further allusions to contemporary events are discussed in Lily B. Campbell, *Shakespeare's 'Histories'. Mirrors of Elizabethan Policy*; P. Reyher, *Essai sur les idées dans l'œuvre de Shakespeare* (esp. p. 272 ff.); E. M. W. Tillyard, *Shakespeare's History Plays*.

[2] Cf. e.g. I, iii, 288; II, i, 5; II, i, 44; II, i, 59; II, ii, 132; III, v, 45; Cf. also commentary on V, ii, p. 201 f.

'Richard III' as a History

The concluding speech again confirms the fact that this play shares certain attitudes with the typical Elizabethan history-play.[1] Not only does the final scene assess a sequence of events from the past in terms of its application to the political present, but the note of patriotic glorification of England so strong in all Shakespeare's Histories (and particularly at their close), is clearly discernible here. Moreover, the idea, which goes back to medieval Christianity, that God's providence works itself out in the flow of historical events, is expressed yet again in Richmond's prayer. And finally, in the light of this last speech Richard's disastrous rise and fall is seen to be more than material for a fascinating character study; just as the historical events of the play contained a lesson for the Elizabethans, so Richard's career was put before the audience as a moral example and a warning. We are shown not only what happened, but what these events meant for the country and for those caught up in them.[2] The ending itself, which contains the promise of a new and better beginning after so much violence, suffering, and malice, pronounces a final moral judgement on the past and assigns it a place in the panorama of history, though it must not be forgotten that *Richard III* is far *less* concerned with moral lessons than were the majority of histories of the day.

Here again we see what so many examples on so many levels have shown us before in the course of this study: there is hardly a contemporary trend of thought, hardly a formal or stylistic convention in the drama of Shakespeare's time which we do not also find in his works. But his superior skill as a dramatist, his new insights into eternal human problems and his grasp of their dramatic potential puts these elements into a different perspective.

[1] Cf. I. Ribner, 'The Tudor History Play: An Essay in Definition' *PMLA*, LXIX (1954), p. 591 ff. Ribner discusses previous attempts (by Schelling, Briggs, Lily B. Campbell, E. M. W. Tillyard, A. P. Rossiter, etc.) to define the history-play.

[2] On this point, see the discussion on the difference between *history* and *tragedy* in Shakespeare in Peter Alexander's introduction to the Collins edition of *Shakespeare's Histories* (1955), p. 8, and the recent article by Nicholas Brooke in *The Critical Quarterly* VII (1965), p. 123 ff.

They become subservient to new ends, with the result that they seem to be both heightened and transformed. Shakespearian scholars over the last three decades have been concerned with pointing out the extent to which Shakespeare's dramas were a product of their time, but whatever may be the justifications for considering his works primarily as documents of Renaissance attitudes and as products of the Elizabethan theatre, this point of view is too limited. But to know about both is important, for only then can one fully understand that other aspect of his work which transcends its historical background and appeals to us directly, even today. It has been the purpose of this commentary to point the way to this understanding.

NOTE ON THE PLAY, ITS TEXT
AND ITS DATE OF COMPOSITION

Richard III concludes the first tetralogy of Shakespeare's Histories which in the three parts of *Henry VI* treat the Wars of the Roses of the fifteenth century with the contention between the houses of York and Lancaster up to the battle of Tewkesbury (1471). Together with the comedies *The Two Gentlemen of Verona*, *The Comedy of Errors*, *The Taming of the Shrew* and the tragedy *Titus Andronicus* the play belongs to the early phase of Shakespeare's work.

Most scholars and editors have taken 1592–1593 as the date of the play's composition. Peter Alexander, however, places the beginning of Shakespeare's career as a playwright in the late eighties, so that according to this theory *Richard III* may have been written about 1590 (see Peter Alexander's introduction to the Collins-Shakespeare, 1951, p. xvi f.).

As has been explained in the introduction, the complex textual problems are not discussed in this commentary. It may be remarked, however, that in spite of the great many variants of readings with which an editor studying the *Quarto* and *Folio* editions is faced, the number of variants which have an actual bearing on the meaning and on the interpretation is very limited. In certain cases of this kind the commentary has in fact touched upon textual problems. Short accounts of the textual problem pertaining to *Richard III* may be found in John Dover Wilson's edition of the play pp. 140–160 and in his lecture 'On editing Shakespeare with special reference to the problems of *Richard III*' (*Talking of Shakespeare*, ed. John Garrett, 1954). Full studies of the text are: D. L. Patrick, *The Textual History of Richard III* (1936); J. K. Walton, *The Copy for the Folio Text of Richard III* (1955). An important new investigation of the problem has been recently undertaken by Kristian Smidt, *Injurious Impostors and Richard III* (1963). The textual problems of *Richard III* have also been dealt with in the following books: P. Alexander, *Shakespeare's Henry VI and Richard III* (1929); E. K. Chambers, *Shakespeare. A Study of Facts and Problems* (1930), vol. I, pp. 226–301; W. W. Greg, *The Editorial Problem in Shakespeare* (1951), pp. 77–88; *The Shakespeare First Folio* (1955), pp. 190–199; A. Walker, *Textual Problems of the First Folio* (1953), pp. 13–36. The latest short article on the problem is by E. A. J. Honigmann, 'The Text of *Richard III*' *Theatre Research, Recherches Théâtrales*, VII (1965), pp. 48–55.

Students interested in the true historical figure of Richard III, who is not identical with the play's hero, may be referred to P. M. Kendall, *Richard the Third* (1955). For a full genealogy of the characters referred to in this play see the genealogical table in J. D. Wilson's edition.

The following Munich dissertations are relevant to certain topics treated in this commentary, but have not been cited in the footnotes of the English version.

M. Braun, *Symbolismus und Illusionismus im englischen Drama vor 1620*, Munich, 1962 (privately printed dissertation)

B. Eber, *Die Apostrophe in der englischen Tragödie des 16. Jahrhunderts*, Munich, 1950 (typewritten dissertation)

Ch. Ehrl, *Sprachstil und Charakter bei Shakespeare*, dissertation subsequently printed in book form; Heidelberg, 1957

T. Eichhorn, *Prosa und Vers im vorshakespeareschen Drama*, Munich, 1949 (typewritten dissertation)

Th. Finkenstaedt, *Die Verskunst des jungen Shakespeare*, Munich, 1955 (typewritten dissertation)

H. Fischer, *Interpretationskommentar zu Shakespeares 'Antony and Cleopatra'* [Act I], Munich, 1957 (typewritten dissertation)

J. Förg, *Typische Redeformeln und Motive im vorshakespeareschen Drama*, Munich, 1955 (typewritten dissertation)

H. W. Gabler, *Zur Funktion dramatischer und literarischer Parodie im elisabethanischen Drama*, Munich, 1965 (privately printed dissertation)

H. Gruner, *Studien zum Dialog im vorshakespeareschen Drama*, Munich, 1955 (typewritten dissertation)

F. Hoffmann, *Die typischen Situationen im elisabethanischen Drama*, Munich, 1955 (typewritten dissertation)

M.–B. von Loeben, *Shakespeares sprachliche Ironie und die Entwicklung seiner Dramatik*, Munich, 1965 (privately printed dissertation)

D. Mehl, *Die Funktion des 'Dumb Show' im elisabethanischen Drama*, Munich, 1960; dissertation subsequently printed in book form: *The Elizabethan Dumb Show*, London, 1965

E. Meierl, *Shakespeares 'Richard III' und seine Quelle*, Munich, 1954 (typewritten dissertation)

W. Riehle, *Das Beiseitesprechen bei Shakespeare*, Munich, 1964 (privately printed dissertation)

B. Schmid, *Form und Gehalt der Großen Rede in Shakespeares Historien*, Munich, 1955 (typewritten dissertation)

A. Schopf, *Leitmotivische Thematik in Shakespeares Historien*, Munich, 1952 (typewritten dissertation)

K. Schlüter, *Shakespeares dramatische Erzählkunst*, dissertation subsequently printed in book form; Heidelberg, 1958

B. Thaler, *Szenenschluß, Szenenanfang und Szenennaht in Shakespeares Historien und Tragödien*, Munich, 1965 (privately printed dissertation)

H. Weinstock, *Die dramatische Funktion elisabethanischer Sprichwörter und Pseudosprichwörter bei Shakespeare*, dissertation subsequently printed in book form; Heidelberg, 1966

A. Wollmann, *Die Personenführung in Shakespeares Historien*, Munich, 1955 (typewritten dissertation)

The following earlier studies by the author have been made use of in this commentary:

'Shakespeare und das Königtum' *SJ*, 68 (1932), pp. 56–79

The Development of Shakespeare's Imagery (1951; 6th ed. 1965)

Wandlung des Botenberichts bei Shakespeare, Sitzungsberichte der Bayer. Akademie der Wissenschaften, Phil.-hist. Klasse (1952)

English Tragedy before Shakespeare. The Development of Dramatic Speech (1961; German version 1955)

Clarences Traum und Ermordung, Sitzungsberichte der Bayer. Akademie der Wissenschaften, Phil.-hist. Klasse (1955)

'Shakespeares erste Dramen' *Geistige Welt. Vierteljahreszeitschr. für Kultur- und Geisteswissenschaften*, I (1947)

'Anticipation and Foreboding in Shakespeare's Early Histories' *ShS*, VI (1953)

'Tradition and Originality in Shakespeare's *Richard III*' *SQ*, V (1954)

'Zur Methodik der Shakespeare-Interpretation' *Sprache und Literatur Englands und Amerikas*, vol. 2 (1956)

INDEX OF NAMES